LABOUR MIGRATION IN
THE POST LIBERALIZATION ERA

LABOUR MIGRATION IN THE POST LIBERALIZATION ERA

EDITORS
Denzil Fernandes & P.O. Martin

CISRS
2019

Labour Migration in the Post Liberalization Era – Jointly published by the Rev. Dr. Ashish Amos of the Indian Society for Promoting Christian Knowledge (ISPCK), Post Box 1585, Kashmere Gate, Delhi-110006 and Christian Institute for the Study of Religion and Society (CISRS), 73, Millers Road, Benson Town, Bangalore - 560046.

© CISRS, 2019

Online Order: http://ispck.org.in/book.php

ISBN: 978-93-88945-03-5

Laser typeset by

ISPCK, Post Box 1585, 1654, Madarsa Road, Kashmere Gate, Delhi-110006 • *Tel:* 23866323

e-mail: ashish@ispck.org.in • ella@ispck.org.in
website: www.ispck.org.in

Contents

Foreword   ix

Introduction   xiii

Impact of Globalization on Urban Slum Dwellers-Migrants From
Rural Areas: A Social Case Study of
Barasat Town, North 24-Parganas District, West Bengal
Notan Bhusan Kar   1

Workers, Identity, Policies and their Position in the Urban Space
Atlanta Talukdar and Deepshikha Malakar   20

Negotiation in Urban spaces:Rural to Urban Migration of Labour
Sukanya Kakoti and Raju Saikia   30

Cityscape for Young Migrant Women:
A Reflection on Intra Domestic Workers in Bangalore
Richard Gonsalves   43

Socio-legal Dynamics ofMigrant Workers in India
Bhumika Sharma and Mamta Kashyap   56

Vulnerabilities of Interstate Migrants in India:
A Case Study of Waste Pickers and Manual Scavengers in Delhi
Ojasvi Goyal   66

Income Generation, Livelihood and Statelessness:
An Analysis of the Current Situation of
Tea Garden Workers of North Bengal, India
Saikat Roy 82

The Making and Unmaking of the
Migrant Labourers of the Marginal Caste
Paul D'Souza 96

An Analysis of the Livelihood Determinants and Vulnerability
of Seasonal Migration in Khohar Village, Rajasthan, India
Aparna Radhakrishnan, Niti Saxena and Vrindaa Sharma 117

Vulnerabilities of Distress Labour Migrants from North
and North Eastern States in South India
P.O. Martin and Smitha Philip 133

Migrant Workers in Sanitation Work: Vulnerabilities
of Inter-state Migrants in India
Ratnesh Katulkar and Paul D' Souza 153

Status of Rural Migrant Workers in Ranchi City
Sweta 173

Politics of Saptial Governmentalities:
Migrants and their Right to the City
Teena Anil 186

Post Liberalization, Dalits and Large Scale Industry:
Experiences of Labour who migrated from
Coastal Odisha to Other Parts of India
Dhaneswar Bhoi and Neelima Rashmi Lakra 205

Graveyard of Inter-state Migrant Workers
on Gujarat's Alang Beach: An Inquiry into
How Migrant Workers Constitute a Community of Fate
    Gopal Krishna   224

Annexure
    Dr. George Pattery SJ   249

Contributors   252

Foreword

At the root of voluntary domestic migration, which we see abundantly in India today, there remains different manifestations of the same causal factor: relative income differentials. The most brutal manifestation of income inequalities occurs as economic compulsions on the supply side of labour markets in developing countries. People flee from poverty, misery, persecution, violence, and deprivation and move across space searching for a secure living and bare necessities of life. There could be other factors inducing migration: demography, decline in productivity and land-man ratios, and natural calamities, endemic to all transitional societies. The Indian sub-continent of the 19th century is replete with episodes of extensive deprivation that resulted in large scale migration of people to different parts of the world: South Africa, the Caribbean and South Pacific islands, South East Asia, Sri Lanka and Mauritius.

The drama keeps recurring to this day. There is a huge volume of internal migration, the pace and intensity of which has only increased in recent years. Workers from the heart-land states of India and the north-eastern region, most notably: Assam, Bihar, Chhattisgarh, Jharkhand, MP, Orissa, UP and Bengal move in large cohorts in search of employment and income-earning opportunities. The factors and forces that have influenced these migratory flows have been in the making for several decades, well before the era of economic liberalization that came towards the closing decade of the 20th century. The extensive migratory movements, currently on, are indicative of two major developments affecting the Indian economy. First, there is a break-through with demographic growth – potentially leading to a dividend in the long run – by way of containing mortality rates in the low-income states of the country. The early stages of such break-through would result in declining land-man ratios, compelling people to migrate. Second, opening up of a vast internal labour market provides employment to those who are disguisedly unemployed in the hinterland. The terms and conditions on which they find employment or take up residence in their host states are matters of abiding concern. The studies in this volume go at length to narrate the scale of intensity of deprivation faced by the migrant workers with special reference to a number of parameters: age, gender, skill content, linguistic and cultural roots, assets, social origins, wages, working conditions, housing; and they pointedly draw attention to their social, financial, cultural, political, and psychological vulnerabilities in different regions of India.

The studies in this volume serve a valuable purpose as they alert us to the urgent need for public interventions through agency of the state aimed to facilitate, supervise and regulate the functioning of markets and to ensure fairness and justice to all migrant workers. Such intervention involves a range of responsibilities. First, recognize and respect the rules laid down at national and inter-national levels to safeguard the human rights of migrants; second, confer the migrants with legal immunity, based on well-defined procedural rules, as they claim access to their legitimate rights and entitlements; and third, create the right institutional safeguards and engage in affirmative action so that all workers can be empowered to protect their interests. To this end, it is time to embark on a policy dialogue focused on the nature and content of state intentions that can be put in place to defend and safeguard the rights and entitlements of migrant workers. An informed policy discourse should be preceded by a conscious effort to understand and analyse the lives and times of migrant-workers. The studies organized by the Indian Social Institute take us towards building the knowledge base required for meaningful policy interventions.

AV Jose
November 2018

Introduction

Labour mobility has been an important fact of the social life of a country. Many people migrate to seek better employment opportunities within the country and abroad. During the post-liberalisation era, Census data suggests that there has been an increase in migration. In 1991, there were 230 million migrants constituting 27.4 per cent of the total population. In 2001, the number of migrants increased to 307.1 million constituting 32.9 per cent of the total population. In 2011, the volume of migrants increased further to 453.6 million constituting 37.5 per cent of the total population. Thus, Census data itself reveals that there is a significant increase in internal migration not only in the volume of migration but also in the proportion of migrants to the total population in India. About 10.2 percent of migrants (46.3 million) people have reported in Census 2011 that they have migrated in search of employment. While a few of these workers migrate to fulfil their aspirations for a better life, a large number of workers migrate due to rural and agrarian distress. Some of the migrants have been forced to migrate due to ethnic or religious conflicts, natural disasters or displacement on account of development projects. A significant proportion of migrants have moved to urban centers and metropolitan cities, which has resulted in the rise in the population living in urban areas from

25.7 per cent in 1991 to 31.1 per cent in 2011. These migrants live in miserable conditions in slums with hardly any basic civic amenities. Worse still, migrants are looked at with suspicion in spite of their significant contribution to the economy of the place of destination. They are always treated as 'outsiders' and the source of crime and social evils in the place. They are also kept out of the public social welfare benefits and other affirmative action by the State to ensure they do not settle in the place of destination. In spite of this plight of the inter-state labour migrants, their issues and concerns have not figured in either academic or policy discourse.

In order to highlight the issues of migrants in India, Indian Social Institutes in New Delhi and Bangalore organised a two day National Seminar on "Labour Migration in the Post Liberalisation Era" from 18-19 August, 2018. The Seminar attracted several academicians, research scholars and faculty from different colleges, institutes and Universities, who presented their papers at the Seminar. This book is an effort to gather the fruits of the Seminar by compiling all the articles written by the participants of the Seminar on the various issues related to labour migration in India.

The articles dwell on issues related to rural to urban migration, their vulnerabilities, the challenges they face in urban centres and the manner in which they negotiate their citizenship rights in urban space. The article titled "An Analysis of the Livelihood Determinants and Vulnerability of Seasonal Migration in Khohar Village, Rajasthan, India" by Aparna Radhakrishnan, Niti Saxena and Vrindaa Sharma is an empirical study of migration of farmers in a remote rural village in Rajasthan. Their empirical findings on a comparative study of migrating and non-migrating farmers reveal that lack of crop diversification, less livelihood options, uncertain climatic conditions, poor market linkages, depleting groundwater tables and exploitation by middlemen affects their livelihood and influences their migration decisions. The article titled "Graveyard of inter-state migrant workers on Gujarat's Alang beach: An inquiry into how migrant workers constitute a community of fate" by Gopal Krishna traces the journey of migrant workers from villages in Gorakhpur, Uttar Pradesh, to the ship-breaking yards of Alang beach, Bhavnagar, Gujarat. He argues that the global economy has marginalised workers so much that migrant workers continue to come to work in the graveyard of foreign ships undertaking dangerous and hazardous jobs, which ends up being their own graveyard. The plight of the migrant tea garden workers in West Bengal was the theme of the article by Saikat Roy titled "Income generation, Livelihood and Statelessness: An analysis of the current situation of tea garden workers of North Bengal, India". He points out that economic liberalisation and the transition to the market economy adversely affected the tea industry in North Bengal and the migrant workers who depend on it for their livelihood. Paul D'Souza analyses the reinforcement of caste-occupation relations among migrant sanitary workers and the process of their assimilation and marginalisation in the city of Ahmedabad in his article titled "The Making and Unmaking of Migrant Labourers of the Marginal Caste." He points out at the contradictory sociological trends of continued exclusion and progressive inclusion of the communities who belong to caste groups engaged in sanitation works in the larger urban society and its socio-economic geography. Ojasvi Goyal analyses the vulnerabilities of migrants in urban settings engaged in precarious employment in her article "Vulnerabilities of Inter-State Migrants in India: A Case Study of Waste Pickers and Manual Scavengers in Delhi." She argues that the vulnerabilities of migrant workers need to be taken into consideration in the formulation of policy and welfare measures for them. The article on "Migrant Workers in

Sanitation Work: Vulnerabilities of Inter-State Migrants in India"
by Ratnesh Katulkar and Paul D'Souza is based on a research
study on migrant workers belonging to communities engaged
in sanitation work in Madhya Pradesh and Chhattisgarh. The
study reveals that discriminatory policies of the State increases
the vulnerabilities of these migrant workers due to the denial
of their rights and public social welfare measures. Teena Anil
discusses the familiar reality of migrants trying to occupy urban
space officially and asserting their citizenship rights in resettlement
colonies in her article titled "Politics of Spatial Governmentalities:
Migrants and their Right to the City." Based on a research study
conducted in the resettlement colonies in Delhi, she argues that
though workers who migrate to cities are treated as 'outsiders'
and live on the margins of cities, they are part of the city and
belong to the city's socio-economic, political and physical space.
The various socio-economic issues faced by daily wage workers
in state offices in Guwahati is presented by Atlanta Talukdar and
Deepshikha Malakar in their article titled "Workers, Identity,
Policies and their Position in the Urban Space." They also analyse
the implementation of public policies for the welfare of these
workers in Assam. The article by Sukanya Kakoti and Raju Saikia
on "Negotiation in Urban spaces: Rural to Urban Migration of
Labour" not only analyses the impact of migration on the lives of
migrant workers in urban centres, but also discusses the various
negotiation processes they undergo with various state and non-
state institutions in order to survive in urban spaces. Richard
Gonsalves reflects on his personal experiences and his empirical
research on migrant domestic workers in his article "Cityscape
for Young Migrant Women: A Reflection on Intra Domestic
Workers in Bangalore." He argues that migrant women remain
in precarious employment, such as part time work, as they have
to juggle between the roles of homemaker and domestic maid.

Sweta's article on "Status of Rural Migrant Workers in Ranchi City" tries to capture the multi dimensional deprivations and vulnerabilities of migrants from rural areas of Jharkhand and neighboring States who flock to Ranchi in search of daily wage employment at various crossroads in the city. She also presents the dismal working and living conditions of these migrant workers in Ranchi. P.O. Martin and Smitha Philip focus on the influx of distress migrants from the North and North-East Indian States to the Southern Indian States in their article titled "Vulnerabilities of Distress Labour Migrants from North and North Eastern States in South India." They argue that these distress migrants are vulnerable to exploitation and face several challenges as they are treated as 'second class citizens' and are denied their labour rights as inter-state migrants and citizens of India. Notan Bhushan Kar argues that globalisation has had an adverse impact on the rural economy of West Bengal resulting in the migration of rural peasants to slums in urban areas. His research article titled "Impact of Globalization on Urban Slum Dwellers-Migrants From Rural Areas: A Social Case Study of Barasat Town, North 24-Parganas District, West Bengal" analyses the struggles of rural migrants in Barasat town in the midst of unfavorable conditions in view of mitigating the sufferings of migrant workers. Dhaneswar Bhoi and Neelima Lakra analyse the changes migrant workers have to undergo in their personal, social, cultural and educational life on account of migrating from rural Odisha to urban centres in India in their article "Post Liberalisation Land Encroachments by Largescale Industry: Evidences of Forced Labour Migration from the Dalits of Coastal Odisha." They argue that liberalisation has forced people leave their agrarian lifestyle in rural areas and live in congested cities prone to pollution and health hazards. The article on "Socio- Legal Dynamics of Migrant Workers in India" by Bhumika Sharma and Mamta Kashyap highlights the various legal provisions that are aimed to protect the rights of migrant workers. In particular, the article discusses the provisions of Inter-State Migrant Workmen (Regulations of Employment and Conditions of Service) Act, 1979, which is the primary legislation that regulates the rights of migrant workers in India.

It is hoped that these reflections of various dimensions and the complexities of the issues faced by migrant workers may trigger a greater debate among academicians so that the issues of labour migration enter the mainstream of academic discourse. It is also hoped that this attempt to highlight the problems of migrant workers may attract the attention of policy makers so that we may have more migrant-friendly policies and legislations governing the country.

Denzil Fernandes

Impact of Globalization on Urban Slum Dwellers-Migrants From Rural Areas: A Social Case Study of Barasat Town, North 24-Parganas District, West Bengal

Notan Bhusan Kar

Abstract

The alarming increase in the number of migrating workers from rural areas during the few decades has resulted in a rapid increase of population in the urban areas all over India. With the advent of globalization, liberalization and privatization during early nineties, there has been an increase in the job opportunities especially in the service sectors and informal sector. Moreover, the subsidies being withdrawn from the agriculture sector as per International Monetary Fund-World Bank imposition, has resulted in making traditional agriculture a non-profitable option. The acquisition of land for various developmental programmes has also resulted in landless, jobless peasants. Thus many marginal and poor peasants have been forced to migrate to urban areas for their livelihood and work as semi skilled and unskilled worker. They work at various service sectors and informal sectors and live in slums. Many spend their nights on pavements. With this crowding, there is an encroachment in various areas and an ever-increasing demand for water, electricity, health, education and other essential commodities.

This has resulted in many social evils like rise in anti-social activities, social unrest etc. This overcrowding has also disturbed the local natural environment. The slums having no proper sanitation have polluted the entire area resulting in many instances of health hazards. The local Govt. institutions like municipalities and corporations are unable to provide civic amenities at this juncture to these migrants. This paper mainly deals with the social study of such migrating urban slum dwellers and in analyzing their struggles against an undesirable environment and formulating strategies to improve their living standard.

What is Migration?

It is the movement of a person or a group of people from one place to another place. Migration can be temporal or permanent, and overall it may be voluntary or forced. As per his/her wish, one can move to settle in another place but forced migration exists when a person is moved against his/her will.

Types of Migration

There are two types of migration:

(a) Internal Migration: This refers to movement within national boundaries, such as between States, Provinces, Cities or Municipalities.

(b) International Migration: This refers to movement over national boundaries. An international migrant is someone who moves to a different country.

Migration pattern in India

There are four migration patterns in India:

(a) Rural - Rural: It is the movement of people from one rural area to other rural place in search of a better job. Generally, an agricultural labourer moves during the harvesting season.

(b) Rural – Urban: It is the movement of people from the countryside to the city. This happen due to urban growth attracting people for a better job.

(c) Urban – Urban: It is the movement of a person or group of people moving from one urban area to another urban area. Generally, specialized job seeker moves for these purposes.

(d) Urban – Rural: It is the opposite movement of rural-urban that people move from urban to rural areas for any kind of their purposes.

For example, Indian women after their marriage generally move with their husband's homeland.

Factors of Migration

(a) Push Factors: Push factors are those that force the individual to move voluntarily, and in many cases, they are forced because the individuals risk something if they stay. Push factors may include conflict, drought, famine, or forceful displacement. Poor economic activity and lack of job opportunities are also strong push factors for migration. Other strong push factors include discriminating cultures and political intolerance.

(b) Pull Factors: Pull factors are those factors that attract the individual or group to leave their home for better economic opportunities, more jobs, and the promise of a better life.

Causes of Migration

People migrate for many different reasons. These reasons can be classified as (a) economic (b) social (c) political and (d) environmental

(a) Economic migration: moving to find work or follow a particular career path.

(b) Social migration - moving somewhere for a better quality of life or to be closer to family or friends.

(c) Political migration - moving to escape due to political harassment or war.

(d) Environmental migration – Due to hazards of polluted environment, person or group of people move to other safe places.

Concept of Globalization

Some people feel that the concept of globalization is the free movement of trade, investment, services and exchange of culture world over. But according to some experts, globalization is integration of nation's economic system with the international market forces. Ironically, some others describe globalization as a strategy of the imperialist forces to loot the 'Third World' countries. In fact, globalization is the mobility of finance capital across the world, particularly of the poor countries. The unprecedented technological progress has enabled the easy flow of finance capital at the fastest speed to any country.

In the process of globalization, the three International Institutions namely, International Monetary Fund (IMF), World Bank (WB) and World Trade Organization (WTO) play a major role. These three organizations in a close collaboration function as the "Intelligence Agencies" on the economic policies of the underdeveloped countries. And lastly, some feel that Globalization stands for the ultimate rights of multinational companies to allocate resources according to their own criteria.

Globalization in India

Globalization, liberalization and privatization started in India during 1991 when the Govt. of India implemented the New

Economic Policy under the directives of IMF-WB alongwith their desired impositions. One such imposition was that the Govt. of India should gradually withdraw the subsidies from the agricultural sector. As a result, the cost of production in cultivation increased manifolds, making traditional farming an unprofitable option for the Indian farmers. On the other hand, land acquisitions in the name of various developmental projects rendered many peasants landless and jobless. According to NSSO (56th round) Report, 40 percent of the farmers have expressed their desire to quit farming. Thus many marginal and poor peasants have been forced to migrate to urban areas for their livelihood. According to the *National Crime Bureau* record, in the ten years period between 1998 and 2008 as many as *2 lakh* farmers committed suicide in India.

Urbanization in India

Urbanization is an indicator of economic development. Employment opportunities attract people to settle in urban areas. The Eleventh Five Year Plan of the Government of India notes that '....the contribution of the urban sector to India's GDP has increased from 29 percent in 1950-51 to 47 percent in 1980-81. The urban sector presently contributes about 62 - 63 percent of the GDP and this is expected to increase to 75 percent by 2021'. The trend of urbanization in India in recent decades is attributed to the economic reforms initiated in the year 1991. India's total population increased about 3 times between 1951 and 2011, but the urban population rose about 4.6 times during the same period. As per the Census of 2011, India's urban population was 40 crores comprising 33 per cent of the total population of 120 crores. The Census of India classified as many as 5661 towns in 2011, which was 572 more than 1991 Census. Out of the total

5661 towns, 3800 are *statutory towns* which means, the towns having municipality, corporation or cantonment board etc., and 1361 are *census towns* which means a town having a minimum population of 5000 with a population density of 400 persons per sq. km., atleast 75 percent of males which are the working population engaged in non-agricultural pursuits.

This rapid increase in urban population has led to a tremendous pressure on civic amenity system like water supply, drainage, solid waste management, transport etc. In many cities, the problems of the traffic congestion, pollution, poverty, social unrest are assuming alarming proportions.

Migration in India

As a consequence of the neo-liberal policies followed by the successive Governments, although there has been serious income disparities and agrarian distress, there has been a vast growth of informal economy which has resulted in rapid migration from rural to urban areas. According to estimates, internal migrants in India are above 450 million; inter-state migrants are above 45 million; seasonal migrants are between 10 t0 30 million adults every year; and circular migrants are above 100 million. The Economic Survey of India (2016-17) estimates annual labour mobility in India to be 5-9 million and inter-state migrant population to be around 60 million. Further, there are 5-6 million Indians migrating from state-to-state each year and 4.5 per cent is the annual growth of inter-state migration. These migrating people work as semi skilled and unskilled worker. Mostly, they work as contractual labour at various service sectors and informal sectors and live in slums. It is to be noted that both the 2011 Census and the National Sample Survey of 2012 estimated that every seventh person in urban India was a slum dweller. According to 2011 census, 42.6

million populations live in slums. This constitutes 15 percent of the total urban population of the country.

Keeping in view the above features a social case study was done in Barasat Town on slums dwellers who migrated from rural areas for their livelihood. The objectives of the study were:

1. Causes of migration and effects of economic globalization on them.

2. The type of works they are engaged in & condition of living and source of livelihood.

3. To suggest a few strategies for their development.

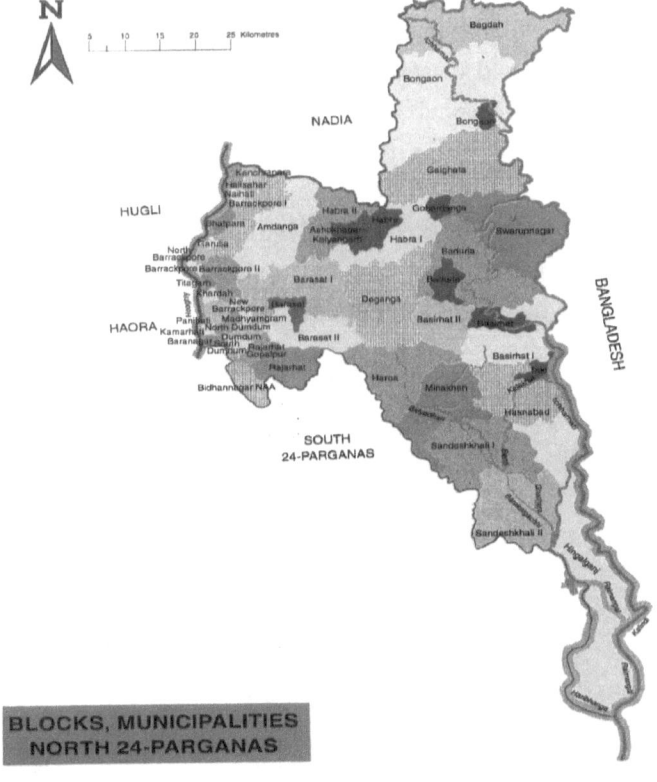

BLOCKS, MUNICIPALITIES
NORTH 24-PARGANAS

Barasat Town : An Overview

Barasat town is located at a distance of about 25 km from Kolkata. The latitude and longitude of Barasat town area is 88.482962 and 22.707002. Barasat is a municipal town established in the year 1869 and now is the district headquarters of North 24-Parganas in West Bengal. Its area is 34.05 sq. km. and has a total population of 2.32 lakh as per census 2011. Males constitute 52 percent of the total population and females 48 percent. The literacy rate is 85.6 percent, it has 159 slums and out of the total population of 55,168, 23.77 percent are living in the slums. The total area of slums is 4.78 sq. km. and the number of families living in slums is 12,957. All the wards in Barasat have slum dwellers. The town is mainly a commercial place with many Govt. establishments and a session judge court with many schools, colleges and a State University. Rapid urbanization of Barasat is due to the demographic explosion and poverty-induced rural-urban migration. The migration is directly or indirectly linked with the effects of globalization. The town which originally had 18 municipal wards in 1991 has now been divided into 32 municipal wards owing to the rapid increase of population. A general information of Barasat Municipality has been shown in table no. I.

Table-I

Barasat Municipality Established in	1869	No. of Wards	32
Population	231521 (Census-2011)	Population of Male	1.18 lakh
Population of Female	1.13 lakh	Minority Population	25875
SC Population	32855	ST Population	1555
No. of Holdings	81880	Electricity coverage	95 percent
Total of Slums	**159**	**Total Population of Slum**	**55168**
Total area of Slums	**4.78 sq. km.**	**No. of Family in Slums**	**12957**

Source : Barasat Municipality

Causes of Migration

Since 1991 when globalization started in India, its adverse impacts affected rural Bengal as it did the other States. According to the data of Govt. of West Bengal in 1990s the food grains production was 5.84 per cent but in 1996-97 this decreased to a mere average of 2.39 per cent. During this period, the cost of production increased due to an increase in the prices of harvesting materials. The increase in prices of irrigation was 147.7 percent and fertilizer was 78.36 percent. The prices of various other harvesting items too increased, resulting in the decline of the production of the food grains. The increase in the cost of production in the agricultural sector forced many farmers to give up their occupation of agriculture as they could not cope up with the ever-increasing prices. They were left with no other alternatives but to look for some other means of livelihood for their survival. In West Bengal too, though land reforms had been implemented, a large number of poor and marginal peasants have been forced to opt for other means of livelihood instead of agriculture. All these people thus moved to urban areas looking for odd jobs for surviving. Most of them are unskilled or semi skilled and whatever jobs they get in urban areas force them to live in slums.

The slum dwellers of Barasat town are mostly migrants from its surrounding rural areas because of the above mentioned reasons. Most of them were poor, marginal peasants and landless agricultural workers when they lived in the villages. The harvesting expenses increased year after year. Most of them fell into debt trap. Some of the poor and marginal peasants committed suicides due to huge debt. The field survey report of *Berachampa village* in North 24-Parganas as given in Table-II clearly shows how the increase in production cost affects the income of a peasant.

The real agricultural Land distribution scenario in rural Bengal

Distribution of vested land

Congress Government (up to '67 election)	3.76 lakh acres
United front government (9 months + 13 months)	2.50 lakh acres
In '77 to 2006	4.26 lakh acres
Total	10.52 lakh acres

Source : Ajit Narayan Narayan Basu, Paschimbanger Krishi Niti, page-64

The total cultivation land of West Bengal is 54.72 lakh hectares. It should be noted, only 10.52 lakh acres which is 7.5% of the total agricultural land in West Bengal. The Left Front Government distributed vested land only 4.26 lakh acres, much less than the previously distributed 6.26 (3.76 + 2.50) lakh acres of land.

And 14.95 lakh of share croppers have been recorded and 11.06 lakh of the land was conferred to them, which is 7.9% of total agricultural land. So, vest land distributed 7.5% + land allotted for operation *barga* 7.9%= only 15.4% of total agricultural land have been distributed in West Bengal. Here 130 lakh agricultural workers in the state out of them 74 lakh agricultural workers are completely landless. In West Bengal the poor peasants' families comprising 55.4% owned only 3.9% land. (*Source : Ajit Narayan Narayan Basu, Paschimbanger Krishi Niti*) A Recent study sponsored by the *State Institute of Panchyats and Rural Development*, found that, on average, 13 per cent of the *pattadars* who received land had lost it and around 14 per cent *bargadars* have been evicted from their *barga* land by 2001.

Table-II
Harvesting Expenses of Aman* Paddy per bigha
(Base Year=2011)

Sl. No.	Harvesting Expenses		Amount (Rs.)
1	Tractor Expenses	@ Rs.150/- per hour × 2=30 hrs.	375=00
2	Agricultural Labour expenses : (a) Resizing field (b) Paddy Plant (roya) (c) Weeding	@ Rs.60/- × 1= @ Rs.60/- × 6= @ Rs.60/- × 2=	60=00 360=00 120=00
3	Seeds cost	@ Rs.200 per bigha	200=00
4	Paddy Cutting, Bundles etc.	@ Rs.60/- × 3=	180=00
5	Carrying charges from field	@ Rs.60/- × 3=	180=00
6	Jharai	@ Rs.60/- × 3=	180=00
7	Fertilizers Charges	@ Rs.10/-x 20 bags	200=00
8	Pesticides Spray	@ Rs. 150/- per lit.	150=00
Total Expenses :			2005=00

Source : Field Survey in Berachampa village of North 24-Pgs.

Approx. 10 jute bags rice are obtained from 1 *bigha* of land (1 bag contains of 60 kg. of rice). These bags have been sold in the open market of this village at an average rate of Rs.600/- per bag. Thus the total earning of a peasant amounted to Rs.600/- x 10= Rs.6000/-. And their expenses amounted to Rs.2005/- or say Rs.2000/-. The net income of a peasant is (Rs.6000-2000)=Rs.4000/- per bigha (1 acre=3.25 bigha). If a poor peasant has 3 bighas of cultivation land, he can earn hardly Rs.4000/- x 3= Rs.12000/- in a year through Aman cultivation and including the other earning from cultivation of aus, vegetables, etc., one can earn around Rs.4000/- per annum. The total income is Rs.12,000+Rs.4,000/-=Total Rs.16,000/-. The monthly average income of a marginal peasant owning 3 *bighas* of land is estimated at Rs.1,334/- only. If a marginal peasant has 1(one) *bigha* of land, then his average monthly income is Rs.445/-. All these negative syndrome forces poverty-induced migration of rural poor peasants to urban informal sectors.

(*Three crops of paddy are grown in West Bengal *aman, aus* and *boro*. Aman is the main paddy crop. Aman and aus are both *kharif* crops and *boro* is a crop harvested in the summer. Kharif crops are sown in the monsoon).

The table no.-III shows the increase of slums & slum dwellers between 1991 and 2011 in Barasat Town.

Table-III

Increase of slums & slum dwellers in Barasat Town

Year	Slums	Slums dwellers
1991	45(28.31%)	10,147(18.39%)
2011	114(71.69%)	45,021(81.61%)
Total :	159(100%)	55,168(100%)

Source: Field Survey and Barasat Municipality

It is clear from the above table that the numbers of slums and slum dwellers have increased in Barasat town after the implementation of the New Economic Policy in India during 1991. Slums increased from 28.31 percent to 71.69 percent and the increase in slum dwellers was from 18.39 percent to 81.61 percent between 1991 and 2011.

The percentage of slum children (6-12 years), primary literacy rate of boys and girls in the slum of Barasat town is shown in the table-IV given below:

Table-IV

Percentage of slum children (Primary) (6-12) to slum population	Percentage of Literacy Rate (Boys)	Percentage Female Literacy (Girls)
11.77	76.53	70.39

Source: Provisional Population Totals, Series-20,
HDR-North 24-Pgs., West Bengal

It is observed from the above table that both boys and girls primary literacy rate is high and one reason may be behind it is the midday meal scheme of the govt. provided in the schools.

Occupational Structure & Living Condition

Globalization, liberalization and privatization though apparently seem to have aided the generation of employment scope in India, but in reality it has acted as a negative factor. Under globalization, survival and existence of the poor are affected adversely. Liberalization which permits cheap import of goods directly or indirectly affects agriculture, handicraft and cottage industries. The rural economy is thus adversely affected and so the poor rural people have to face the consequences. The benefits of liberalization generally accrue to only those who acquire new skills. It is unlikely that common man and the poor will benefit from liberalization. Privatization causes retrenchment of workers. Most of these cities using capital intensive technologies cannot generate employment for these distressed rural poor. So there is a transfer of rural poverty to urban poverty. Poverty-induced migration of illiterate and unskilled labourer occurs in cities and towns in India.

Barasat town is no exception, it is also facing the same problem of migration as the other cities and towns in India. Most of the rural migrating poor people live in slums. Usually the slum dwellers are mostly involved in labour-based work in the informal sectors. Very few are engaged in the organized sector as they do not possess any formal training to procure decent jobs.

Table-V

Occupations of slum dwellers in Barasat town

Various Occupation	(In Percent)
House maid, night guards etc.	12%
Daily Labourer	55%
Petty Businessmen	5%
Rickshaw puller & Driver	20%
Vendors	8%

Source : Field Survey

From the above table, it is found that the majority of the workers among slum people are engaged as daily labourers (55 percent), followed by rickshaw pullers and drivers (20 percent). Among the slum community, 12 percent are engaged in different types of services. Most slum women are engaged as house maids, males are engaged as nights guards, security guards etc. 8 percent are engaged as vendors like vegetable sellers, train hawkers etc. This shows that the trend of employment from different sources is mainly based on hard physical working capabilities. Here in particular, most of the rickshaw pullers stay in *jhuggies*, owner's workshops or below staircases, on footpaths, under hanging balconies on the roadside, in the rickshaws or even in open space. The stressful life with no rest day coupled with unhygienic living conditions and limited food results in poor health of most workers. Diseases like tuberculosis, asthma, hernia, weak eyesight and underweight are common. They have no medical insurance or access to health care facilities. Many families whose kids used to go to school earlier have been forced to drop out simply because they have no affordable income. Most of the Barasat slum houses are very small and are usually made of mud and bamboos. Some are also made of *Tin* in different wards. The environment of the slums is very congesting and unhygienic. The inhabitants suffer from inadequate service of civic amenities. As they need to cook in order to feed themselves and their families, they have to cook in the same room where they live using either coal, cow dung, kerosene or wood as fuel which further pollutes the environment resulting in various health hazards. Another vulnerable aspect of the slums is the women trafficking and smuggling of goods. The highly porous West Bengal-Bangladesh border is used for smuggling goods. In some of the areas the trafficking is done by utilizing women and even the minors are inducted in this profession. As per police record in 2009, 8 cases of anti-human trafficking were registered. The number of victims that were rescued was 6 and 5 traffickers arrested in the police raids.

Social Impact on Migrant Families

The following adverse social impact has been observed by field survey in the slums of Barasat Town:

1. *Decline in Joint Family System:* Due to migration the joint family converted to nuclear families. This is a general feature noticed in most of the slums.

2. *Landlessness:* Rural Bengal, being a farm dominated society with agriculture as the main occupation, migrants from rural to urban slums, are obviously detached from land.

3. *Joblessness and increase in the proportion of workers:* When people are displaced from their habitat, they lose their means of livelihood. Creation of new jobs or alternative sources of income for them becomes very difficult since the migrants do not possess any skill to learn new methods of earning their livelihood. Hence those who were owners of the means of

production before migration have now become daily wage earners.

4. ***Homelessness:*** Loss of house and shelter remains a permanent feature for most of the migrant families.

5. ***Food insecurity:*** Migration increases the risk of chronic food insecurity. Migration deprives the ousters from their former resource of livelihood rendering them landless. As a result, the displaced families have to buy everything including food items from the market.

6. ***Loss of access to common property:*** For the oustees, particularly, the landless and poor people, loss of access to common property (common properties, water bodies, grazing land, etc.) leads to a major deterioration in their income and livelihood levels. As a result, the resettlers do not get fuel wood and other minor forest produce, which they used to collect from their rural old habitat.

7. ***Social Disintegration:*** Migration has dismantled production systems, kinship groups and family systems are often scattered and cultural identity of the people is under threat. Social and community networks that help people to cope with poverty through exchange of food and clothing, mutual help with farming, building houses and caring children are disrupted.

8. ***Increased Morbidity and Mortality:*** Loss of ancestral and homestead land, less access to health care facilities, the psychological trauma caused thereby and the food insecurity together often leads to serious diseases. In fact, lack of food, safe drinking water, unhygienic living and environmental degradation has a serious impact on the health of the migrant families.

The following data also shows the conditions of migrants in Barasat Town:

- 65% of the migrants from rural to slums of Barasat Town living in poverty conditions, resulting in a high incidence of communicable and non-communicable diseases.

- Over 35% of the slum households do not have access to electricity.

- About 55% of the households do not have an accessible source of safe drinking water.

- Almost 35% of the migrant families do not have access to a sanitation facility.

- Average Monthly Consumption Expenditure of the displaced families (average 4 persons) is Rupees 2000/- only.

(Source: Field Survey)

Other Urban Impact on migrants

The brunt of urbanization has been felt by these poor migrants in Barasat town also. For the extension of Metro Rail, eviction notice has been served to those people living slums in beside the railway tracks. No adequate compensations or alternate arrangement for their rehabilitation has been offered to them. The large numbers of constructions of Malls, Restaurants, and Shopping Complexes etc., have been welcomed by the richer section but the poor people are unable to cope up with this culture. Thus the void between the richer section and poorer section has widened. This division has given rise to many socio-economic problems. The slum dwellers and rural migrants being the poorest are facing a great crisis where their very existence is at stake.

Conclusion

It can be concluded that the New Economic policy which is associated with Globalization is mainly responsible for poverty, migration, peasants' distress etc. In India there are two types of Indians: 10 percent is the elite group of the total population, while 90 percent live an existence of utmost poverty. The report of *National Commission for Enterprises in the Unorganised Sector* says, 77 percent of Indian population live on rupees 20/- or less per day. The withdrawal of food subsidies, drastic reduction in the benefits of the Public Distribution System, rise in prices of essential commodities, taxes on common people, concessions given to big business houses, etc. are a few examples of the attack of globalization on the common people in India. So it should be the prime task of common people to intensify the struggles against globalization and pressurize Govts. to withdraw the conditions imposed by IMF-WB.

Both Central and State Governments have launched several programmes such as Urban Basic Services for the Poor (UBSP), Comprehensive Slum Improvement Programmes (SCIP), National Slum Development Programme (NSDP) and Basic Minimum Services (BMS) with a view to alleviate urban poverty including environmental improvement of the slums and socio-economic development of the poor in recent years. But it is not sufficient. Govt. should take initiative at the local level with intensive methods to sort out the problems and take various measures for the implementation of plans and prgrammes to solve it. Employment opportunities should be generated for the slum people. Civic amenities should be improved so that it can be provided to all the urban people including the slums dwellers. Integration of rural and urban economy can be achieved by emphasizing agro-based industries where the raw material would be processed in rural economy and then transferred to urban economy through industries. Urban planning and housing with human face should be implemented for slum people. *Land Reform Programmes* should be continued by the Govt. taking all the necessary steps for helping the peasants in order to minimize rural migration. A careful and proper planning is needed for urban development.

References

1. *Economic Survey,* Govt. of West Bengal, 1991-92 & 1999-2000.

2. Website of North 24-Parganas.

3. *Economic and political weekly*, April, 28, 2012.

4. *Economic Survey,* Govt. of India, 2011-12.

5. *Urban Development*, fifth five year plan (2007-12) Planning Commission, Govt. of India.

6. *IASSI Quarterly Journal*, January-March-2008.

7. Bhattachariya, Bela; *Calcutta Slums: A Study of slum dwellers*, Classical Indica, Calcutta(1989).

8. Bureau of Applied Economics & Statics, Govt. of West Bengal, 2003-04.

9. Various newspapers published in Bengal.

10. Barasat Municipality-various Bulletins and Website.

Workers, Identity, Policies and their Position in the Urban Space

Atlanta Talukdar and Deepshikha Malakar

Abstract

With the Independence of India, industrialisation, globalisation, and urbanisation took place across the country. This change brought in changes in every aspect. Industries and various organisations (both international based as well as national) were set up in all parts of the nation. This led to the demand for man power and it increased along with time as the production level increased. This led to inter-state as well as the intra-state migration of people from rural to urban and to town to cities for better jobs, better livelihood and for their better future. But the works were divided according to educational qualifications, technical skills and in many cases, on caste based division. These factors created some problems for the workers because the majority of the workers were from the rural areas with less experience or technical skills. Many workers were less qualified because they couldn't afford to receive higher education. All these factors have created a hierarchy and class divisions among the workers and stagnation has been build up. The high class workers were benefitted from all whereas the lower workers were being exploited and were deprived of their needs. This paper would try to understand the various socio-economic issues and problems faced by the daily wage workers in the state offices in Guwahati, Assam. This paper also seeks to   understand the present identity of the workers in the workplace as well as in the society and their position in the present urban space; also whether the policies put forward by the government of India for the safeguard of the workers in their work place are being followed.   Finally, this paper also tries to understand the means of livelihood amongst the workers.

INTRODUCTION

With the advent of Independence of India, industrialisation, globalisation and urbanisation took place across the country. This change brought in changes in every aspect. Industries and various organisations (both international based as well as national) were set up in all parts of the nation. This led to the demand for man power and it increased along with time as the production level increased. This led to inter-state as well as the intra-state migration of people from rural to urban and to town to cities for better jobs, better livelihood and for their better future. Migrants continually face difficulties in becoming a full part of the economic, social, cultural and political lives of society. They are often treated as second-class citizens facing numerous constraints including inadequate housing and a lack of formal residency rights, low pay, insecure and hazardous work, limited access to state-provided services such as health and education, discrimination based on ethnicity, religion, class/gender (UNESCO/UNICEF, 2012).

The migrants live a life of deprivation, dislocation and therefore disentitled and disenfranchised. They are perhaps the most faceless, voiceless and invisible group in a city's populace (Jha & Pushpendra, 2016).

The North-East Indian state of Assam has also experienced migration from different states, mainly to the sprawling city beside the mighty river Brahmaputra. When the British came to Assam, Guwahati was not a healthy centre of the State. In 1808, Hamilton and Mc. Koch said about Guwahati as a very underprivileged and the unhealthiest station in Assam (Barpujari, 1992). In 1836, a town improvement committee was established in Guwahati by the British and from this period onwards the growth of modern Guwahati started.

Guwahati experienced a massive population increase in 1971-81 and 1981-91, as a large number of people migrated into the city. The migration was social and economic in nature. People who were facing extreme poverty and hardship came to Guwahati for survival from various parts of Assam for employment opportunities and a better life. There was also a flow of people from other states to earn livelihood in different economic activities. There has been migration from Bihar, Andhra Pradesh and Punjab since the colonial period (Desai et.al. 2014). As the town became the administrative headquarters, it grew in size and aroused a need to build and maintain a sanitation system to safely dispose of sewage and garbage. The local community/caste unaccustomed to doing such work and their reluctance made colonial authorities bring people or safai Karmachari who belong to Dalit communities from other states of India to do such works. Without proper sanitary facilities and equipment, it was required of safai Karmachari to essentially work as manual scavengers. The very nature of their work created a certain stigma and compelled them to live in isolation in small colonies with very poor facilities often called Dalit colonies. They worked as daily wage workers and got very less remuneration which is not at all sufficient to have a healthy livelihood. With the increase in population in these colonies by internal growth and in migration, the condition within these confined areas deteriorated. Government's housing provision and other facilities made some improvement in these areas, but still its environment remains unhealthy and highly congested.

Humans are entities whose identities depend essentially on the various relations in which they stand in the real world (Wilde, 1988). Migrants are productive residents who labour for their survival – they are the 'city makers' who play a critical role in sustaining the city (IGSSS, 2012). Rather than being recognised for their contribution to the city, the homeless migrants are being treated as the 'other', the 'outcast', the 'unclean'. Dalits, who play a major role in cleanliness of the city Guwahati, are the most underprivileged, unsafe and discriminated.

OBJECTIVE

1. To study the socio-economic issues and problems faced by the Dalits.

2. To understand their identity in the workplace as well as in the society and their place in the present urban space.

METHODOLOGY

The study has used qualitative research method in order to get the insight and perspectives of the study. This methodology as used as it was useful in providing the meaning, experiences, attitudes and perspectives of the research.

Tools of Data Collection

In conducting this research, the area of investigation and the research objectives determine the method that the researcher follows. The research method consists of how the researchers collect; analyses and interprets the data in the study. Both primary and secondary would be collected for the research.

For the primary data:

• In-depth interviews (a technique designed to bring out a detailed picture of the participant's perspective on the research topic.) With participants were conducted by posing questions in a neutral manner, listening attentively to participants' responses, and asking follow-up questions and probes based on those responses. In-depth interviews are usually conducted face-to-face and involve one interviewer and one participant.

• Focus group discussion was also used to explore the participant' perception and opinions about their place in the urban setting and knowledge about the various policies.

Secondary data was collected from books, journals, government websites and government published reports and newspapers.

Sampling and Study area

Purposive sampling which is a non-probability form of sampling was used to collect the data. The goal of purposive sampling is to sample cases/participants in a strategic way, so that those sampled are relevant to the research questions that are being posed (Bryman, 2008).

The study area for the research was Guwahati. Sample size was 30. The subject chosen for survey concerns the life and identity of Dalits and their place in urban setting, which has been subjected to social persecution,   iniquitous oppression and ruthless dissemination.

DATA ANALYSIS

The first Dalit colony as per records in Guwahati Municipal Corporation was located in the M. C. Road, where at present Kamrup Academy School and the Chenikuthi Middle English School are situated. But as the adjoining areas developed into a neighbourhood of the affluent and powerful, the colony was relocated in the Morashali area near Nehru Stadium. Then, it was an isolated place where garbage and raw sewage was dumped and occasionally served as a cremation ground. Later, the government's housing provision and other facilities made improvement substantially in the area, but still, it is definitely perceived as a slum with an unhealthy environment and highly congested.

In the 1970s, a number of the families moved to a new colony that was established in the Fatasil Ambari area of the city. Over time, several such areas have sprouted across the city sheltering people engaged in institutions and organisations like the railways, university, hospitals, and Govt. offices etc., employed as *Safai Karmachari*. But they have faced the same situation. Their condition has not uplifted. The workers are mainly the Dalit people working as the daily wage workers in the government offices. This group of people comes under SC category but they have not benefited from the facilities provided by the government. The economic condition is very poor. There is a Government Lower Primary school within the area and many private schools and colleges are located in nearby areas.

There is no government housing complex. Most of the houses are Assam Type *pucca* houses, whereas some *kuccha* houses are also found in the area. People constructed the houses in a very congested manner and most of them have 2-3 rented houses. The sources of water include public water supply tap, well etc. some people also collect water from broken water supply pipelines. Electricity is available in all the households, though many of them are unauthorised. Sanitation facility is not hygienic in the area. Only some household have their individual toilet facility. Most of them use common toilets between 4 to 6 household, but no proper septic tank system is available. Sewage and solid waste system of the area are very poor.

From the present study, an annual income of a household has been estimated by calculating the total income of all the members of a household.

Table No. 1: Annual Income (Source: Fieldwork)

Sl. No.	Total Annual Income	No. of Families
1	5000-10000	14
2	10001-20000	14
3	20001-30000	2
4	30001-40000	0
5	40001-50000	0
6	50001-above	0

From the table above, it is clear that the income of the workers is very low. With this low wage, it becomes difficult for the workers to maintain their livelihood. They take up loans from their friends or from informal institutions known as *Sansay Samittee*. The women also work as sweepers, daily wage workers in the offices to support the family. Regarding the nature of employment of the employed population, the majority are engaged as wage workers. It is followed by an engagement in household activities, which is found among the female members only. Some people are engaged in sweeping/ cleaning. In part time domestic work, most of the females are engaged, some are engaged as shopkeepers/ vendors, others are engaged in private jobs, as drivers, plumbers and some engaged as barbers.

The family of each worker consists of 5-6 members. As their economic condition is not well, they do not get many opportunities in regards to education; they do not get access to better health facilities and so on and so forth. The educational level is very low. Hardly a few have attained a bachelor's degree. A majority of the workers are only high school pass.

Having migrated to the urban space, the workers thought that they would get a better life style and better job opportunities but stagnated in the same position with no identity of their own. Their living condition is very poor. They live in semi-*pucca* houses with bare minimum facilities for sustenance.

CONCLUSION

The Dalits are being separated and are being discriminated in various dimensions such as demography, gender, levels and patterns of urbanisation, occupational patterns, ownership of land, rural labour, employment and unemployment rates, employment under reservation in the public sector, incidence of poverty, literacy and education, health status and access to the health care facilities, access to civil amenities and the status of civil rights, their engagement in government or civil society. The issues of poverty, social exclusion, and marginalisation of Dalit's one to be given importance in solving them.

This Community being a Scheduled Caste has received only a few benefits like scholarships but irregularly, and the amount they receive is very less. The Government also provides rice and other basic needs at subsidized rates to the Below Poverty Line list but it is not sufficient for them. The Dalit community faced a lot of problems and are still facing the same present. They do not have any kind of social, political, educational or economic security. They face a problem of double burden in the society. Dalit movements were carried out demanding equal status in the society with equal rights as others. It was only after Independence when Dr. B. R. Ambedkar drafted the Indian Constitution, that included the Dalits under the Scheduled Caste, they got a new identity and a new status. The reservation system was introduced for the minority groups like the Scheduled Tribes (Hill), Scheduled Tribes (Plains); Scheduled Castes; they were made available for the upliftment of the discriminated groups. Various policies, schemes, scholarships are being introduced in favour of them. But if we see at the grass roots, many groups like the Dalits have not benefited from these facilities. Due to the discrimination faced by them, they do not get proper jobs in societies. They are left with the jobs that are not done by the others and their income is too low to support their family.

Thus it can be seen that though they have migrated from their native places to other parts of the country for better livelihood and status option and for the better economic condition they are still suffering in daily existence. Though the income has risen, it is not up to the level for their sustenance. They are still deprived of the governmental policies. There has been very little change in the three parameters of their socio-economic condition and as a result, the community faces problems in the life style and the upcoming generation is not in a better position and their status in the society is not uplifted.

REFERENCES

Barpujari, H.K. (1992). *"The Comprehensive History of Assam Vol.II Medieval Period: Political from Thirteenth Century A.D. to the Treaty of Yandabo"* 1826. *Publication Board Assam.*

Bhagat, R.B. (2017). "Migration and Urban Transition in India: Implications for Development". *International Institute for Population Sciences.*

http://www.researchgate.net/publication/319619776

Desai, R., Mahadevia, D., Mishra, A. (2014). 'City Profile: Guwahati'. Working Paper, Centre for Urban Equity(CUE).

Gait, E.A. (1906). *A History of Assam.* Thacker, Spink & Company.

Jha, M.K., Kumar, P. (2016). "Homeless Migrants in Mumbai: Life and Labour in Urban Space," *Economic & Political Weekly, Vol.51(26-27):69-77.*

UNESCO/UN (2012). *Social Inclusion of Internal Migrants* in India. New Delhi.

http://www.census2011.co.in/census/city/191-guwahati.html

Negotiation in Urban spaces: Rural to Urban Migration of Labour

Sukanya Kakoti and Raju Saikia

ABSTRACT

Migration is not a new phenomenon in the history of humankind, people migrate for various reasons over a period of time. It is seen that urge for money or better livelihood is one of the key factors in the mechanism of migration from times immemorial. This paper focuses on the migration of the unskilled laborers from the rural areas to the urban areas in India. Urban spaces are always considered as one of the ultimate destinations for the unskilled labor force for better livelihood. The paper will explore the various problems faced by the migrant workers in the urban spaces and how they negotiate with those problems. It will also look into what are the changes that they have to encounter when they migrate to the urban areas. The paper will consider the unskilled labors in the informal sector. The paper will also analyze the effect of the migration on the lifestyle of the migrant laborers in the urban spaces. In the paper, using material from published sources on the subject and analyzing available secondary resources, an attempt has been made to outline the negotiation process from the part of migrant laborers as well as from the part of urban spaces in the modern times.

KEYWORDS- Labour migration, Rural to Urban migration, Urban Space, Livelihood.

Introduction

Migration is a continuous process, people are migrating from one place to another and migration has shown an unbroken upward trend in the recent decades. Migration is a global phenomenon which includes both external and internal migration. It is estimated that there are around 244 million international migrants and 763 million internal migrants across the world.[1] From times immemorial, human beings were continuously migrating. Movement of people has been happening on an everyday basis. Migration is moving from one politically well-defined area to another. In the process of migration, one generally leaves behind their familiar environment and enters an unfamiliar world. Several factors like culture, ethnic boundary and structural restriction become a hindrance to the mobility of the people. At the same time, mobility may also bring enhanced opportunities in many forms (Banerjee, 2011). Migration is also one of the factors for the demographic changes across the world. The term in-migration and out-migration are used to denote the migration within the country. Similarly, the term immigration and emigration are used to refer to moves between countries (C.Das & Saha, 2012). Migration within the country and across the intranational border has an impact upon the native and the host places. Both the places have to face their own part of a negotiation with the upcoming change.

In the contemporary time and in the era of globalization, the pace of urbanization is increasing paving the way for migrant workers for their livelihood. It is observed that urban areas are usually regarded as the ideal place for the large span of the workforce. And this phenomenon is not specific to a particular country or region, it is similar in almost all the counties. The kind of migration vary from country to country, the motive and purpose of migration in developing and developed countries are different but urban spaces always remain the ideal. In this era, the process of migration is also one of the agents of demographic change. Migration is an agent of population change as well as it distributes the population over space. Though migration brings change it is not an invasive process rather it is participatory in nature (Hall, 2015). Migrant workers add to the existing work force in the urban space. The unskilled laborers constitute the large span of migrants to the urban areas. Those who are unskilled among them are mainly engaged in the informal sector to earn their living. The ultimate aim of the migrants is to earn money in the urban areas and support their family. It is a common phenomenon that urban areas require many people in their informal sector. Though the informal sector does not contribute much to the larger economic growth of the country in urban areas, they occupy a very special place. The informal sector is a very important part of urban areas, this sector has a huge contribution toward the people of urban areas.

Understanding Migration and Rural to Urban Migration

Migration can be categorized in various ways. Some of the categories of migration are based on political boundaries.[2] Migration based on political boundaries are further classified into internal and international migration. Internal migration is the migration occurring within a country from crossing political boundaries, either within a state or between states, whether urban to rural, urban to urban, rural to rural, or rural to urban. International migration is the migration occurring across country boundaries. Others are based on movement patterns,[3] which further includes step migration, circular migration, and chain migration. Step migration means migration initiating from a small settlement and moving to a larger one in the urban hierarchy over the years. This includes a pattern of closer, not too destabilizing migrations from a person's place of origin to an ensuing destination. Cyclical migration experiences between an origin and a destination with at least one migration and return. Chain migration is the migration of families at different stages of the life cycle from one location to the next, who subsequently bring people from their home location to this new place. In the chain migration, a chain of people constantly moves from place to place, supported by those who migrated before them.

Lastly based on decision-making approach,[4] these approaches include voluntary migration, involuntary migration, reluctant migration and forced migration. Voluntary migration is based on a person's free will, initiative and desire to live in a better place and to improve their financial status, among other factors. Involuntary migration is based on a person being forced out of their home due to certain unfavorable environmental and political situations. Reluctant migration is when a person is put in a situation that encourages relocation or movement outside their place of residence. Forced migration is when a person is unable to return home (refugee) or undergoes a legal procedure to qualify as a refugee in the host country (asylee) or is forced to leave their home due to a conflict or development but does not cross any boundaries (internally displaced person [IDP]) (Migration and Its Impact, 2017).

In the context of this paper, the rural to urban migration is taken into consideration. Within the internal migration of labor, rural to urban migration holds a very important place. In the migration studies, migration is to an extent is related to the development process. The regional disparity in development can be considered as one of the reasons of rural to urban migration of unskilled labor. The unequal distribution of resources and lack of opportunities plays the basic role in the migration of labor from rural to urban areas. Most of the migrant workers from rural areas consider migration as a survival strategy which extremely affects their life and their family behind them. They face a kind of transformation in the process of migration which is very new to them and it affects everyone related to them (Ajaero & Onokala, 2013). The process of migration was existent in every time period and also in every region of the world. The main aim of migration was for a favourable condition for livelihood. With the coming of industrial age, the pattern of migration started evolving. People started migrating to the industrial areas from the remote areas in search of jobs. Cities and towns act as an attraction for the laborers in the rural areas. Factors such as low income, poverty, low unemployment opportunities, lack of education, and health facilities act as the push factor for them to migrate to urban areas (Longchar, 2014).

Rural agriculture is the only source of income for the unskilled labor. Most of the time they do not have their own agricultural land and work in others field. Agricultural income is seasonal, and during out season they remain unemployed, this plays a big push factor for the rural laborers to migrate towards urban areas. Rural to urban migration is the most common phenomenon among the rural laborers. Understanding the mechanism of this migration and how they deal with change is the real question. Migration literally means adjustment with the new environment, new way of life and with new sets of challenges. There is a huge difference between rural and urban space and the transformation that they face in the whole long process is the key question in the migration studies. Understanding the pull and push factor from rural to urban migration is not enough but what happens afterward and what is the role of the state in the process is important.

Migration and urbanization

Migration not only has the impact upon those who migrate but it also has a huge impact on the regions to which they migrate. Migration plays a key role in the expansion of the areas and also in the redistribution of the population. Migration creates the regional disparity of population distribution and to an extent results in the urbanization of areas. It is a common notion that urban areas attract migrant workers but at the same time migration of labor expands the urban areas. It is predicted that over the period 2011-2050, the world urban population will increase from 3.6 billion to 6.3 billion. The increase in population will be seen in cities and towns of developing and less developed countries. Some of the reasons for the increase in the urban population can be categorized in three components, firstly the natural increase in urban areas, secondly reclassification of rural areas as urban areas, and thirdly net migration from rural to urban areas (Chandrasekhar & Sharma, 2014). As the paper focuses on the rural to urban migration of labor in India, more emphasis is on the net migration from rural to urban areas.

The census of India defines an internal migrant as a person residing in a place other than his/her place of birth (Place of Birth definition) or one who has changed his/her usual place of residence to another place (change in Usual Place of Residence or UPR definition). In the context of India, rural to urban migration has contributed around 20 percent of the increase in urban population and other 80 percent is because of other reasons like natural increase. The total population of India constitutes 1.21 billion according to Census 2011. Internal migration in India constitutes around 309 million which constitutes around 30 percent of the population according to the census of 2001. According to the NSSO 2007-08, it is estimated that the number of internal migrants is 326 million population. Some of the leading states in the internal migrants are Uttar Pradesh, Bihar, Rajasthan, Madhya Pradesh, Andhra Pradesh Chhattisgarh, Jharkhand, Odisha, Uttarakhand and Tamil Nadu, whereas key destination areas are Delhi, Maharashtra, Gujarat, Haryana, Punjab, and Karnataka. Migration in India is of two types: (a) Long-term migration, resulting in the relocation of an individual or household and (b) Short-term or seasonal/circular migration, involving back and forth movement between a source and destination. According to NSSO 2007–2008 it is estimated that short-term migrants vary from 15 million to 100 million (Faetanini & Tankha, 2013).

Migration and urbanization are directly related to the process of economic development of a country. Modern urbanization began with the advent of the Industrial Revolution and the rapid urbanization of industrial areas went hand in hand. Migration from rural areas remains the sole reason for the rapid urbanization at that time (Altvater, 2005). In the case of developing countries like India, large part of migration is related to the stagnation of agricultural growth, and stagnation of agricultural growth is directly related to the low income among the labors in rural areas. This results in huge migration from rural areas in search of better livelihood. These outmigrants from rural areas are largely absorbed in the urban informal[5] economy (Kundu, 2007). These laborers mainly engage in rag-picking, vegetable vending, woodwork, pottery, handicraft, basketry, jewelry-making, leatherworking, weaving, sewing and furniture-making, tailoring, food catering, domestic work, shoe polishing and etc. They earn income according to their limited skill. The informal sector absorbs a large span of unskilled labor and supports their livelihood. The scope of the informal economy in rural areas is very limited in nature. Since the density of population in rural areas is very low and they do their required work themselves only except for a few. All these reasons lead to the migration of labors to the urban areas.

Migration is a process of structural transformation and it leads to the diversification of population in urban areas. The structural transformation of the urban areas is not the only consequence of migration but it largely impacts the life of the migrant workers. There are many challenges that the migrant workers have to face in the urban spaces. The lifestyle of the migrant workers takes a total U-turn after coming to the urban areas. The environment of rural and urban areas has vast differences and the migrants have to negotiate every step with the changes in urban areas. It is not only the migrant workers who have to negotiate but the urban spaces also have to negotiate with migrants.

Migrant workers and Negotiation in Urban Space

Internal migration constitutes a flooding of the population in the urban areas. With the increasing density of population in urban areas, the challenges for the migrant workers also increases. From the time they migrate to the urban areas, they have to negotiate every step. Starting with finding a job till finding a roof is a challenge for them. The main aim of the migrant workers is to earn money for better livelihood. It is a wrong notion to explain livelihood in terms of income earning. Livelihood is associated with many other activities such as gain and retaining access to resources and opportunities, dealing with risk, negotiating with the social relations etc (Beall & Kanji, 1999). Being in the informal sector of the economy, the migrant workers are excluded from many basic amenities of life.

Internal migration patterns and dynamics intersect with two developments in India's current human development context. Firstly, the rapid urbanization and the growth of second-tier cities and towns and increase in the levels of migration cause cities to face many socio-economic and environmental challenges. This process creates urban poverty and creates inequalities in access to income and services, which creates the social exclusion from the part of the urban population. Secondly, the expansion of rights-based approaches which ensure that basic services are accessible to all citizens (Faetanini & Tankha, 2013). Analysis of both the dynamics shows that they are the complete opposite of each other to each other. And this is the point where the need for migrants to negotiate in the urban spaces arises. Though there are some policies for the welfare of the marginalized group they are not specific to migrant workers.

Due to lack of analytical refinement in the way that internal migration is defined, the delivery of services for migrants is hampered. Migrants continually face difficulties in becoming a full part of the economic, cultural, social and political lives of society in the urban areas. Most of the time they feel excluded from the economic, political, cultural and social lives of the urban society. Internal migrants face various problems such as lack of political representation, inadequate housing and a lack of formal residency rights, low income, insecure or hazardous work, limited access to state-provided services such as health and education, discrimination based on ethnicity, religion, class or gender, extreme vulnerability of women and children migrants to trafficking and sex exploitation (Faetanini & Tankha, 2013).

The increasing flow of migrants has both positive as well as the negative impact on the urban space. Growing sums in urban areas are the result of migration from the rural areas. To regulate the unregulated growth of slums in the urban areas is a challenge in itself. The more the inflow of migrants, less will be the space for their accommodation, which in turn leads to the creation of the slums. Slums lack many basic amenities of life, health and hygiene in slum areas are issues to be addressed. Slum areas many times do not have drinking water facilities, basic sanitation etc. Often informal sector of the urban areas is considered important in the urban areas, but the rapid inflow of migrant workers is a challenge for the urban space (Singh, 2016). When a person migrates from a rural area to an urban area, they have to intermix with people belonging to diverse culture and background. No doubt intermixing helps in creating a composite culture, but in the initial period, it is a challenge for the migrant to intermix. Sometimes, living with people from the different cultural group can create a social vacuum and a sense of dejection among individuals (Bala, 2017). To ensure the betterment of the migrant workers, the urban spaces should become inclusive in nature as the number of migrants increases. It will require adequate and affordable housing, health and education service, infrastructure and sanitation facilities. The government should make proper welfare policies for the protection of the migrant workers.

Migrants are looked as 'outsiders' by the local host administration, and as a burden on systems and resources at the destination. They are marginalized in the urban spaces and have to face many social injustices. Most of the time they have to live in fear. In India, migrants' right to the city is denied on the political defense of the 'sons of the soil' theory, which aims to create vote banks along ethnic, linguistic and religious lines. Exclusion and discrimination against migrants take place through political and administrative processes, market mechanisms and socio-economic processes, causing a gulf between migrants and locals (Faetanini & Tankha, 2013). When they face ill treatment as outsiders, it becomes very difficult for them to manage the situation in an unknown place. Most of the migrant workers are from rural areas where they have shared very close bonding with their kin, the situation is very different in urban areas. They meet new people with whom they do not have a close bonding. The migrant workers have to negotiate with the urban space in every step and with time those negotiations become their part of life. And also from the part of urban spaces, the same is true.

Conclusion

Migration of workers from rural to urban areas is unstoppable and it will continue in the future also. Urban areas attract the migrants as the remote areas have fewer opportunities for earning income. The important question that arises is that of the inclusion of the rural migrants in the urban areas. Are urban areas equipped enough to include the migrant workers as part of their urban social life? What is the role of the state in regulating the urban spaces for the migrant workers? From the part of migrant workers, they have to negotiate with the urban spaces in many ways and vice-versa. But is it the sole responsibility of the migrants to face the problem in the host areas or do they require some help in their initial period is the basic question. It is the migrant workers who face the challenges and they do have support from the government. There are many welfare policies for the marginal population of the country but they do not actually cover the migrant population. Understanding the negotiation from the part of migrant workers should be a matter of discussion. Migration is a universal fact but basic amenities are also the basic right of every human bring. And every migrant should also get the same facilities as the other people in the host place.

Bibliography

Ajaero, C. K., & Onokala, P. C. (2013)." The Effects of Rural-Urban Migration on Rural Communities of Southeastern Nigeria". *International Journal of Population Research.*

Altvater, E. (2005). "Globalization and the informalization of the urban space". *Research Center on Development and International Relations*, 1-25.

Bala, A. (2017). "Migration in India: Causes and consequences". *International Journal of Advanced Educational Research*, 54-56.

Banerjee, A. (2011). "Mobilities and Spaces: Gendered Dimension of Migration in Urban India". In S. Raju, & K. Lahiri-Dutta, *Doing Gender Doing Geography: Emerging Research in India* (pp. 89-109). New Delhi: Routledge Publication.

Beall, J., & Kanji, N. (1999). *Households,Livelihood and Urban Poverty.* London: London School of Economics and Political Science.

C.Das, K., & Saha, S. (2012). *Inter-state migration and regional disparities* in India.

Chandrasekhar, S., & Sharma, A. (2014). "Urbanization and Spatial Patterns of Internal Migration in India". *Indira Gandhi Institute of Development Research*, 1-39.

Faetanini, M., & Tankha, R. (2013). *Social Inclusion of Internal Migrants in India.* Delhi: UNESCO.

Hirway, I., Singh, U. B., & Sharma, R. (2014). *Migration and Development Study of Rural to Urban Temporary Migration to Gujarat.* Ahmedabad: Centre for Development Alternatives.

K.Vinayakam, & Sekar, S. P. (2013). "Rural To Urban Migration in an Indian Metropolis: Case Study Chennai City". *Journal Of Humanities And Social Science*, 32-35.

Kundu, A. (2007). "Migration and Urbanisation in India in the Context of Poverty Alleviation". *International Conference and Workshop on Policy Perspectives on Growth, Economic Structures and Poverty Reduction.* Beijing.

Longchar, M. (2014). "Rural-Urban Migration and its Impact on the Urban Environment and Life in Nagaland". *Transactions*, 101-107.

M.Hall, S. (2015). "Migrant urbanisms: ordinary cities and everyday resistence". *Sociology*, 853-869.

(2017). *Migration and Its Impact.* World Economic Forum.

Muthusamy, A., & Ibrahim, M. S. (2016). "Problems Faced by Informal Workers in different Sectors in India". *Indian Journal of Applied Research*, 37-40.

Singh, G. (2016). "Surging Internal Migration in Punjab: Emerging Policy Issues". *International Journal of Engineering Technology, Management and Applied Sciences*, 158-168.

Singh, H. (2016)."Increasing rural to urban migration in India:A challenge or an opportunity". *International Journal of Applied Research*, 447-450.

Endnotes

[1] World Economic Forum Report, 2017

[2] Based on political limits and the boundaries crossed, such as districts, counties, state borders and international boundaries, further identified as the places of origin and destination (World Economic Forum Report, 2017).

[3] Based on classifying people according to their social status, travel points and periodicity (World Economic Forum Report, 2017).

[4] Based on classifying migration as voluntary or involuntary, given certain socio-political factors (e.g. the fear of ill-treatment attributed to race, religion, political affiliation, nationality or association to social groups; flight from war; conflict involving arms; civil war; natural or man-made disasters; famine) or developmental factors (e.g. substantial infrastructure projects, including airport, road, dam or port construction; the administrative clearance of urban projects; mining and deforestation; the creation of conservation parks/reserves and other biosphere related initiatives, among others) (World Economic Forum Report, 2017).

[5] The informal sector had to be defined in terms of characteristics of the production units (enterprises) in which the activities take place (enterprise approach), rather than in terms of the characteristics of the persons involved or of their jobs (labour approach).

Cityscape for Young Migrant Women: A Reflection on Intra Domestic Workers in Bangalore

Richard Gonsalves

Abstract

This paper attempts to analyze the city as a space brimming with opportunities for development of self and livelihood. It views the cityscape as a milieu that despite the cultural discrimination and xenophobia, houses tremendous potential for the migrant workers. The analysis is located in the cultural context of Bangalore which has developed in leaps and bounds as the city of migrants. This holds true not only for the technocrats in the organized sector but also for the migrant populace in the unorganized sector.

It is the workforce of young migrant women employed in the domestic work that this paper explores. Most of the women are intra state migrants who move to Bangalore on a seasonal basis. These women find employment either at the construction sites or in the domestic household of the cosmopolitan Bangalore. This paper engages at a theoretical as well as realistic level with the term seasonal employment and how the nature of the employment empowers as well as disempowers women. Even though these women are in a state of mobility, the sphere of domestic work proposes avenues for self-improvement and livelihood. The urban space that alienates the women migrant worker and presents many sexual threats also provides the apparatus for autonomy and self identity. Domestic work and housekeeping are the most viable options for these women since they are in a state of flight. Since most of the women hail from the families of farmers that depend on natural resources, there is no fixed and stable source of livelihood. Hence, they migrate to the urban space seasonally. These women deliberately choose a part-time work, which allows them to juggle between home and the world, country and city.

The paper employed empirical research and personal experiences to theorize the travails of the migrant women in domestic work. The informal nature of the labour, that many a times renders them helpless and exploited, also allows them to conveniently switch between their roles as domestic maid and homemakers.

Keywords: Autonomy, Migrant Women, Domestic work, unorganized sector, livelihood

This paper centers on a study of the young migrant women employed as domestic workers in the cosmopolitan space of Bangalore city. It is not only documentary but analytical in nature and studies the predicament of these workers from a sociological perspective. Alongside, the paper also attempts to see whether this intra state migration can possibly stimulate a new discourse on the notion of self-development and female autonomy. It employs empirical research and personal experiences to theorize the travails of the migrant women in domestic work. The paper commences with a discussion on labour and development post-liberalization and its repercussions for the unorganized sector. It then moves on to show how this cosmopolitanism has addressed the life issues of young domestic workers in the rural sector. The paper, then, chronicles the socio-economic circumstances that force migration and studies certain specific cases of some women domestic workers in Bangalore. The paper concludes by reflecting on the possibility of autonomy that migration is capable of offering. In other words it raises the question Does it empower and enable women in any way or do they remain entrapped in the patriarchal arrangement?

City Space post liberalization

The space of the city assumes special significance because the entire process of building capacities and potential rest on the mobility and access to education, healthcare, markets and places of recreation. I believe an understanding of the social character of spaces is imperative to investigate the larger context of migration and labour and so I begin with a discussion of the Bangalore city that has emerged as the new IT capital post liberalisation that has propelled migration not only in the formal but informal economy as well. Post-liberalisation, the city has witnessed booming industrialisation, trade, commerce, automobile, textile and hundreds of start ups that have sprouted across the city. The city's economic landscape is marked by diverse professions and vocations. This has also fuelled migration both internal as well as external. What this paper attempts to map is the internal migration in the context of informal economy. To the migrants in the unorganised sector, Bangalore acquires the status of a myth and often becomes a character.

The city represents a change. It doesn't offer a definite type of community life but several kinds of 'lives' and living. It is a milieu that absorbs every kind of life and creates an accommodating space for everyone. It is modern, hopeful, liveable, local, cosmopolitan and most importantly a caste-less space to the imagination of an intra state migrant. The transition from country to city symbolises dissolution of caste-based hierarchies, or at least an attempt to transcend them. What the discourse of development hides is the subtle and nuanced form of caste and gender based oppression which pervades both formal and informal economy. In the context of Bangalore, the city's demography has changed from a city of locals to a city of migrants.

The proliferation of multinationals which has informed inter-state migration has also created an increasing need for work force in the unorganised sector. The informal segment has developed a parallel to the formal segment of a work force in leaps and bounds but paradoxically remains without an organisational or state support. The booming IT world of Bangalore employs many unskilled rural migrants from Gulbarga, Raichur and Bidar who remain scattered and work without any social and legal protection. It is this populace of rural migrants that the paper engages with and attempts to capture the implications of migration for women employed as domestic work force.

Domestic Work: Skilled or Unskilled?

Domestic work has been one of the oldest as well as the emergent form of labour in India. The phase of liberalisation has not only revamped the city of Bangalore in terms of employment opportunities but also offered new consumption practices. The public spaces of market, malls, pubs and clubs are being equally accessed and consumed by both men and women alike. This is so since the new age woman in the phase of liberalisation located in urban world upgrades herself of these benefits and keeps abreast of these development provisions to realise her ambitions. The advent of globalisation in the Indian subcontinent has introduced a new market dynamics, thereby, bringing about the consumer culture that has entailed production of new spaces and identities. Here I am specifically referring to shopping malls, gymnasiums and clubs. These spaces have reinvented the middle class woman as the 'consuming woman,' one who partakes of the logic of consumerism enunciated by these new spaces in the public domain. This consuming woman allows herself to be tempted by the glamour of the market who splurges and spends on herself. She accesses these spaces for leisure and consumption without any specific purpose of buying household things.

Hence, the space of domesticity which contained her and at the same time provided her sustenance is now passed on to the domestic workers. As women negotiate more with the public space, the sphere of domesticity needs a new caretaker. In fact, the ability to engage with the public world on terms equivalent with men is premised on the presence of domestic workers. This is where the domestic workers come into the picture. Domestic work has been overwhelmingly feminised and there are many factors behind this peculiar tendency. The sphere of domesticity has been understood as the natural condition of women's social existence. The household chores, cooking, cleaning, taking care of the children and elderly have been socially and religiously mandated as the sacred duty of a woman. The private space of domesticity is where a woman belongs and she should seek fulfilment there. Needless to say that domestic labour goes unsung, unrewarded, undervalued and most importantly, unpaid or under-paid.

What makes the migrant women consider domestic work as a viable labour? First and foremost, it is the element of class and caste. Caste defines their choice of profession and binds them to it. These women get tied down by the occupations related to removal and cleansing of filth and dirt. Also, most of the women who choose this form of work are from economically disadvantaged sections and are either illiterate or semi-literate. Moreover, they are not in possession of any special skill and are rated as 'unskilled.' Domestic work is the only skill they possess. Hence, it is an inadvertent choice. There are a host of other factors also that determine their choice of domestic work. The paper explores them as the argument progresses.

Gendered Migration

There has been a propensity to view internal migration as essentially a male activity. Since migration is associated with ideas of aspiration and progress which are chiefly a male prerogative, women's issues are overlooked with women as residual or dependents in the process of migration. Therefore, it is important to center on the narratives of migrant women and adopt an intersectional approach to gendered migration. The migrant women that this paper studies belong to the rural parts of north Karnataka, namely, Bidar, Raichur, Gulbarga and Dharwad. Most of them fall into the age group of 20 to 30 and are young mothers. In the context of these women, migration is decided by the male members and they remain voiceless. However, that does not, by any measure, imply that they do not act in migration. The imagined male perspective of hope and anticipation triggers migration but women act as much as men when it comes to lived experiences. They are not passive movers. Even though marriage remains the predominant reason for migration of women, the increase is also because of increase in gender specific patterns of labour. As discussed earlier, the emergence of multinational culture and transformation of Bangalore, participation of women outside and changing patterns of consumption practice have resulted in the demand for women-centred service such as domestic help.

Migration is followed by immediate challenges of finding employment and livelihood and it is not just the men who are confronted with this challenge, women too experience the same amount of pressure to find work in an alien land. Migration is accompanied by change as well as turbulence for both men and women. The focus, in this paper, is on how migrant women construct their identity in an alien land, the problems they encounter and the strategies they adopt to make life liveable.

In most of the discourses on migration, women have been represented as victims of migration. The impulse has been to view their migration as associational or forced. I reiterate, even though migration for the intra migrant domestic workers is not voluntary it is not a static movement also. Migrant women are not a homogeneous category characterised by submissiveness and containment in the household sphere. The paper seeks to take a departure from this inadequate representation of intra migrant women as dependents.

Instead, it analyses the component of agency in the context of women on the move. The complex experience of intra migrant women problematises the notion of agency and presents it in fluid and myriad ways. The migrant woman's experience is coloured by both agency as well as constraints. The new land presents her with new avenues but there is a baggage of the past, a linking with the native land not only in terms of rituals, customs and cultural practices but also responsibilities towards the native land. Meenakshi Thapan argues, "There is not only fluidity in the experience and construction of identity but also in the manifold ways in which there is a 'back-linking' with the past, the country of origin, whether this is in terms of rituals, practices and values, relationship and family ties, or even the idea of country that is carried to the new land."[1] At the same time, the migrant woman's presence in the new land is constrained by structures of the new land, the laws and regulatory regimes. Hence, the migrant woman's identity is a fluid one which informs her daily existence, personal experience. How does this mixed experience help her in constructing her identity is the thrust of this paper.

This paper attempts to capture this fluid state of intra migrant women's identity through an exhaustive analysis of their life in Bangalore city. This analysis is based on personal interviews, meetings and some studies carried out on their life in the urban milieu. The cases studied will exemplify the duality of these women's existence and how they negotiate with various kinds of power structures on a regular basis.

Intra-migrant Domestic Workers in Bangalore

The argument in this paper develops by linking trials, dilemmas and conflicts of the young migrants from northern districts in Karnataka, to mobility in the cosmopolitan city. The fieldwork, which is the primary source of analysis and inference, takes a small sample of this migrant women populace. It provides vignettes of their experience and attempts to understand how these women incorporate their aspirations in to the larger familial goals. The districts of North Karnataka that these migrant women hail from are characterised by rural distress. Raichur, Gulbarga and Bidar are districts that have been perennially plagued by agrarian distress. Rural life in these districts is that of impoverishment and deprivation. The prime occupational engagement for low class and caste people is agriculture since they are illiterate and follow the traditional caste set up. Most of the agricultural labourers have little landholdings and since north Karnataka is highly prone to drought, these farmers always live in uncertainty. For instance, Raichur is marked by contradictions. There is a stark contrast between the rain-fed dry areas and dam-dependent areas. One is characterised by barrenness and the other fertility. All this makes north Karnataka a semi-arid land.

The migrant women from these districts do not migrate out of their own accord. Their migration is associational. It is the men who decide to move for social and financial security. They move to sustain the lives of their husbands in the city and look after their everyday needs. The women interviewed reside in the areas of Krishnappa Garden and Suddagunte Palya which are on the peripheries of the city. These places have been converted into IT parks and have the presence of sky-rocketing apartments and swanky multinationals. Krishnappa garden witnesses paradoxical co-existence of IT park and slums. It has a large population of migrants from north Karnataka who have been staying for the last thirty years. The slum that they inhabit earlier belonged to BEML company and was used as a garbage dumping ground. The male migrant workers inhabited this area and later their families too moved in. Most of the male migrants work as construction workers. The migrant women folk, in question, fall in the age group of 20 to 30 and are often young mothers. The most convenient work for them is domestic work and housekeeping since it allows them to shuttle between home and the world.

The other area of study that is Suddagunte Palya also houses a large number of migrant populations. The slum inhabited by the migrant families is closely located to RMZ park, another IT hub. It is also situated near a drainage with railway tracks crossing the migrants' area. The location of the drainage and railway lines is one of the reasons for the migrant families to move into this place. It assists them in their daily chores. The young migrant women in this place, just like the women in Krishnappa Garden, made an associational movement from rural to the urban world. It was found that migration of women was closely related to the migration of men which hints at the determining role played by the family in the lives of the migrant women.

Domestic work seems to be the most feasible form of employment for them. Their own involvement in their house leaves them with little avenues to explore options other than domestic work. Moreover, motherhood ties them to their infant which proves to be a constraint for them. The world of domesticity is all they have to explore. The spate of IT parks and posh apartments provide them employment which is part-time and informal in nature. The migrant women replay their roles as caretakers and perform the same tasks in the house of the employer. The temporary nature of their employment is not only due to their commitments to their own home but also due to the affinity with their native land. These migrant women are always on the move. They juggle between country and the city on account of looking after the native land and the sick and the elderly. They move back to their native land for a few months during the harvest season or festivals. Even elections define their movement. What Rapport and Dawson say holds absolutely true for these young migrant women, "home is conceptualised in fluid terms, as neither being here nor there,...rather, itself, a hybrid, it is both here and there-an amalgam, a pastiche, a performance."[2]

These migrant women domestic workers fluctuate between native land and the host city, making both the places their home and re-defining the idea of home as a mobile and fluid entity. What makes them juggle between these two worlds is their cultural baggage and duty towards their native land. Since north Karnataka is partly arid, these women move back to their native place during the harvest season and stay there till the agrarian job is done. The commitment to land makes their employment in Bangalore city seasonal.

These women are more mobile and fluid than their male counterparts. While men choose to stay in the city owing to their job, women move to perform not only agrarian tasks but cultural duties as well. They shift to their native places to conduct rituals and participate in festivals and, by doing so, keep the family culturally rooted. In fact, they also network with people sharing the same ethnic features and make their area an ethnic enclave. They carry their indigenous traits wherever they go.

What we find is that despite the duality of their existence, migration proves to be an empowering experience for these young migrant women. The enabling aspect of their migrant existence is that it allows them to earn livelihood independent of their husbands. Some migrant women even confessed that their husbands do not have any knowledge that they are working as domestic workers. This helps them to save some money for themselves and their children, which their husbands would have otherwise spent. These women negotiate with the power structure in their own distinct ways and manipulate the patriarchal system to attain some amount of economic independence. The paper argues that the idea of autonomy and selfhood need to be seen from the lens of social class. Women appreciate and acknowledge different experiences and situations based on their social class backgrounds. What may appear to be a stifling condition to an upper class woman, may be deemed enabling and empowering in the case of a lower class woman. For these women, city offers an escape from the overt form of caste oppression. That caste-based oppression re-enacts itself in another ways, is a different story altogether.

Though these women migrated on account of their husbands' decision to migrate, they have exercised their agency in choosing the decision to stay in the city. Despite the constant physical movement from urban to rural, they do not give up on working in the city. There are other factors associated with these that impede their autonomy. The most important being the aspect of safety and sexual harassment at the workplace and the slums where they dwell. The seasonal and part-time nature of their employment, doesn't entirely keep them immune to these threats, but allows them to avoid it. It is veritably true that these domestic workers

are regularly exposed to abuse and assaults. The women domestic
workers combat it on a daily basis by networking with other
domestic workers in the same area and coin tactics to protect
themselves from such threats.

Conclusion: Domestic work and Globalisation

Domestic work, though pushed to the margins and, seen as outside
the ambit of capitalism, is actually located at the heart of capitalism.
The traditional social arrangement granted the public sphere to
men and private to women and projected the home as an enclave
outside the forces of the market. It was depicted as a pure and
idyllic space that remained outside the logic of capitalism where
the male wage earner could return to rejuvenate himself. Women
sustained the domain of home and children as they were placed
at the heart of this arrangement. It was for them that the male
earner laboured. However, home is not away from the capitalistic
arrangement but participates in it. The family is well integrated
into the capitalistic arrangement as the site of consumption. In
the present era of globalisation and Bangalore being the linchpin
of capitalism, this consumption has increased manifold with the
women taking on careers and adopting the ethic of the market.
Hence, the domestic workers' covert participation in the global
market and their unacknowledged contribution to the social
reproduction has been absolutely essential for the functioning of
the system. This paper is an effort to understand such women's
migration goals in the context of agency and selfhood. Their agency
and selfhood are attained within the larger rubric of family and
household given their precarious situation.

References

Rapport, Nigel and Dawson Andrew. *Migrants of Identity: Perceptions of Home in a World of Movement*. Oxford: Berg. 1998

Thapan, Meenakshi. *Transnational Migration and the Politics of Identity: Women and Migration in South Asia*. Sage Publications. Delhi. 2005.

Personal Interviews

Mahadevamma, Kallappa (2018, June 24).

Lakshmi. (2018, May 15).

Ramadevi, Sita. (2018 March 19).

Manjamma, Erappa. (2018 July 3).

Field visit

1. Krishnappa garden, Bangalore. (2018, May 15).
2. Suddagunte Pallya, Bangalore. (2018 July 3).

Endnotes

[1] Meenakshi Thapan, *Transnational Migration and Politics of Identity* (Sage Pvt Publications: 2005), p. 8.

[2] Nigel Rapport and Andre Dawson, *Migrants of Identity: Perceptions of Home in a World of Movement* (Oxford: Ber, 1998) p. 25.

Socio-legal Dynamics of Migrant Workers in India

Bhumika Sharma and Mamta Kashyap

Abstract

Migration of workers is a universal phenomenon. The origin of migration can be traced to the origin of human kind. Migration in India has largely been fuelled by push and pulls factors - the increasing regional disparities, rural - urban disparities and urban bias in economic planning. Inter-State Migrant workmen (Regulations of Employment and Conditions of Service) Act , 1979 is the primary legislation to regulate the rights of migrant workers in India. Though a number of other laws also have some provisions in this regard, it is interesting to note that how the position of migrant workers has been transformed post 1979.

Globalization too has an impact on the conditions of workers in India. Indian economy is moving fast and creating more job opportunities. The migration of labour from one state to another as well as within the state itself has led to problems on various accounts. On this premise, the present study tries to explore the role played by legislations in regulating the issues concerning migrant workers in the country.

A doctrinal method of study has been adopted here. The objectives of the present study are to enumerate the reasons for increase in the number of

migrant workers in the country and to highlight the legal provisions that
confer benefits on the migrant workers. The study would in the end come
up with possible suggestions.

Key Words – *India, Migration, Legal, Society.*

1.   INTRODUCTION

Concept of Migration

Migration is a form of mobility in which people change their
residential location across defined administrative boundaries for
a variety of reasons, which may be involuntary or voluntary, or
a mixture of both.[1] The decisions on whether to move, how,
and where are complex and could involve a variety of actors in
different ways.

The pattern of growth under globalization has led to changes
in the pattern of demand for workers and consequent changes
in labour market structure. There has been an overall growth in
certain sectors, and this has generated a certain type of demand
for workers. Second, the premium which the employers place on
flexible labour and reducing labour costs appear to them to be
higher than the gains that could accrue to them from a dedicated
and long-term labour force.

Internal Migration

Internal Migration refers to movement from one household to
another household in a different compound, home or homestead
within the Demographic Surveillance Area (DSA).[2] Movement
from one household to another household within the same
compound, home or homestead is not classified as internal
migration and it is treated separately from internal migration.[3]
Internal migration occurs when a registered member of the DSA
migrates from his/her current household to join another household

or form a new household in another location within or between places in the DSA.[4]

Internal migration not only involves much poorer segments, it impacts on the economy as a whole, on sending and receiving regions, and on the migrants and on their families also arguably much more than on international migrants.

Statement of the Problem

The researchers have selected the topic of the study firstly because migration of labour is a global concern and secondly under Indian economy, the migrant workers are a disadvantaged class.

- Migration for employment and its linkages with development has now emerged as a global issue which affects most nations in the world. It is high on the international, regional and national policy agendas. Through their labour, migrant workers contribute to growth and development in their countries of employment. Yet, the migration process also poses serious challenges. Many migrant workers, especially low skilled workers, experience serious abuse and exploitation. Women, increasingly migrating on their own and now accounting for almost half of all international migrants, face specific protection problems. In the face of rising barriers to cross-border labour mobility, the growth of irregular migration, and trafficking and smuggling of human beings constitute major challenges to protection of human and labour rights.

- A serious data gap on the extent, nature and magnitude of internal migration exists in the country. Despite the fact that approximately three out of every ten Indians are internal migrants, internal migration has been accorded a very low priority by the government, and existing policies of the Indian state have failed in providing legal or social protection to this vulnerable group.[5]

Objectives of the Study

- To discuss social conditions of migrant workers in India,
- To enumerate the legislations in brief to protect the rights of migrant workers in India,
- To give suggestions to improve the conditions of migrant workers in the country.

Research Methodology

A Doctrinal method of study has been adopted here. The researchers have used secondary sources such as books, reports, legislations etc. in computing the findings.

2.   LABOUR MIGRATION IN INDIA: A SOCIAL REALITY

Definition of a Migrant

- The Census defines a migrant as a person residing in a place other than his/her place of birth (Place of Birth definition) or one who has changed his/ her usual place of residence to another place (change in usual place of residence or UPR definition).
- The NSS confines itself to the UPR definition.

Census collects data on the age and sex of the migrant, reason for migration, its duration, place of origin, and the industry and occupation of the migrant; the results are available up to the district level. The NSS also collects additional data on items such as the consumption expenditure of the migrant's household, educational attainment, activity, industry and occupation of the household at the place of origin, as well as remittances.

Definition of Resident

In both the surveys, a resident is defined as one who has been staying in a location for six months or more (except newly born infants).

Dearth of Data regarding Migrants in India

Data on internal migration in India is principally drawn from two main sources – the decennial population Census and the quennial migration surveys carried out by the National Sample Survey Office.

One of the main lacunae of both the Census and NSS surveys is their failure to adequately capture seasonal and/or short-term circular migration, and their coverage is best for permanent migrants and reasonably adequate for semi-permanent migrants.[6]

Indian system suffers from the problem of internal migration. In recent years, several changes in India are likely to have impacted the pattern and pace of migration. The growing spatial inequalities in economic opportunities have necessarily also impacted the pace and pattern of migration.

Disadvantages faced by Migrant Workers

Lack of formal residency rights; lack of identity proof; lack of political representation; inadequate housing; low-paid, insecure or hazardous work; extreme vulnerability of women and children to trafficking and sexual exploitation; exclusion from state-provided services such as health and education and discrimination based on ethnicity, religion, class or gender.[7] In the absence of proofs of identity and residence, internal migrants are unable to claim social protection entitlements and remain excluded from government-sponsored schemes and programs.[8] Children face disruption of regular schooling, adversely affecting their human capital formation and contributing to the inter-generational transmission of poverty.[9] Further, migrants are negatively portrayed as a "burden" to society, discouraged from settling down and excluded from urban planning initiatives.[10] Most internal migrants are denied basic rights, yet internal migration is given very low priority by the government in policy and practice, partly due to a serious knowledge gap on its extent, nature and magnitude.[11]

Contribution of Migrant Workers

Migrants bring back to source locations a variety of skills, innovations and knowledge, known as 'social remittances', including changes in tastes, perceptions and attitudes, such as for example, a lack of acceptance of poor employment conditions, low wages and semi-feudal labour relationships, and improved knowledge and awareness about workers' rights. Migration may provide an opportunity to escape caste divisions and restrictive social norms, to work with dignity and freedom at the destination.

Points of Migration

The leading source States of internal migrants include Uttar Pradesh, Bihar, Rajasthan, Madhya Pradesh, Andhra Pradesh Chhattisgarh, Jharkhand, Odisha, Uttarakhand and Tamil Nadu, whereas key destination areas are Delhi, Maharashtra, Gujarat, Haryana, Punjab and Karnataka.[12] There are conspicuous migration corridors within the country: Bihar to National Capital Region, Bihar to Haryana and Punjab, Uttar Pradesh to Maharashtra, Odisha to Gujarat, Odisha to Andhra Pradesh and Rajasthan to Gujarat.[13]

3.   LEGISLATIVE FRAMEWORK VIS-À-VIS LABOUR MIGRATION IN INDIA

A number of legislative provisions exist in India to secure the rights of the migrant labour and workers as follows-

Sl. No.	Legislation	Objective
1.	Workmen's Compensation Act, 1923	To provide compensation for injury by accident for the payment by certain classes of employers to their workmen.
2.	Payment of Wages Act,1936	To regulate the payment of wages to certain classes of employed persons
3.	Minimum Wages Act, 1948	To provide compensation for fixing minimum rates of wages in certain employments
4.	Immoral Traffic (Prevention) Act, 1956	To provide compensation for the prevention of immoral traffic
5.	Contract Labour (Regulation and Abolition) Act ,1970	To regulate the employment of contract labour in certain establishments and to provide for its abolition in certain circumstances and for matters connected therewith.
6.	Bonded Labour System (Abolition) Act , 1976	To provide for the abolition of bonded labour system with a view to preventing the economic and physical exploitation of the weaker sections of the people
7.	Equal Remuneration Act, 1976	To provide for the payment of equal remuneration to men and women workers and for the prevention of discrimination, on the ground of sex, against women in the matter of employment
8.	Inter-State Migrant Workmen (Regulation of Employment and Conditions of Service) Act, 1979	To regulate the employment of inter-state migrant workmen and to Provide for their conditions of service

9.	Building and Other Construction Workers (Regulation of Employment and Conditions of Service) Act,1996	To regulate the employment and conditions of service of building and other construction workers and to provide for their safety, health and welfare measures
10.	Unorganised Workers Social Security Act, 2008	To provide for the social security and welfare of unorganised workers

The above legislations secure the rights of migrants directly and indirectly.

UIDAI signed a Memorandum of Understanding (MoU) on 29 July 2010 with the National Coalitions of Organisations for the Security of Migrant Workers. The MoU outlines the framework of the UIDAI-Coalition partnership for ensuring inclusion of migrants in the unique identification project, and ensuring they are issued a secure and unique identification number. This includes developing strategies for enrolment such as special enrolment drives for migrants alongside spreading communication and awareness about Aadhar within the migrant communities

4.   CONCLUSION AND SUGGESTIONS

The intensity of migration is expected to increase in the future as a response to economic crises, political instability and global environment change.

Migrants continually face difficulties in becoming a full part of the economic, cultural, social and political life of the society. Regulations and administrative procedures exclude migrants from access to legal rights, public services and social protection programmes accorded to residents.

Internal migration is, by its very nature, a cross-sectoral theme. It involves a majority of women, and men and children, young and old, migrating in family or alone, on a long or short term basis, for work, for marriage, or both; it touches the entire spectrum of the human life: education, labor, citizenship, gender, children, health, nutrition, voting; it is an urban and rural phenomenon. A holistic approach in addressing the multiple challenges associated with internal migration is yet to be developed, which requires the interaction of several departments and ministries at central and state level governments.

Suggestions (as per UNESCO/UNICEF's Ten Key Principles for Better Inclusion of Internal Migrants, 2011-12)

- We should promote positive political discourse and avoid a prejudiced, negative portrayal of internal migrants;

- We should start awareness for a better understanding of internal migrants' positive contribution to society;

- We should adopt a human rights-based approach for internal migrant inclusion in society;

- We should develop gender-sensitive and age-sensitive policies and practices for internal migrants;

- We should create portability of social protection entitlements for internal migrants;

- We should upscale successful innovative practices for a better inclusion of internal migrants;

- We should revise and strengthen data collection techniques for the Census to fill knowledge gaps, especially those related to circular and seasonal migration and women's migration;

- We should mainstream internal migration into national development policy, and regional and urban planning;

- We should ensure policy coherence on internal migration and its cross-cutting impacts; and

- We should ensure democratic participation of internal migrants in society;

Endnotes

[1] *Social Inclusion of Internal Migrants in India* at 4, UNESCO, New Delhi, June 2013.

[2] INDEPTH Resource Kit for Demographic Surveillance System, available at http://www.indepth-network.org/Resource%20Kit/INDEPTH%20DSS%20Resource%20Kit/Internal_in-out_migration.htm

[3] *Ibid.*

[4] *Ibid.*

[5] *Social Inclusion of Internal Migrants in India* at 4, UNESCO, New Delhi, June 2013.

[6] *Ibid* at 10.

[7] *Ibid* at iii.

[8] *Ibid.*

[9] Ibid.

[10] Ibid.

[11] Ibid.

[12] *Internal Migration in India Initiative*, Policy Brief, UNECSO 2012, available at 2http://www.unesco.org/new/fileadmin/MULTIMEDIA/FIELD/New_Delhi/pdf/Policy_briefs_full_low_01.pdf

[13] *Ibid.*

Vulnerabilities of Interstate Migrants in India: A Case Study of Waste Pickers and Manual Scavengers in Delhi

Ojasvi Goyal

Abstract

The ascending garbage hills on the outskirts of Delhi is an illustration of human impact on the environment. Stray dogs, storks and other creatures are forced to quest in dumps for their survival and so are some humans. As per the corroborative evidence, more than one lakh waste pickers rummage through piles of filth to earn a living in the capital city. A majority of them are migrants from rural and tribal areas of West Bengal, Odisha, Bihar or eastern Uttar Pradesh. The labour movement from rural to urban areas in India has been push type (crisis led) rather than pull type (development led) due to lack of opportunities in the backward regions. As India stands at the crossroads of defining development trajectories, the urban growth fundamentalism has brought inextricable externalities for the interstate migrants, which has been largely ignored in the policy discourse. The paper critically analyses the vulnerabilities of interstate migrants in India with special emphasis on waste pickers and manual scavengers. An in-depth analysis of social, financial, cultural, political, psychological and health-related vulnerabilities is projected here. The impact of imposition of GST on scrap items is studied and how it has substantially reduced the earnings of waste-pickers. A comprehensive data based study is conducted to analyse the employment trends in the informal sector and its impact on economic growth. Statistical tools and Secondary data is used for the same. The Paper presents an overview of the existing government policies and laws for the upliftment of interstate migrants in India. The need to include their vulnerabilities in the policy matters and reach a consensus on the same is highlighted.

Introduction

The tone and tenor of interstate movement professes a strong correlation between poverty and migration. The would-be migrants are often lured by the fact that urban wages would be adequate to ameliorate the financial stress of their families but the stark reality of urban spaces often goes unnoticed. The implicit and explicit costs of moving to cities are huge, as are the barriers to entry in the formal sector which demands high quality education and skills. The socially deprived class of migrants get engaged in casual work such as leather manufacturers, rickshaw pullers, in construction, brick kilns, textiles, mines, etc. Waste pickers and manual scavengers rank lowest in the hierarchy of urban informal employment. Apart from abysmal, unhygienic living conditions, the social stigma attached to their occupation is extremely stressful. Plummeting resources to meet the daily needs and mounting debt pushes the migrants towards deprivation. The term **Rag-picker** is used for someone who makes a living by rummaging through refuse in the streets to collect material for salvage. In **Delhi**, most of the waste pickers were migrants from neighbouring states. That is, 33% from **West Bengal**, 22% from **Uttar Pradesh** and 13% from Bihar.

In **Jammu** city also most of the rag pickers (81%) hailed from **Bihar** state. The rag pickers were distributed all over residential and commercial areas for their work. Ragpicking has a positive impact on urban spaces with a weak waste management infrastructure. In India, the economic activity of ragpicking is worth about ₹3200 crore. India was also found to have a near-90% recycle rate for PET bottles, which could probably be attributed to ragpicking, given a lack of solid-waste management and under-developed waste collection and recycling culture in that country. Manual scavenging refers to the practice of manually cleaning, carrying, disposing or handling in any manner, human excreta from dry latrines and sewers. It often involves using the most basic of tools such as buckets, brooms and baskets. The practice of manual scavenging is linked to India's caste system where the so-called lower castes are expected to perform this job. Manual scavengers are amongst the poorest and most disadvantaged communities in India. In 1993, India banned the employment of people as manual scavengers. In 2013, a landmark new legislation in the form of the Manual Scavengers Act was passed which seeks to reinforce this ban by prohibiting manual scavenging in all forms and ensures the rehabilitation of manual scavengers to be identified through a mandatory survey. Despite progress, manual scavenging persists in India. Evidence suggests that in 2018, there are 53000 manual scavengers across 12 states in India. There has been a fourfold rise in their number from the last official count. There has been a substantial increase in the incidence of migration from rural areas over the past three decades. The marginalised and disadvantaged sections resort more to migration as compared to the better off sections. Most of the internal migration remains outside the coverage potential of the secondary data. About 314 million people in India could be described as 'ever migrant' in 2001 as per the data of Registrar General and Consensus Commissioner. However, in India the majority of migrants are women who move out of their villages due to marriages. Migration rates are positively related with educational attainment, social group status and per capita consumption. The poor and vulnerable migrants are largely employed in the informal economy.

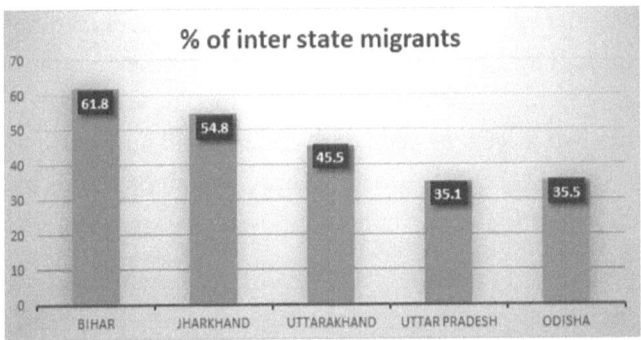

Source: Shrivastav 2011

A decline in short duration migration is also observed. The presence of poorer migrants in cities seem to be shrinking as the cities are becoming more unfavourable to marginalised migrants. The economic and non-economic costs of moving to cities are prohibitively higher as are the barriers to formal employment markets. But the result is not precisely less migration but circulatory and seasonal migration.

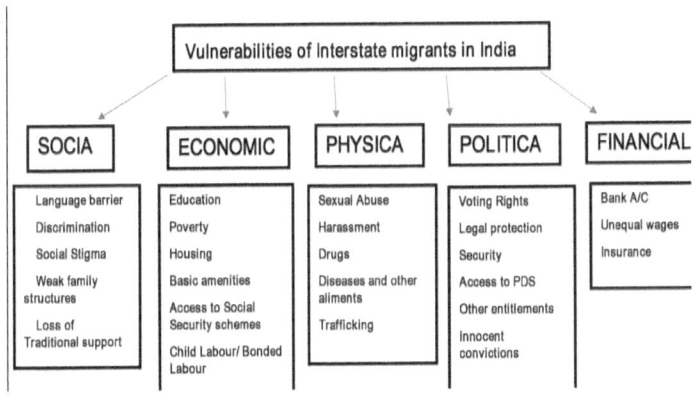

Source: Author's Work

Bustamante (2011) points out that "migrants are inherently vulnerable as subjects of human rights from the time they leave home to initiate their migration. In other words, any human being is less vulnerable at home than right after he leaves it to become a migrant. The same applies to the sociological extension of the notion of home to a community of origin. The same person that migrates had more resources, both material and human, to defend and/or protect, himself, when he was at home, prior to moving elsewhere, than after the outward movement had taken place."

According to Derose et al (2007), vulnerability is shaped by many factors, including political and social marginalization and a lack of socio-economic and societal resources. Varennes (2003) states that "living in host states where they (migrants) may not master the official language(s), are unfamiliar with the workings of the legal system and administration, detached from traditional support and family networks, exposed to a society with ways of life or cultures which they may find at times alien, they may face trials that can leave them disoriented and disturbed." Thus, vulnerability of the migrants arise because of living in a place which is different in culture, language, social settings, legal protection, entitlements and consumption habits from their native places and the loss of the traditional support system they enjoyed before migration. Waste picking is often a family enterprise. It offers flexible working hours (especially important for women) and a high level of adaptability. It is easily learned and requires no education and little training. And for many of the poorest people around the globe, it is one of the only livelihood options.

Waste workers however, are often subject to social stigma, face poor working conditions, and are frequently harassed. Though these aspects are usually discussed in the context of international migration, the situation is more or less the same when migrants cross borders of states within large countries like India. In view of the host state's failure to acknowledge their presence, interstate migrants are barely considered in policy making in the state where they live. It is also possible that their voices may not be heard in the states of their origin. The widely held feeling among local community that they are 'outsiders' adds to their vulnerability. In the Indian federal system, people derive their entitlements through the fundamental rights conferred on them by the Indian Constitution and the various laws enacted by the Union government and the state governments. Apart from these rights and legal protection, people are eligible to make use of various programmes/ schemes executed by the central and state governments. Most of the central government schemes are applicable throughout the country. Even in central government schemes, the benefits reach the people through the state or local government. Unless otherwise specified, such benefits are available only to the permanent residents of the respective state. In such a situation, the interstate migrants lose their entitlements when they cross borders of their native state. For instance, a migrant labourer from states like Bihar, Orissa, West Bengal or Assam who has been availing rice or wheat and other provisions at subsidized price through the Public Distribution System (PDS) in the home state is unlikely to benefit from the PDS in Delhi. Thus, the migrants have to depend solely on the open market and become more vulnerable to the price differences in the open market compared to the local community. In the open market, some instances where migrants were asked to pay more than what is demanded from the local population were also reported. Waste pickers require adequate space for sorting and storing collected materials. In the IEMS, 59 per cent said inadequate space is a problem. Without storage, material cannot be held until it can fetch a higher price; unsheltered materials can be degraded or ruined by weather.

Macroeconomic trends like inflation and recession impact waste pickers. The rising cost of living and the increasing numbers of waste pickers, including migrants, were the most cited problems affecting all waste pickers in the IEMS study. The global recession hit waste pickers hard. Research conducted by WIEGO and its Inclusive Cities partners found the economic crisis caused a marked drop in the demand for and price of waste. At the same time, newly unemployed people entered the profession. Within value chains, waste pickers are in a disadvantaged position. Most in the IEMS study reported difficulty negotiating better prices from buyers, and focus groups in almost every city ranked exploitative or dependent relations with buyers among the most significant negative drivers. Waste pickers provide recyclable materials to formal enterprises. More than three quarters of waste pickers in the sample say their main buyers are formal businesses. Between one quarter and one half also supply recyclable materials to informal businesses, private individuals and the general public. Social stigmatization compounds waste pickers' difficulties – 97 per cent of waste pickers in Bogota and Durban said social exclusion was a problem in their work; 76 per cent in Nakuru experienced social exclusion. However, waste pickers' organizations help counteract social and legal exclusion. Harassment is a significant problem. Treated as nuisances by authorities and with disdain by the public, waste pickers are usually ignored within public policy processes and may even be arrested or physically assaulted. They may face exploitation and intimidation by middlemen, which can affect their earnings. Overall, 47 per cent of waste pickers surveyed in the IEMS indicated that harassment was a key issue affecting their work. In Bogota and Durban, the problem was reported by over 80 per cent of waste pickers. Women engaged in this occupation typically earn less than men and often face other forms of inequality. In 2012, the Latin American Waste Pickers' Network (Red Lacre), the National Movement of Waste Pickers in Brazil (MNCR), and WIEGO opened a dialogue about gender in the context of waste picking or informal recycling. Read more about the origins of the project, and access resources and tools that resulted from it. Handling waste poses many health risks. Informal waste pickers are exposed to contaminants and hazardous materials, from fecal matter and medical waste to toxic fumes and chemicals. Those who work at open dumps face risks caused by trucks, fires and surface slides. Some must take collected waste home to sort or store, introducing dangers to the home. A lack of worker protection and poor access to health care aggravate these risks. Waste pickers also endure ergonomic hazards such as heavy lifting and repetitive motion, and may experience back and lower extremity pain. Through its Social Protection Programme, WIEGO has done work on occupational health and safety (OHS) for waste pickers. One facet of the project involved the design of more ergonomically appropriate equipment.

In India, working with the waste pickers' union KKPKP and the Self-Employed Women's Association (SEWA), new pushcarts were designed and tested. Waste pickers using the new carts could carry an extra bag of refuse worth about 20-25 rupees in earnings. One woman reported saving 400 rupees in medical expenses after using the SEWA equipment. A similar situation exists in accessing the benefits of Rashtriya Swasthya Bima Yojana (RSBY), a health insurance scheme for poor12 families implemented throughout the country by the Central government. At an annual fee of Rs. 30, the scheme provides for annual coverage for inpatient care of up to Rs. 30,000 7 to five members of a family. To cater to the needs of the workers belonging to BPL families who migrate, there is a facility to split the card which is given to RSBY beneficiary

families. The smart card issued under the RSBY can be split at
the time of first issue or subsequently at a district level office. But
the families of migrant workers appear to be not making use of
this facility and therefore are unable to avail the benefits of the
scheme. Thus, in practice, the portability of benefits of RSBY
scheme remains an issue. Usually, benefits of the schemes run
by individual state governments are available to persons having
resident status in the respective state. Migrants, in general, do not
have resident status in the destination state. Migrant labourers are
not covered by this scheme also as they are not eligible for state
specific schemes. It is clear that many of the entitlements one
has in his home state are unavailable once he crosses borders of
state even when they are within the same country. This is despite
the fact that the Indian federal system envisages full portability
of the benefits across the country at least in the case of central
government schemes. It appears that there is a need for better
coordination between the governments in the host state, states
of origin and the central government to make sure that the
entitlements of inter-state migrants are not lost on account of
migration. The initiative to provide unique identity to citizens
which is underway in India may help to address the issue by
synergizing it with entitlements of the citizens so that migrant
labourers can enjoy their rights wherever they are.

Language Barriers One of the major problems that migrant
workers face when they reach Delhi is related to the differences
in the languages spoken by the migrant workers and that of the
host society. As noted earlier, though migration is between regions
within the same country, language spoken by the migrants and the
local people are different. The official languages of the country are
8 Hindi and English. This is different from the language spoken
by people in West Bengal (Bengali), Orissa (Oriya), Bihar (Hindi)

or Assam (Assamese). All these languages belong to the Indo-Aryan language family while Malayalam is a Dravidian language. Being unable to speak to the local community or the service providers in their language makes them vulnerable on many occasions as may be seen later. In view of the newly emerging situation of having to meet the requirements of people speaking different languages, the local trading community and private service providers have slowly started speaking Hindi. The migrant workers speaking Oriya or Bengali have started learning Hindi after coming to Delhi. The private sector also has started to respond to the situation in many other ways. For instance, films in Hindi language are shown in the migrant concentration areas. Health and Safety of Migrants are vulnerable because of crowded and unhygienic living conditions and inadequate provisions for their safety at the worksite. The limitations to access health care due to language barriers, lack of time, lack of knowledge about the public provisioning of health care etc. exacerbates their vulnerability. However, one advantage the migrants have in Delhi is that they may be able to benefit from the relatively better health system and health care seeking practices in the state. The presence of a public health care system which is responsive to the needs of the migrants is a necessity in states which have significant presence of migrant population. Such a system should be sensitive to the cultural, linguistic and social backgrounds of the migrants. Treatment is expected to be made available from the government hospitals almost free of cost to residents of Delhi who are poor which is ascertained by the hospital authorities on the basis of the type of a ration card they hold. With no ration card, these migrant labourers are not eligible for free/subsidised treatment in government hospitals. But it appears that public health system has slowly started responding to the requirements of the migrants. In some of the government hospitals, health care is provided to the migrant workers free of cost. But they may have to buy some of the medicines and conduct tests from labs outside the hospital for which it is paid from their pockets. Inconvenient timings of the government hospitals may be one of the reasons why they depend more on private hospitals. If they have to consult a doctor in a government hospital, they have to forego work for the day which the migrant workers usually do not want to in their quest for maximizing the earnings. Migrants depend more on private clinics and hospitals compared to public hospitals. They prefer to consult physicians who can communicate with them at least in Hindi. The temporary nature of their employment and stay limits the chances of being covered by preventive care. However, of late, the public health system in the state is slowly realising the implications of not addressing the health issues of the migrant population as it has started affecting the health of the local population also.

POLICIES AND PROGRAMMES

Whether and how informal waste pickers are included in municipal waste systems varies greatly. Worldwide, most waste pickers are not recognized for their contributions and do not have access to state-sponsored social protection. Where waste pickers are organized, this is changing. Membership-based organizations and other progressive entities are helping cities recognize the vital role waste pickers play, and encouraging authorities to design more progressive policies. Cities like Belo Horizonte, Brazil, Lima, Peru and Pune, India are developing policies that integrate waste pickers into waste collection and recycling.

The **Inter-State Migrant Workmen (Regulation of Employment and Conditions of Service) Act, 1979** is an Act of the Parliament of India enacted to regulate the condition of service of inter-state labourers in Indian labour law. The Act's purpose is to protect workers whose services are requisitioned outside their native states in India. Whenever an employer faces shortage of skills among the locally available workers, the Act creates provision to employ better skilled workers available outside the state.

An exclusionary policy environment harms livelihoods. In Bogotá and Durban, more than 89 per cent in the IEMS sample said regulations and by-laws regarding waste are a problem.

A supportive policy environment positively impacts waste pickers' livelihoods. The Belo Horizonte municipality partners with waste pickers and their organizations, providing infrastructure, subsidies and worker education. Despite some concerns raised (such as deteriorating infrastructure) during the IEMS focus groups, 63 per cent said they get positive support from the city. Replacement of repressive policies with inclusive policies focused on legal backing, redistributive measures, social recognition and the strengthening of waste picker organizations is crucial.

A list of Centre/State Acts on Migrant workers:

- Bonded Labour System (Abolition) Rules, 1976
- Building and Other Construction Workers (Regulation of Employment and Condition of Service) Act, 1996
- Building and other Construction Workers (Regulation of Employment and Condition of Service) Rules, 2002
- Building and Other Construction Workers' Welfare Cess Act, 1996
- Building and Other Construction Workers' Welfare Cess Rules, 1998
- Contract Labour (Regulation and Abolition) Act, 1970
- Contract Labour (Regulation and Abolition) Rules, 1971
- Child Labour (Prohibition & Regulation) Act, 1986

- Employees' Provident Funds & Miscellaneous Provisions Act, 1952
- Equal Remuneration Act, 1976
- Inter State Migrant Workmen

WAY FORWARD AND RECOMMENDATIONS

Since waste pickers are not recognised under Indian laws, they face numerous forms of discrimination. Their basic rights are repeatedly violated disregarding their contribution to society. Waste pickers are often targeted and harassed by police and anti-social elements as they are seen as vagrants and thieves. Waste pickers are not legally permitted by state municipalities to collect, segregate and sell waste from garbage dumps across the country, and they are deemed to be committing theft under the Indian Penal Code, 1860. Supriya Routh, in her book, *Enhancing Capabilities Through Labour Law: Informal Workers in India,* found that most waste pickers who were interviewed for a study in 2011 had been taken into police custody at least once in their lives and had been booked for petty cases. Routh's study also found that non-recognition had made migrant waste pickers ineligible for government schemes, in addition to facing insurmountable difficulties in obtaining ration cards, electricity and water facilities. This had a significant negative impact on their standard of living as well as on their mental and physical wellbeing.

Due to constant exposure to putrid and hazardous wastes, waste pickers are vulnerable to skin diseases, musculo-skeletal ailments, respiratory disorders, cuts and needle wounds. But due to non-recognition, waste pickers are often excluded from various government health schemes. Moreover, their jobs are highly insecure. A 2011 study by Chintan, a non-profit advocating for the rights of waste pickers in Delhi, found that after the Municipal Corporation of Delhi privatised waste collection, approximately 50 per cent of waste pickers lost their jobs or experienced a drastic fall in their incomes. Waste pickers previously had an informal sharing system that allowed a large number of them to collect waste within the same area. However, post-privatisation, fewer people were able to earn a living from the same volume of waste. Similarly, a study conducted in Punjab in 2016 also found that privatisation had a negative impact on their access to wastes as well as their capacity to earn a livelihood. The Municipal Solid Waste (Management and Handling) Rules passed in January 2000 (but came into effect in January 2004) under the Environment Protection Act, 1986 by the Ministry of Environment and Forests of the Government of India, after directions from the Hon. Supreme Court of India in the Almitra Patel case, mandating a comprehensive policy for collecting, handling and managing solid waste. The Rules direct the municipalities in 41 Class I municipalities to extend their mandatory responsibility (collection from common points) and undertake measures for door-step collection of waste and citizens' education for source segregation.

Although the Rules do not make a specific mention of waste-pickers, they are explicit in offering a wide range of choices to the municipalities in the systems that they may want to adopt depending upon local conditions. Contracting out the system of doorstep garbage collection, partly or fully, to both local and multinational operators is the most popular because there is a strong lobby that believes that privatisation of garbage collection is cheaper and more efficient. Frequently these measures displace waste-pickers as the contracting party now has direct control over the waste and its disposal.

The challenge before the waste pickers is to intervene in the development of waste related polices to ensure their 'voice' and 'representation'. They need to shape a policy that takes into account the livelihood and survival needs of this section of informal workers and which provides for decent work within this sector. It is also important that this intervention emphasize the need for integration of traditional structures of waste picking and management with the new technologies and business models. Thus appropriate use of technology needs to be emphasized in shaping the policy for waste management in the country. More specifically, some of their demands include:

a) There is no clear policy for waste pickers or even efforts to legislate to protect the rights of the waste pickers, in India.

b) The right to waste and access to waste, need to be envisaged in a holistic solid waste management system that gives due recognition and protection to the waste picker.

c) An integrated waste management system, in which segregation at source enables better management of waste and provides employment with better working conditions to waste pickers, needs to be mandated by law for all local bodies across the country.

Efforts in several parts of the country, notably Delhi, Pune, Ahmedabad, to unionise the workers into cooperatives and simultaneously introduce a system whereby waste pickers collect at source recyclable waste from houses, institutions, shops and establishments. Groups working with waste pickers have been demanding that the waste pickers be integrated into the door to door collection scheme so that it guarantees their access to scrap; improve their working conditions; improve their earnings; and transform the status of the occupation from scavenging to service provision.

REFERENCES

http://www.wiego.org/informal_economy_law/waste-pickers-india

https://www.downtoearth.org.in/news/a-law-for-waste-pickers-60103

https://open.uct.ac.za/bitstream/handle/11427/24492/thesis_hum_2016_peres_teresa_sandra.pdf?sequence=1

https://www.jstor.org/stable/41921808?seq=1#page_scan_tab_contents

Income Generation, Livelihood and Statelessness: An Analysis of the Current Situation of Tea Garden Workers of North Bengal, India

Saikat Roy

Abstract

The tea garden workers of North Bengal region of West Bengal possess double subalternity being workers as well as their identity of being marginalized, as most of them belong to the tribal community. The tribal workers living in a stateless situation are studied in the background of adopted plantation livelihood, economic condition and identity issues. After economic liberalization and enforcement of free market structure, the situation of the tea garden workers have tremendously deteriorated particularly in the context of income generation as well as livelihood issues of tea garden workers. These workers are hardly in a position to speak about their real situation, on the other hand there is no such positive initiative from the part of the state to address their condition. As a result there is a migration flow towards tourism industry in the hill side and other metropolitan cities for income generation.

In this context the paper tries to locate the situation of the migrant tea garden workers as well as governmental response.

Key words: *Income generation, Livelihood, Subalternity, Statelessness, Tribe, Worker, Tea Garden, North Bengal.*

Introduction

Economic compulsion of the workers and the in-consequent domination by the capitalist is the characterising principle of all capitalist production yielding surplus value and normal profits by a process of realisation. But capital, whether in advanced or backward capitalism, has always attempted to pay wages at below value by various means of extra-economic compulsion, with or without the backing of the state. Historically, capital has even created extreme forms of such extra-economic coercion, as in the brutality of the modern slave system in the Americas, the West Indies, Cuba, South Africa, etc. Once slavery was finally abolished through protests, revolts and war (but even before that in the Dutch colonies) a new form of slavery, the plantation system came into being that mainly safeguarded super-profits in indigo, sugarcane, rubber, tea, etc. The strongest survivor of that system is in the tea industry of North East India. The hills of Darjeeling, the Terai plains (Darjeeling district) and the sub- montane tracts of the Dooars (Jalpaiguri district) -all annexed within a few decades—were mainly forest and sparsely populated. The Company, spurred on by the hope of monopolising the sale of tea world-wide, started to make large land grants to all would be British planters without charging any land revenue. British investors, both from among the local functionaries of the company and from the UK., who did not know anything about planting and manufacture of tea, could rely on a new corporate entity, the managing agency. The individual gardens or cluster of them belonging to the same owners were incorporated in England.

Now the problem was to find the large number of workers needed for the estates. The local populations in these regions

refused to work in the plantations once they realised that life in
the estates was a form of slavery more onerous that any suffered
under the Ahoms or other chiefs. It was then that recruitment
focused on the tribal populations from the mainly eastern part
of the central Indian plateau- Jharkhand and Chotanagpur —to
work in the increasingly proliferating number of estates in the
Terai and Dooars of North Bengal. The overwhelming majority
of the latter shared a wide ranging socio-cultural ethos in their
homeland and which can be called the Jharkhandi ethos. But they
spoke various languages belonging to the Mundari subset of the
Austro-asiatic group of languages and also several languages of
the Dravidian group.

Migration and exlusion of labour force in the capitalist system

A brief journey into the theories of modern state market nexus in the
capitalists' world is necessary to place the state-market relationship
in India in perspective. Power or governance in India is fast taking
the shape of biopower and the market is reproduced in social and
cultural spheres. It is in this task that the state penetrates into the
social and cultural spheres and also in the individual and social
psyche. It appropriates the existing cultural symbols and creates
new symbols. It is, therefore, absolutely essential to understand
the changing equation between economy and power or the rules
to 'bio-power' in order to explore the integrationist mechanics of
the liberal-democratic Indian state.

India in post-war II period pursued welfareism of a kind
and at the same time increasingly performed the function of
reproduction of the order and the damage-repairing work by
periodically coming up with welfare programmes to support the
victims of exploitation, and even by coming up with bail-out
packages for the 'capital-in crisis' in the line prescribed by Keynes.
In the Nehruvian model of national development, this was also

followed by the latter regimes until the early eighties, when the state in the pre-globalization period combined capitalized growth with 'welfare packages' for the vulnerable in order to defer the legitimating crisis.

The liberal-democratic order in India made an elaborate arrangement for the integration of its otherwise "excluded" and marginalized sections into the order through schemes like democratic decentralization, land reforms, capacity building programmes right to education, forest rights act, tribal sub-plan, the policy of protective discrimination, granting of regional autonomy and formation of regional development authority, special welfare programs for the marginalized and poor people including the SCs and STs and so on. This was clearly in line with the liberal model of development where (a) the state makes arrangements for the protection of the victims of the market forces; (b) reproduces and prepares the labour force for the market, and (c) ensures peace and stability to facilitate smooth sailing of the manufacturing and business activities. But the growing market leaves a negative impact on the welfare character of the state and its ability to arrest the resulting exclusion and marginalization, particularly of the vulnerable sections like the *adivasis* who have very little control over material resources and skills. When the market rules reign supreme, the *adivasis* who have not experienced much of capacity building stand the risk of further exclusion.

Adivasi labour force in Terai and Dooars region
The *adivasi* (tribal) population in north Bengal is largely constituted of the migrants from the chotanagpur region of central India, who moved out of their original abode in the second half of the 19th century because of exploitation by the *dikes* (aliens), land loss, loss of forests rights, imposition of land rent, and colonial oppression, particularly in the post-Santhal rebellion period. The expanding

tea gardens in the Dooars and Terai regions (along with parts of Assam) offered them livelihood although they found themselves in another exploitation and oppressive economic and power arrangement. The expanding *zamandari* estates in the districts of the region, particularly in Malda, and Dinajpur districts in the latter half of the 19th and first of the twentieth century also accommodated these migrants, primarily as tenant-cultivators. The expansion of rail links later also encouraged migration of tribal labour force from central India. The migration flow stopped by 1940s when the tea gardens stopped expanding and the land management system underwent major transformation after the abolition of tribal *zamindari* system in the1950s. In the Dooars and Terai, the surplus labour force, ejected from the tea garden, took hold of the fallow land when lack of education (and skill) made them depend on agriculture and tea almost exclusively.

Trends in income generation, economic condition and livelihood

Tribal economy, largely defined as subsistence economy, is based on agriculture in four districts of north Bengal, namely Cooch-Behar, north Dinajpur, Malda, and on tea in Jalpaiguri and Darjeeling districts. Census data over the years have shown that the percentage share of cultivators (owning cultivators) has declined sharply in these districts with corresponding rise in the number of agriculture laborers. By reading these two trends together, one can discern the massive land alienation the tribal population in the region has experienced. And this happened despite the government efforts to protection of tribal land and despite the much acclaimed redistribution of land among the landless *adivasis,* as a part of land reform programmers. (See, Roy 2008: 41-42; Roy 2009).

Another trend in tribal economy has been a decline in significance of household industry over the years. In the districts, the share of the 'main workers' engaged in household industries hover around 0.5 to one percent in 2001 (Roy 2008: 42). The 'the other workers' category that includes jobs in tea garden workers in the offices or other organisd sector, did not grow expectedly. Interestingly, such growth is higher only in Darjeeling and Jalpaiguri districts where the *adivasi* work force is primarily engaged as tea garden workers; the growth of jobs in other districts has been then 0.5 percent annum. And even in Jalpaiguri district which accommodates most of the tea gardens, the growth of jobs has been only 16 percent in four decades.

The slow growth of jobs in 'other workers' category has to be understood in the stagnation and the planters 'refusal to recruit in permanent worker category. The strength of permanent work force in number of casual workers has been a feature of the tea gardens such that the strength of male workers has declined while there has been a marginal increase in the number of female workers both in the permanent and casual categories- a feature that can be termed as 'feminisation of workforce' (Roy 2008: 46-48). The increase in work participation as 'other workers,' although meagre, is not only a positive development the *adivasis* of north Bengal have achieved. Four factors are primarily responsible for the economic plights of the *adivasis* in the region: a) meagre control over material and human resources, b) their incapability to take advantages of the market opportunities, c) inadequate state support, and d) exploitative presentation of the market group which control them. The increase of control over the material and human resources could have enhanced their 'capacity' to take greater advantages of market opportunities and to thwart the penetration of the more powerful exploitation forces. But what the state has done so far is to initiate some relief-work here and there and some reservation which have failed to enhance the quality of tribal life. The low rate of literacy (while total ST literacy is 43.4%,

ST female literacy is only 29.15% in west Bengal in 2001), high rate of dropout at the school level and very little spread of higher and technical education have hampered the process of human resources development over these years (see Roy 2008: 26-27). The presentation of the outsiders into the tribal belt with the spread of communication and including market crisis created by the tea garden owners including distinct strategy of casualisation and the threat of closure as a measure to deprive the tea workers and weaken the trade union movement have conversely brought miseries for the *adivasis.*

Work situation of Adivasi people in the tea gardens of Terai and Dooars region

By the time of Independence, there was a rudimentary healthcare system, primary schools with mud-floored structures for all classes and one teacher; improvements in the roads infrastructure (thanks mainly to war preparations), and railways were constructed mainly for hauling tea and grains, etc.

But the enclave nature of the economy and the extreme domination of the management remained. The domination was now not in the form of policing the workers and juridical powers of the management. The *sardars* referred to above and a small number of their relatives and friends were slowly elevated to a layer of people who did the ground level management under orders from the management, allowing the top layers to retreat from conflict situations. This layer now has a name—sub-staff. This layer of management, with a wage difference with the workers and with many special privileges, was/is not socially very distant from the workers. This was their strength and the measure of their efficacy while carrying out the unpleasant orders of higher management. They could/can utilise kin/community/tribe/ caste differences to divide and rule for the management. But such differences are vanishing fast under the cudgel of the capitalist work process.

Since 1951, many benign laws have been passed for the benefit of tea workers and many good laws have been extended to the estates such as on the payment of wages, compensation for injury at work, pensions and gratuity, minimum wages etc. These were in the main due to the unionisation process that began in the late forties and picked up a very strong momentum in the early fifties. But for the lack of strong inspectorates and the judicial process remaining out of the reach of the workers due to illiteracy, poverty and the rapaciousness of most lawyers, none of these laws are as a rule implemented properly or at all.

The work situation in the tea belt of North Bengal is facing lots of troubles following the issues of collapse of tea gardens, wages, basic facilities directly affecting the economic condition of the *adivasi* people of the region. The concentration of the tribes in remote areas with less income opportunities, negligible hold on the material resources, neglect of the development of human resources in terms of education and technical skill, decline of traditional crafts, crises in tea industry and agriculture are some of the apparent factors that explain the problems of livelihood of the tribal population of north Bengal.

Till today, electricity has not reached tribal villages. In Terai-Dooars area tribals are mainly tea gardens workers. Closure and lock-out of tea gardens has become everyday news. At present there are nearly twenty closed tea gardens. And about 95,000 workers are suffering from starvation. They are deprived of their provident fund, gratuity benefit and medical facilities. They have no BPL cards, as they receive ration from tea gardens. Role of trade union leaders is dubious. Often they passively helped the tea gardens owners to declare lock-out in lieu of financial benefit.

In Terai-Dooars region malnutrition, starvation deaths, diseases, joblessness, child trafficking have become a regular feature. Government financial assistance to the workers of closed tea garden workers is not regularly paid. As a result the workers are forced to work elsewhere as daily wage labourers. In some cases the nature of work offered is unsuitable to the tea garden labourers, specially the women workers of the tea gardens are not accustomed to hard laborious work. There is also legal complication to distribute financial assistance to all workers of the closed tea gardens. As per existing rules, those who have no PF account are not entitled to get allowance. So a huge number of workers of closed tea gardens are yet to receive allowance.

Besides closure and lock-out, tea garden workers are afraid of another danger. In 1997, the West Bengal Government gave permission to establish Housing Complex on the 406.64 acre plot of Chandmoni Tea estates land. As a result plantation workers were evicted and they were employed under the construction company. The Workers of Sikarpur, Dagapur and Matigara tea estates which are situated on the outskirts of Siliguri are afraid of eviction anytime soon. Already the owner of Matigara Tea Estate is following the path shown by the Chandmoni Tea Estate. Matigara Tea Estate has already uprooted tea plantation on a huge area. Naturally the workers of these gardens are afraid of losing their jobs.

Since 2005, under the umbrella of Akhil Bharatiya Adivasi Vikas Parishad (ABAVP) the *adivasi* people started raising their voice against the situations they are facing everyday. The *Parishad* is a Delhi-Based NGO 'which was formed for the social and cultural uplift of the adivasis in the country' (Bhowmik 2011:

27). The organisation has its root in Adivasi Bikas Manch of the trade unions and political parties to overcome them, have resulted into loss of faith in their effectiveness. Since then the ABAVP is struggling for the betterment of the work situation of the Adivasi people.

In a memorandum dated 29. 01. 2009 submitted to the then Chief Minister of West Bengal the *Parishad* highlighted the following issues:

1. That all the closed/ locked out tea gardens must be opened immediately and all the sick tea gardens must be revived without delay for which the govt. both central and state must come forward with adequate financial package for taking necessary action into the matter immediately.

2. That no tea garden should be declared closed/ lock out without prior approval of the concerned district magistrates.

3. That all the holidays in tea gardens must be declared as paid holidays.

4. That the hospital facilities should be provided to all the garden workers irrespective of permanent or casual including ex-workers.

5. That all the tribals residing/ working in tea gardens must be included in the list of BPL card holders and accordingly the BPL cards must be issued to them immediately.

6. That the surplus/ vested land of the government of West Bengal in tea gardens areas of Dooars and Tarai should preferentially be distributed among the *adivasis* of tea gardens.

7. That all the private tea gardens must be taken into the purview of government undertaking for overall development of the tea gardens and the *adivasi* workers as a whole.

8. That the adequate representatives from this *parishad* in the matter of labor welfare and development of tea gardens must be taken into consideration in the committees of management of the tea gardens as per provisions under the plantations labour act 1951 as amended from time to time.

9. That all the welfare/ development schemes of government under CAPART, DRDA, IRDP, NREP, LAMPS, JRY, REEOP, WBSC/ST development finance corporation self-employment program and lay etc. must be given to the *adivasis* of tea gardens similar to the tribals of panchayat areas irrespective of panchayat jurisdiction.

10. That the need-based wages as per minimum wages act 1948 with West Bengal rules as amended from time to time must be given to the workers of all the tea gardens.

11. That all the country liquor/ foreign liquor shops running in the tea garden and the ITDP areas must be closed forthwith.

Despite continuous actions there was no remarkable change in the situation of Adivasi laborers. They are still facing the problems of wages, locked tea gardens, housing and other government facilities.

Till 2014, a great number of memorandum have been submitted to the government offices but there is no remarkable change to be noticed. In the memorandum submitted to Chief Minister Mamata Banerjee dated 12. 02.2014 the ABAVP focused on the following issues:

1. The Adivasi Society in Tea gardens is the victim of abject poverty due to the insufficient wage and non-implementation of the Plantation and Factory Act etc.

2. Closed/locked out tea gardens be opened with permanent solutions. Sick tea gardens may be revived without delay for which the both central and state government must come

forward with financial packages for taking necessary action into the matter immediately.

3. No tea garden should be declared closed/locked out at the whims of tea management and without prior approval of the concerned District Magistrate as these have become a practice of management to blackmail the tea workers to bow before management and not to raise any legal demands.

4. The tea garden workers are still landless and homeless for one and half a century. Although other poor landless people of West Bengal have got land *patta,* the tea workers have been left in the lurch.

5. The housing facilities of tea gardens are on Govt. lease land, which have been allotted to them. The State Govt. may allot those lands/ plots to them permanently.

6. The wage of tea workers must be framed as per the guidelines of Minimum Wage Acts as workers have been receiving lesser wage than fixed under minimum wage acts and suffering in abject poverty for decades due to the apathy of tea industries.

7. Holiday in tea gardens must be declared as paid holiday as workers are taking rest on the basis of labour laws.

8. Labour Department of West Bengal has not been able to monitor the flaunting of various Labour Acts, including hospital facilities in tea gardens. Therefore, the Govt. should come forward and extend its own health service to the tea garden labourers and Govt. may impose CESS on the tea industries for the health services.

9. All tribals residing/ working in Tea gardens may be included in the list of BPL card holders and accordingly BPL cards may be issued to them immediately.

10. Surplus/ vested land of the Govt. of West Bengal in Tea Garden areas of Dooars and Terai should preferably be distributed among the Adivasis of Tea Gardens.

The picture shows that in the last 5 years the work situation of the *adivasi* people in the Terai and Dooars region has not seen noticeable changes. They are still fighting with the same problem as they were 5 years ago.

Conclusion

When the 'protector' state is in a mood to recede and the market is on the rampage, it is quite natural that the powerless and voiceless people who live on the margins would find themselves more vulnerable. Being a part of the neo-liberal market the *adivasis*, with animal control over material and human sources and culture capital, are engaged in fierce survival battle as dominant sections with much greater control over resources not only do not give them much economic and socio-political space but often intrude into whatever small space they occupy. With very little effort to human resources development initiative, the *adivasis* cannot reap the benefits of the policy of protective discrimination or the special development initiatives of the state.

The state, armed with its welfare package, does try to do repair works here and there, but ends up extending support to the liberal market. With very little control over human resources the *adivasis* cannot access the benefits of the policy of protective discrimination or the special development initiatives undertaken by the state periodically. The corrupt yet inefficient bureaucracy and the *panchayat* functionaries come in their way to reap the benefits of development initiatives. The over –exploitative arrangement in the tea gardens and loss of land (because of division of holding among the heirs and alienation by the manipulative and resourceful neighbours) perpetuate their marginalised existence in the region.

The market uncertainty, the penetration of the forces of globalisation and crisis in the tea gardens make them even more vulnerable as a social category. Being a part of such a depressing reality, the *adivasis* in the region are now showing signs of losing confidence in the ability of the state and other systematic organs to protect them.

References

Ahamad, Imtiaz, Ghosh, A. Partha, Reifeld Helmut, ed., 2000. *Pluralism and Equality*: *Values in Indian Society and politics*, Sage Publications, New Delhi.

Bhawmik, Sharit, 2011. 'Wages and Ethnic Conflicts in Bengal's Tea Industry,' *Economic and Political Weekly*, August 6, 2011: 26-29.

Dasgupta, Jyotindra, 1998. 'Community, Authenticity and Autonomy: Insurgency and Institutional Development in India's North-East', in Amrita Basu and Atul Kohli (eds.), *Community, Conflict and the State in India,* Oxford University Press, Oxford.

Pandharipande, R. V., 2002. "Minority matters: issues in minority languages in India". *International Journal on Multicultural Societies*, 4 /2.

Rajan, Nalini., 2002. *Democracy and the limits of Minority Rights*, Sage Publications, New Delhi.

Roy, Sanjay K., 2008. *Work Participation of Tribal Women and Marginalization*: The Case of Tribes in North Bengal, Levant Books, Kolkata.

Roy, Sanjay K., 2009. 'North Bengal Tribes in Development Perspective' in *Journal Anthropological Society*, 44: 5-27.

UNDP (United Nation Development Programme)., 2004. *Human Development Report* 2004: Cultural Liberty in Today's Diverse World. New York: UNDP.

Xaxa, Virginius., 2008. "State, Society, and Tribes: issues in Post-Colonial India", Dorling Kindersley (India) Pvt. Ltd, licensees of Pearson Education in South Asia, New Delhi.

The Making and Unmaking of the Migrant Labourers of the Marginal Caste[1]

Paul D'Souza

Abstract

The migration from rural areas to urban centres in search of employment opportunities is common among the Marginal Caste, making it one of the urbanized caste communities. An empirical study of the Marginal Caste in the city of Ahmedabad shows two important trends: 1) The migration status based on the number of years residing in the city indicate marked differences in the 'settled-residents' and 'recent migrants' among the Marginal caste in the city. The 'settled migrants' have claimed space in socio-religious spheres in the city along with occupational and residential space. The story differs for the 'recent migrants' on many counts as they have not been able to occupy similar socio-economic and residential spaces in the city like the 'settled-residents'. 2) The occupational history of the migrants and their families belonging to the community shows a drastic shift in occupation. The shift is from 'work not related to sanitation' in rural areas to 'sanitation related works' in the city. There is no substantial occupational mobility visible among the Marginal caste; on the contrary, there is a further marginalization of those engaged in sanitary works in the urban labour market.

In this context, the paper unfolds the dynamics of urban labour market revealing the process of making and unmaking of the Marginal Caste in the city and how the very process of urbanization and the state have played a significant role in establishing the members of the Marginal Caste as sanitary workers in urban labour market in both, organized as well as informal sector. Firstly, it shows that instead of secularizing caste-occupation relations, urbanization has now only reinforced the same but also strengthened the caste economy. Secondly, the process of assimilation and marginalisation of the Marginal Caste in the city reveals the existence of two seemingly contradictory sociological trends, i.e. continued exclusion and progressive inclusion of the Marginal Caste in the larger urban society and its socio-economic geography. The existence of this paradoxical trend challenges the modernity of urban India and the development induced paradigm of urbanization.

1.   Gujarat and its urbanization

One of the major characteristics of modernized Gujarat is its urbanization. Gujarat is the third most urbanized state of the country and is steadily transforming into a predominantly urban society. According to 2011 census, the total population of Gujarat is 60 million, which includes the urban population of more than 27 million distributed in 278 urban centres. The population of urban Gujarat has increased by more than five times during the first eight decades of the 20th century. It has increased from 2.03 million in 1901 to 10.60 million in 1981 and 18.93 million in 2001. The level of urbanization in Gujarat during the 20th century has always been higher than the country as a whole. Over the years, the share of urban population has gone up to 38 per cent in 2001 and has reached to 42.6 per cent in 2011.

A large number of urban centers in Gujarat are concentrated in the industrialized corridor from Mehsana in the north to Vapi in the south located along the Ahmedabad-Mumbai railroad link.

This "golden corridor" has contributed to the rapid economic growth and economic prosperity of the state. The development of small-scale industries all over the state and large-scale industries in certain areas, has generated employment potentials causing rapid rural–urban migration (Shahi 1989: 92). The uneven development in Gujarat has resulted in large-scale migration by poor households from poorer regions to nearby urban and rural areas in search of livelihood and to escape social oppression. Industrially developed and urbanized centers provide conducive environment to migrant workers to improve their livelihood. Providing a detailed mapping of the inter-regional migration between the period 1961-81, Visaria and Kothari (1984) clearly show a strong association between the level of development and in-migration within the state. Another study by Amita Shah (2002) also indicates the direction of inter-regional migration, mainly from rural to urban areas. Evidently, the incidence of rural-urban migration was higher in Gujarat than in the rest of India.

2.   Ahmedabad city – A reflection of the state

The city of Ahmedabad is the symbol that evokes images of modernity that have far reaching implications across urban India. The city of Ahmedabad founded in 1411 as a new capital for the *Sultans* of Gujarat by Ahmed Shah, known as the Walled City, earned its special place in the twentieth century India. Its title as the "Manchester of India" gave it the status of a Westernised and industrialised city of India with a capitalist outlook with entrepreneurship in textiles. The Gandhi Ashram in Ahmedabad became the national headquarter of India's freedom movement; the cosmopolitan modern institutions like world class institution of space science - Physical Research Laboratory, India's premiere business school - the Indian Institute of Management and The National Institute of Design have secured a prominent place in modern globalized world pointing towards the future of India; two most experimented coalitions in Indian politics after independence, i.e. the KHAM strategy for a political coalition of the Congress party and the coalitions of the BJP on the basis of Hindutva, became the "laboratories" for the national politics of India. The laboratories also became ground for explosion of caste-based rioting in 1985-86 between Marginal Castes and upper castes, and religion-based riots between Hindus and Muslims in 2002, one of the worst riots in India. Ahmedabad was the epicentre of these explosions that changed the communal, social and geographic landscape of the city.

Along with historical growth and development, the city has developed key social characteristics showing two sides of Ahmedabad. The modern city continues to hold on to the traditional Ahmedabad; caste and religious communities with distinct culture and life style. The city of the businessman is also the city of industrial working class. The city that looks at the future with global outlook is also the place of the poor and the marginalized living below the poverty line; the city that dreams of "slum-less city" accommodates more than 40 per cent of its population in hundreds of slums and *chawls*. In spite of economic development, the city is lagging behind on many fronts, leaving a large majority at the margins of urban life. The socio-religious and communal segregation and polarization is the culture in which the city lives now; symbolically the river Sabarmati divides the city into two.

Ahmedabad, which is the *de-facto* state capital, accounts for over 23 per cent of the total urban population. Spatially, the Ahmedabad Municipal Corporation (AMC) area has grown from 5.72 sq. km. in 1887 to 190.84 sq. km. in 1991. At present, the total area of the mega city is 464.16 sq. kms. As per data released by the Government of India for Census 2011, Ahmedabad is an Urban Agglomeration coming under the category of Million Plus UA/City. Although Ahmedabad city has a population of 5,577,940; its urban / metropolitan population is 6,361,084. Administratively, the city of Ahmedabad is divided into six zones comprising of 64 election wards. The Central Government declared this city as a 'Mega city' in 2005. In 2006, the Ahmedabad Municipal Corporation (AMC) included 17 other municipalities and 30 Gram *Panchayats* in its jurisdiction. Thus, the city is one of the largest "corporation cities" of the state. In many ways Ahmedabad is the microcosm of the state, representing the modern state of Gujarat with all its development and deprivations.

3.   The Urbanized Marginal Caste

According to 2001 census, the total population of the Marginal Caste in the State of Gujarat was 407,083, accounting for 11.3 per cent of the total Scheduled Caste population. A higher percentage of the Marginal Caste lives in the urban areas than in the rural. The urban population is much higher in the districts which have major cities of the State i.e. Ahmedabad, Vadodara, Rajkot, Junagadh, Surat, Jamnagar (except the case of Bhavnagar) than the rural population in respective districts. This makes it amply clear that all the cities have witnessed a high migration of the Marginal Caste because of employment opportunities as sanitary workers in the Municipal Corporations and local bodies. Twenty one per cent of the total population of the Marginal Caste in the State is concentrated in Ahmedabad district of which 80 per cent lives in the city of Ahmedabad alone. The composition of the population of the Marginal Caste living in Ahmedabad shows that the metropolitan city is instrumental in providing livelihood as sanitary workers not only to the large rural population of the Marginal Caste of the district but also from other parts of the

State. The city is one of the largest "corporation cities" of the state employing the highest number of members from the Marginal Caste for sanitary functions.

Urbanization and Changing Occupational Status in Urban Labour Market

Urbanization has modified the traditional occupational structure and has brought about a considerable degree of occupational mobility and change. An intensive study conducted among the Marginal Caste in Ahmedabad reveals the process of conversion of its members as sanitary workers in the city. In order to assess the occupational mobility among the respondents, an inquiry was made into the last occupation held by members of the respondent's family over three generations. This included grandparents (generation 1), parents (generation 2), and the respondent and the spouse (generation 3).

The distribution of three generations by occupational categories (see chart 1) shows that they were engaged in mainly four types of occupations: 1) 'Work not related to sanitation' in rural areas - agriculture related work/daily wage labour/traditional occupations; 2) 'Work not related to sanitation' in city - rag pickers/labour work/ assisting jobs/skill-based works/professional jobs/petty business 3) 'Sanitation related work' - organized sector; 4) 'Sanitation related work' - informal sector.

The generation-wise distribution of the consolidated occupational categories shows that nearly 44 per cent of the first generation members – the grandparents of the respondents were engaged in agriculture-related works and traditional occupations like basket-making or rope-making back in rural areas. Those of them who migrated to the city were engaged in 'Sanitation related work' (37 per cent), largely in the informal sector. The first generation members remained employed with the above two types of occupations and very few among them diverted to other 'work not related to sanitation'.

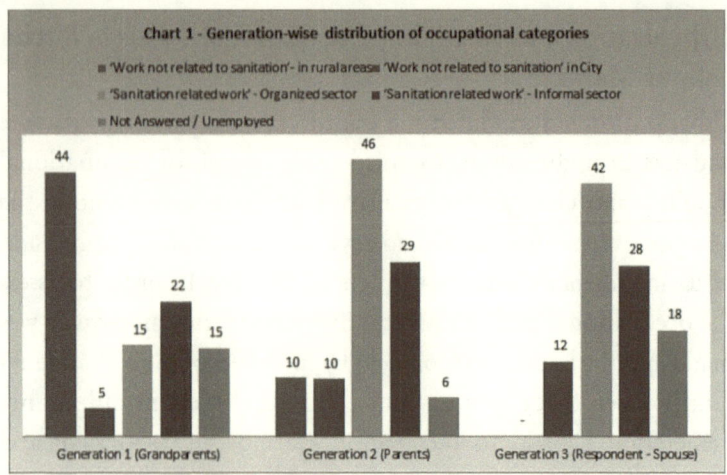

A significant shift is indicated among the members of the second generation – the parents of the respondents. Of the total, 75 per cent of the members were engaged in 'Sanitation related work'. It is important here to see the historical development of the occupational shift among the members of the Marginal Caste in the city. The number of those employed in organized sector, by the state as sanitary workers from this generation is highest (46 per cent) among all three generations. Similarly, a large number of members who migrated to urban areas during this time could not be absorbed in organized sector and neither could they find opportunities in other work not related to sanitation. Thus, 29 per cent of them from this generation take recourse to employment in informal sector as sanitary workers.

Along with this shift, another small but significant shift is being indicated, where nearly 10 per cent of them have moved to 'work not related to sanitation' of which 7 per cent of them have taken up lower level occupations like rag picking and causal labour. This once again indicates the non-availability of either the 'Sanitation related work' or other higher-level occupations. Only 10 per cent of the respondents' parents were engaged in agricultural and traditional occupations back in the rural areas.

The members of the third generation are all in the city and obviously no one is engaged in occupations like agriculture or traditional occupations in rural areas. As many as 70 per cent of them are engaged in 'Sanitation related works' largely dominated in organized sector. Most of those who are now settled residents of the city have become the sanitary workers and workers in informal sector to some extent in the city. However, a significant change observed in this generation is that 7 per cent of them take recourse to lower level 'work not related to sanitation'; and nearly 5 per cent of them divert themselves to higher-level 'work not related to sanitation'.

The occupational status among the members of Marginal Caste in the city of Ahmedabad indicate the significant role of the very process of urbanization and the state[2] have played towards establishing the members of the Marginal Castes as sanitary workers in urban areas (see also Vijay Prashad 2000; Gooptu 1996). The occupational history of the three generations of the family members of the respondents shows a drastic shift in their occupational patterns, from work not related to sanitation to sanitation related works. One observes that the members of the Marginal Castes from rural areas who were predominantly agricultural labourers in the rural economy are assimilated in the urban labour market as sanitary workers, first largely in the organized sector in local bodies and then in the informal sector. The processes of urbanization, and to a certain extent the policies of the state, have been instrumental in diverting a specific caste group to the work related to sanitation in the cities. The city was thought to be a place where employment in any occupation would be free of caste. Instead, the data emphasizes that the urbanization process has reinforced caste-occupation relations and strengthened the involvement of the Marginal Caste in work related to sanitation.

In rural India, the sanitation work was entrusted to a menial servant, who as a rule belonged to the lowest caste and lived on the outskirts of the village. There were a few families in each village taking care of these functions in the villages. Their duties were multifarious. Apart from work related to sanitation, they kept the village meeting-houses clean, patrolled the villages at night, acted as messengers to the headmen, served as referees on matters affecting the village boundaries, guarded the crops, assisted in agricultural operations, attended on Government officials who visited the village, and carried palanquins and torches at festivals (Matthai 1993; Franco et al 2004).

The problem of night-soil and its management was perceived seriously in the urban areas as the same was seldom perceived seriously in the villages (Chaudhary 2000; Chaplin 1997). This contributed to rapid out-migration of the Marginal Caste from rural to urban areas. In fact, 'in the colonial period they were brought into urban areas to perform the works related to sanitation and became an urban community' (K.P. Singh 1998). With the rise in urbanization after 1960s, the number of sanitary workers increased in urban areas. The task force constituted by the Planning Commission, in its report submitted in 1991 had estimated the number of "scavengers" for the year 1989 as 4,00,949 individuals, out of which 3,33,729 were in the urban areas and 67,170 in the rural areas. This shows that about 83 per cent of "scavenges" were in the urban and only 17 per cent in rural areas (see also The Ministry of Welfare, Government of India, Annual Report, 1995-96). The term "scavenger" is used throughout the government records and has gained official, legitimate use. It is defined as 'a person engaged in or employed for manually carrying human excreta or any sanitation work' (National Commission for *Safai-karmachari* Act 1993).

Although they are employed in the organized as well as the informal sector, the state is the largest agency which employs and pays over a million sanitary workers (Macwan 2001). The field investigation done through sample study in the city of Ahmedabad indicate that 75 per cent of the respondents were engaged in work related to sanitation of which around 60 per cent of them were employed in the organized sector[3] as sanitary workers and 40 per cent of them were engaged in the informal sector[4] in works related to sanitation. In urban areas, all functions related to sanitation are carried out mostly by the members of the Marginal Castes. Another important change marked in the pattern of their employment in the towns and cities was that to a large extent, they ceased to be servile labourers and servants of the higher castes and worked instead as paid municipal employees (see Gooptu 1996). They have, therefore, become sanitary workers and a niche has been created for them in the urban areas. They have become indispensable in all public places, institutions, factories, hospitals, cinema houses, business establishments and NGO offices, anywhere where there are cleaning jobs to be done (Fernando 2004). Thus, with urbanization, those engaged in sanitary works are bestowed with more secular (neutral) and official status, the *Safai-karmacharis*. Some social scientists refer to them as 'professionals of the city' (Vivek 1998) and in places

such as the Delhi Municipal Corporation they have been called
"*SwasthyaKamdar*" (the health workers).

4.   The Making and Unmaking of the Marginal Caste

The Marginal Caste living in the city of Ahmedabad is not a
homogenous group. There are marked socio-economic and cultural
differences among them. The classification of the respondents'
migration status based on the number of years residing in the city
divides the entire population into two groups, i.e. the 'settled-
residents' and 'recent migrants'. The 'settled-residents' are those
who are more permanent inhabitants of the city, living in the city
for 50 years or more. As many as 35 per cent (105) of the total
respondents fall into this category. The 'recent migrants' are those
who have come to the city over the recent years from different
parts of the state and are not yet fully settled in the city. As many
as 65 per cent, (195) of the respondents have been living in the
city for less than 50 years. The data points out that the inflow
of the migrants to the city is continuous, although at a declining
rate (see chart 2).

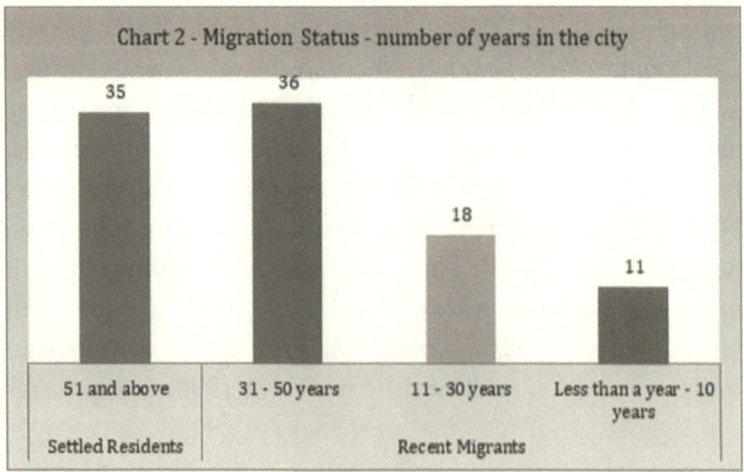

Settled Migrants and their Assimilation in the City

The history of the Marginal Caste in the city of Ahmedabad can be traced to over two centuries. A few facts, collected from the settled residents reveal that their forefathers (ancestors) migrated from villages of neighbouring districts two centuries ago and settled down in and around Ahmedabad. The established population does make a distinction between themselves and the members of the community who migrated later to the city after Independence, calling them outsiders or villagers while considering themselves 'native-residents' or city-dwellers.

Around the turn of the century, the mill owners, started to build *chawls* (walk-throughs) for housing their workers. These were narrow, dead end alleyways lined with one or two room dwellings, which the workers could rent at a low rate. In 1889, the city authorities also started providing factory workers with these kinds of houses, as part of a building plan that closely resembled the 'coolie lines' constructed on plantations and in mining enclaves. These single-storey barrack-like tenements, grouped along narrow streets around the mills, became increasingly popular in the twentieth century (Breman 2004: 33). There are a number of such traditional *mohallas* and *chawls*, divided according to caste and religion within the limits of the old city.

Many of them were settled in old villages at the outskirts of the city and those who migrated later on from different regions of Gujarat found some place in various traditional localities in the city. There were a number of typical traditional *Harijan Mohallas* and *Chawls* of Dalit communities within the limits of old and the walled city well-established since a few generations. It is said that there were twelve traditional *Bhangi Mohallas* corresponding to the twelve gates of the city wall. The walled city of Ahmedabad followed a radial pattern of streets with twelve gates (Nayak 2003).

One could locate some of the *Mohallas* situated at the broken outer wall of the old city even today and now part of the main city. However, some of the traditional *mohallas* that were established at the outskirts became part of the city after the extension of its geographical limits.

The residential pattern of the Marginal Caste in the city of Ahmedabad showing caste-based segregated community clusters is not an exception. Such patterns are found in most cities where settlements were divided up according to caste and religion (Brenam 2004). Around 6 per cent of the total households (577 households) of the Marginal Caste identified are located in traditional *mohallas* and *chawls*. These *mohallas* are mostly occupied by the 'settled residents', a majority of whom found patronage in traditional *jajmani* system (known as *gharaki*) of employment in housing localities, colonies and textile mills.

As the years passed by, the textile mills were closed and the patronage shifted to Ahmedabad Municipal Corporation who employed them as sanitary workers in the city. With this the 'settled residents' occupied a specific, exclusive space in the city's economic and social life. This was well expressed and maintained by the fact that the municipal authorities later on (1940-50) provided housing, commonly known as "slums quarters" and "health quarters" to sanitary workers employed in the Corporation. The quarters later became synonymous with the sanitary workers. Such residential quarters were also provided for employees of the railways, the military staff, hospital staff and various educational institutions and public undertakings. Most of the quarters are built in localities from where the employees can be easily transported to the places of work. As many as 2700 identified households (29 per cent) are located in quarters. Such residential facilities are not provided any more.

Over the years, the 'settled residents' living in *Mohallas* and quarters have begun to move out to housing colonies with their improved economic conditions. Housing colonies are residential localities consisting of row-houses or bungalows built and owned by individual families. This has given rise to more than thirty colonies occupied by the Marginal Caste mostly concentrated in the extended areas of the city. Nearly 13 per cent (1238 households) of the identified population of the Marginal Caste lives in these colonies. Most of the colonies of the Marginal Caste are located close to other Dalit groups or upper caste population. In that sense colonies provide secular spaces (localities free of caste restrictions) in the city. The better style and standard of living of the members in these colonies also indicate socio-economic upward mobility of the residents.

Thus, the 'settled residents' accounting for nearly 48 per cent of the identified households are concentrated mostly in the main city, *mohallas*, quarters and colonies in extended city. Occupationally they have better share in permanent employment in organized sector, especially as sanitary workers. Thus, the occupation of the Marginal Caste has played an important role in gaining access to housing and with their improved economic conditions they have been able to occupy better housing and more permanent space in the city.

Along with occupational and residential space the settled migrants have claimed space in socio-religious spheres in the city. *The Ahmedabad Samasth Bhangi gnatipanch* is a well-organized caste council of the 'settled residents' of the Marginal Caste in the city of Ahmedabad consisting of fourteen traditional *mohallas*. Traditionally the Ahmedabad city *gnatipanch* was divided into three *panches* (before 1926), viz. 1) Kalupur *panch* 2) Majedia *panch* 3) Char *mohalla panch*. Sometime later it was unified into one and was named *Ahmedabad Samasth Bhangi Gnatipanch*. All the members accept and bind themselves according to the constitution drafted and approved by the general body in 1995. However, membership to the group is restricted to those considered as the 'native residents'. The community organization has provided a city-level identity to its members and has established a centrally located space as its office and a temple which has a long history to its account.

The 'settled residents' celebrate two important socio-religious events i.e. *Chhadi Mahotsav* - the annual religious festival on the day of *Goganavmi* and the a*nnual city procession (Nagar-yatra), celebrating the Valmiki jayanti*, which is now known as the mini *rath-yatra* in the city among the Marginal Caste. This clearly asserts for place and has in fact managed to claim urban space in the central part of the city. These processions and annual celebrations are perceived by the members of the Marginal Caste as means to enhance the visibility and identity assertion of the community. They derive significance through the demonstration of the collectivity of the Marginal Caste in public sphere i.e. the main city area, with the support of a few political leaders, religious heads and government authorities. The city has provided space to the Marginal Caste, however small and insignificant it may look, to claim their right to the city.

'Recent Migrants' and their Marginalization in the City

The recent migrants belonging to the Marginal caste who consist nearly 52 per cent of them have not been able to occupy similar socio-economic and residential spaces in the city like the 'settled-residents'. The story differs for the recent migrants on many counts. The inflow of the migrants coming to the city and a large number of them finding a house in slums seems to be a pattern as part of the urbanization process. The recent migrants are mostly spread out over a vast geographical area in slums at the periphery living continuously in "transit localities" as they have not been able to claim more permanent and better housing in the geography of the city. Although some of those living in slums have occupied the place since 30 years and have built their own *Pacca* houses, they continue to live in poor economic conditions.

The in-formalization or the casualization of the labour, well demonstrated in an extensive study on the workforce of the closed textile mills of Ahmedabad by Breman (2002; 2004) is amply proved by the conditions of recent migrants of the Marginal caste in the city of Ahmedabad.

- **In-formalization of labour:** Of the total 300 respondents, 39 per cent (87) are engaged in the informal sector as sanitary workers. Many of the recent migrants work in private residential areas largely on contract basis. With ever-growing urbanization and emerging residential and commercial complexes and institutions of all types, the number of private contractors taking up sanitary work has increased manifold in recent years. The sanitary workers in informal sector are not sure how long their employment under a particular labour contractor would last. Similarly, the "hire and fire" principle being practiced by the labour contractors as per their wishes in order to improve the system does not guarantee the continuity in job for too long. Although, some of them are permanent and non-permanent workers in AMC or in *Gram-panchayats* and *Nagar-palikas* in AUDA (Ahmedabad Urban Development Authority) area, the employment in the organized sector has become a distant dream for a large majority of them who migrate to the city in search of livelihood.

- **Privatization of Sanitation work:** Privatization has changed the employment situation in sanitation work over the last one decade or so. So far the sanitary work has remained the responsibility of the state and the local bodies. The Corporation as well as semi-government or government aided institutions have shifted to privatization of sanitary work. As a result of privatization, one of the most common phenomena among those working in informal sector as sanitary workers is either part time employment or underemployment.

- **Weakening bargaining power**: The inflow of migrants belonging to the Marginal Caste to the city is continuously increasing. On the other hand, entry of the members of the other caste groups in the sanitation works mainly found in informal sector, especially in private hospitals, dispensaries, offices and institutions has further increased. This has resulted in the insecurity of employment among sanitary workers belonging to the Marginal Caste in the urban labour market. The increase in the number of labourers has reduced the bargaining power of the sanitary workers in the informal sector.

The unemployment, underemployment and casualization of the workforce, especially among migrants and young generation of the Marginal Caste once again confirms that the Marginal Caste who had monopoly over the sanitation work in the organized sector are losing hold over the urban labour market of the work related to sanitation over the last one decade or so. A large number of them, not being absorbed in the formal sector fall back to the informal sector and when found with no alternatives of employment the members of the Marginal Caste have taken recourse to rag-picking and other lower levels jobs, which are socially rejected in the urban labour market. This clearly is an indication of the marginalization process of labour. 'In most cases, waste-picking is driven by unemployment and poverty' (Choudhary 2003).

5.   Conclusion

With the growth of urbanization, an estimated 32 per cent of the population now lives in the Indian cities. The speedy urbanization and emergence of cities have made the transition of traditional colonies into modern ways easier and rurality into urbanism much faster. The prevalence of caste in urban India in all its manifestations has disproved the claims that caste is primarily a rural phenomenon and that it cannot survive the urban structures and dynamics. The traditional institution of caste did not disappear; in fact the city opened up new fields for its operation and provided space for shaping new identities in democratic India (Srinivas 1996; Beteille 2002). The large population migrated to the cities from rural India expected better openings to claim and gain space in urban India, not only in physical but also in socio-economic and political spheres.

The paper unfolds the dynamics of urban labour market revealing the process of making and unmaking of the Marginal Caste in the city and how the very process of urbanization and the state have played significant role in establishing the members of the Marginal Caste as sanitary workers in urban labour market in both, organized as well as informal sector. Firstly, it shows instead of secularizing caste-occupation relations, urbanization has now only reinforced the same but also strengthened the caste economy. Secondly, the process of assimilation and marginalisation of the Marginal Caste in the city reveals the existence of two seemingly contradictory sociological trends, i.e. continued exclusion and progressive inclusion of the Marginal Caste in the larger urban society and its socio-economic geography. The existence of this paradoxical trend challenges the modernity of urban India and the development induced paradigm of urbanization.

References

Appasamy, Paul; Guhan, S.; Hema, R. et al. 1996. *Social Exclusion from a Welfare Rights Perspective in India*, International Institute for Labour Studies and United Nations Development Programme, Research Series, 106, Geneva: ILO Publications.

Beteille, Andre. 2002. 'Hierarchical and Competitive Inequality', *Sociological Bulletin*, 51 (1), March, Pp. 3-27.

Breman, Jan. 2002. 'Communal Upheaval as Resurgence of Social Darwinism', *Economic and Political Weekly*, Vol. 37 (16), April, Pp. 1485-88.

Breman, Jan. 2004. *The Making and Unmaking of an Industrial Working Class*, New Delhi: Oxford University Press.

Chaplin, Susan E. 1997. '*Scavengers: Still Marginalised*', *The Administrator*, Vol. XLII, January-March, pp. 123-151.

Chaudhary, B. Kumar. 2003. 'Waste and Waste-Pickers', *Economic and Political Weekly*, Vol. 38 (50), December, Pp.5240-42.

Chaudhary, S.N. 2000. *Occupationally Mobile Scavengers*, Delhi: Har- Anand.

Franco, Fernando; Macwan, Jyotsna and Ramanathan, Suguna. (eds.), 2004. *Journeys to Freedom – Dalit Narratives*, Kolkata: Samya.

Gooptu, Nandini. 1996. 'Urban Poverty and the Politics of Caste and Religion in Early 20th Century North India: Implications for Development Practice and Research', *Oxford Development Studies*, Vol. 24 (3), Pp. 221-240.

Louis, Prakash. 2004. 'Editorial', *Social Action*, Vol. 54 (4), Pp. iii-v.

Macwan, Martin. 2001. *Kadach Jait Ae Vavnsh Na Pan Hoi (Caste May Not Be Race)*, Vadodara: Parivartan Trust.

Matthai, John. 1993. *Village Government in British India*, Delhi: Low Price Publications.

Nayak, Debashish. 2003. 'Revitalizing Our Walled Cities', *Seminar*, 530, Pp. 31-36.

Prashad, Vijay. 2000. *Untouchable Freedom: A Social History of a Dalit Community*, New Delhi: Oxford University Press.

Shah, Amita. 2002. "Uneven Development and Migration: Insights from Micro Initiatives" in Ghanshyam Shah; Mario Rutten and Hein Streefkerk (eds.), *Development and Deprivation in Gujarat*, New Delhi: Sage Publications.

Shahi, U. P. 1989. *Urbanization in Gujarat: A Geographical Analysis*, Gorakhpur: Institute for Rural Eco-Development.

Singh, K.P. 1998. *The Scheduled Castes*, Vol. II, Pp. 235-8.

Srinivas, M.N. (ed.), 1996. *Caste: Its Twentieth Century Avatar*, New Delhi: Penguin India.

Visaria, Pravin and Devendra, Kothari. 1984. "Migration in Gujarat: An Analysis of Census Data", Ahmedabad: Report Presented at Sardar Patel Institute of Economic and Social Research.

Vivek, P. S. 1998. *Scavengers: Exploited Class of City Professionals*, Mumbai: Himalaya Publication.

Endnotes

[1] Here the "Marginal caste" refers to the *Bhangi* or *Valmiki* caste community, the lowest of all in the traditional caste hierarchy, closely associated with those engaged in menial jobs, particularly manual scavenging and sanitary services.

[2] The term 'state' includes all those institutions that have public character (government departments, municipal corporations, and educational institutions receiving grants from the state governments like school, colleges, and hospitals) (see Franco et al 2004).

[3] The organized sector of employment, as it is known in India, comprises all those employed in government, local authorities, public sector enterprises, quasi government bodies, etc. to which statutory labour laws relating to conditions of labour apply (Appaswamy, Paul. Et al. 1996.Pg 53). Scavengers employed in Ahmedabad Municipal Corporation and other local bodies like Nagar Palikas and Panchayats, railways, public hospitals, government run and aided educational and other institutions fall into this category. Scavengers working in private housing societies, private institutions and offices, areas that are not directly under government control and those working under contractors come in the purview of informal sector.

[4] The informal sector or unorganized sector has no clear cut definition but the National Commission on Labour in India 1966 described it as 'those workers who have not been able to organize in pursuit of a common objective because of constraints such as casual nature of employment, ignorance and illiteracy, small size of establishment per person employed, scattered nature, etc. The unorganized sector does not have clear-cut employer-employee relationship, employment guarantees and lacks most forms of social protection and security (Louis 2004: iv). Scavengers working in private housing societies, private institutions and offices, areas that are not directly under government control and those working under contractors come in the purview of informal sector.

An Analysis of the Livelihood Determinants and Vulnerability of Seasonal Migration in Khohar Village, Rajasthan, India

Aparna Radhakrishnan, Niti Saxena
and Vrindaa Sharma

Abstract

Seasonal migration is a common phenomenon in Khohar Village of Rajasthan. Yet, its challenges and consequences are mostly unexplored. This study examines the livelihood vulnerability of migrants and non-migrants analysing the determinants responsible for decision-making on seasonal migration. This paper unlike most previous works investigates the gender differentials of migration through research. It attempts to give a holistic view on seasonal migration wherein the entire family leaves for agricultural labour work to Punjab and Gujarat every year. As the migrants are purposively selected from the population, Heckman Probit model was used to estimate the variables that contribute to the decision to migrate. Qualitative methodology was used to analyse the gender perspectives on migration. Empirical results yield that compared to large and small farmers, medium farmers have higher livelihood vulnerability due to low livelihood diversification index and low crop diversification index. Probit model shows that there are significant differences in the socio-economic variables of migrating and non-migrating farmers. In Khohar village, unstable climate, poor market linkages, depleting groundwater table and influence of middlemen are the primary factors that contribute to the socio-economic instability that lead to significant differences in the livelihood variables of migrating and non-migrating farmers.

Introduction

Migration is an ubiquitous reality in India. Kingsley Davis in his pioneer work in 1951 argued that Indians are less mobile (Davis, 1951). However, this has come out to be far from being true. Over the years with India's successful growth pattern and subsequent urbanisation, the number of interstate, intrastate as well as international migrants have been increasing with people shifting their livelihood base permanently or temporarily usually for better economic prospects. The high economic disparity between regions and the limited scope of opportunities available in rural areas drives labour to increasingly migrate to urban setups. Migration comes with its own set of opportunities and challenges varying as per the nature of migration, the location and other various social and economic aspects. It is a common phenomenon in India as Indians engage majorly in internal migration with the number of internal seasonal migrants estimated to be more than 100 million (Deshingkar and Akter, 2009). Over the last couple of decades, migration seems to be accelerating in India with the annual rate of growth of labor migrants rising to 4.5 percent per annum in 2001-2011 from 2.4 percent in the previous decade (Ministry of Finance, 2017).

Most migration flows from rural to rural areas at 47.4% while rural to urban migration which is assumed to be quite common increased only marginally between 2001 and 2011 from 21.8% to 22.1% respectively and migration from urban to urban rose from 15.2% to 22.1% (Census of India, 2011).

Better employment opportunities and higher wages are one of the common reasons for migration apart from marriage, natural calamities and migrating for prosperity among others. Labour migration includes all individuals who are currently employed, unemployed or seeking employment in the place of destination (ILO, 2015). Migration can be of various kinds and does not necessarily result in better standards of living. The people worst affected are the ones lying at the bottom of the hierarchy, that is the seasonal migrants defined as "A worker employed in the unorganized, informal labour market, engaged for 3 months or more at a work destination, away from his/her native rural block." (Aajeevika Bureau, 2014). Roughly 70 to 80 million workers in the country are seasonal migrants, making it 15 to 20 percent of India's workforce. Female labour migration seems to be on a rise as well. It witnessed a 101 percent increase between 2001 and 2011, and female migration because of business increased by 153 per cent which is four times more than the rate for men (GoI, 2017). Migration should always be a choice; however, when it happens out of necessity, which is the case for maximum rural migrants in the country, it is responsible for some challenges and hardships the migrating families and individuals essentially face which ultimately affect their livelihood.

The State of Rajasthan has a majority of its rural population actively involved in the wage labour market as its sole means for survival. It has an increasing number of migrants contributing to its economy, with around 5.79 million of them being from rural areas where grinding climatic conditions along with low rainfall and proneness to drought makes many of them move out and look for work in other locations in the country (Aajeevika Bureau, 2014). However, the increasing number of migrants and their increasing contributions to the economy are met by a simultaneous deterioration in their livelihood conditions. The seasonal migrants remain almost invisible to the society and to the government with no efforts made to improve their low and unstable wages and harsh living conditions as they continue to survive on the fringes of the economy.

In the last few decades, empirical works on the reasons and significance of migration in many developing countries has been recorded (De Haan, 1999). However, until today the migration pattern of the people of Khohar, a small village in the Alwar district of Rajasthan has not been recorded identifying the major determinants in a gender angle. Out of the total 154 households of Khohar, about 50 migrate on an average every year. The village has a problem of acute water shortage and also witnesses large-scale seasonal migration of entire families and individuals to nearby states where the migrants work as daily wage labourers. Therefore, the present study was designed to obtain an in-depth look view of the cause of migration and how strong the role of gender plays in the situation. This will help understand the migrating trends in detail and in return, resolve the local issues effectively.

Methodology

A. *Data and Study Area:* The following study was conducted in Khohar, a village located in the Ramgarh tehsil of Alwar district, Rajasthan. Situated near the Aravali mountain range, Khohar stretches upto 372 hectares in area and has a population of close to 800 people. It is largely an agrarian economy with 154 households in total of which 125 are landholders. Land under cultivation is approximately 113 hectares (farmers of Rajasthan report land units in *bigha* which is equal to one third of an acre). The cultivated land is spread within the 500-hectare square range from check dam. The soil of the area is light in texture, particularly sandy, sandy loam and clay loam. The upper hills are mostly barren. The district area is mainly underlain by alluvium of Quaternary age which forms the principal ground water reservoir. Some amount of groundwater is found in fractures, joints and crevices of hard rocks found as strike ridge in the district. The groundwater in the upper zone is known to exist down to 70 m depth and holds water under phreatic condition. The aquifers at greater depths are confined to semi-confined. Situated in a hot and dry region with no natural water source in the village, Khohar has a huge issue of water scarcity, as a result of which the village witnesses' seasonal household migration every year.

B. *Sample Selection*: Rajasthan is one of the largest states in the country with 75 percent of its population living in rural areas (Census of India, 2011). Migration, seasonal or permanent is a common phenomenon in the state due its water problems and climatic conditions that add to the plight of the residing population. Khohar was chosen as the area for this research because of rampant seasonal migration of families evident in the village compared to the rural areas surrounding it. For the study, purposive random sampling was undertaken to focus on migrating households in the village.

C. *Collection of Data:* The study adopted a mixed method approach to examine the livelihood vulnerabilities of migrants and non-migrants in Khohar and to analyse the determinants responsible in influencing the decision to migrate. It also investigates the gender differentials in migration through qualitative research, studying men and women perspectives on migration. Quantitative data from all 154 households in the village was collected with the help of a structured interview schedule, surveying the entire population and covering the socio-economic, agricultural and migration details of each household. Qualitative information on gender perspectives on migration was collected with the help of Focused Group Discussions (FGDs) and Key Informant Interviews (KIIs) with a sample representative of the migrant population in the village. Five FGDs were conducted with 6-7 members each comprising of adult female migrants (25 to 60 years old), adult male migrants (25-60 years old), adolescent female migrants (15 to 19 years old), adolescent male migrants (15 to 19 years old) and with aged female family members of migrants (50 to 75 years old). Details regarding their migration patterns, nature of job at destination, challenges faced during migration and the effect on their livelihood were discussed with the participants.

D. *Analytical Method*: As the migrants were purposively selected from the population, Heckman two step model was used to estimate the determinants of household migration decision and total annual income of the household at the farm household level. Heckman model was used to avoid the sampling bias. Household migration decision is the selection dependent variable which is a dummy variable taking value 1 as households that are migrating, that is, households with migrant population and 0 for households without migrant population.

$$M = \alpha_0 + \sum \alpha_K X_K + \varepsilon$$

$$I = \alpha_0 + \sum \alpha'_K . X'_{K'} + \varepsilon'$$

Selection model

M is the probability of the variable indicator of the sign of the selection criteria, that is the decision to migrate or not.

X_K represent the independent variables of the selection equation identification and those of the income equation respectively.

Income model

I represent the migratory income. The inverse mills ratio itself evaluates as the ratio of probability and cumulative density functions from the selection equation. Heckman (1979) argues that this function is a monotone decreasing function of the probability that an observation is selected into the analysed sample.

Results and Discussions

Table 1 represents the demographic and socio-economic characteristics of the sample farm households of the study area. The socio-economic status of the villagers varies considerably between migrants and non-migrants. The education status of household head is the major socio economic variable, that significantly varies between migrants and non-migrants. The migrants have a tendency to discontinue education and migrate, resulting in an increased migratory income of the family. Thus from childhood, they receive partial education resulting in a skewed value of education variable. The land owned by migrants are very small with less access to irrigation water, therefore the agricultural income and the total income is less. None of the migrants has their own bore well, hence the total time spent in a day to collect water was more for migrants compared to non-migrants. The non-migrants are the land owners and the influential persons of the village so the social participation index is high for them. As the adults and children migrate and work, the dependency ratio is almost comparable for both migrants and non-migrants.

TABLE 1: Socio-economic Characteristics of the Respondents

Variables	Migrants (n=47)		Non - Migrants (n=103)	
	Mean	Standard Deviation	Mean	Standard Deviation
Education Status of Household Head	3.68	3.88	5.19	3.68
Total Family Members	5.02	1.56	5.81	2.26
Income from Agriculture	8173.33	15686.98	27888	55942.60
Total Annual Income	74549	75441	164161	172979
No. of Agriculture Equipment Used	0.17	0.64	1	3
Land Size	0.79	1.11	2.48	5.22
Total time spent in a day to collect water	166.77	108.06	88.50	58.92
Number of Livestock	2.91	5.64	3.65	8.51
Dependency Ratio	0.30	0.21	0.33	0.22
Social Participation Index	18.08	18.77	26.01	22.80

Gender Perspectives on Migration and its effect on livelihood
The Focused Group Discussions (FGD) yielded tangible differences between the perspectives of male and female migrants. The FGDs were made on the basis of assets component pentagon of Sustainable Livelihood pentagon (DFID, 1999).

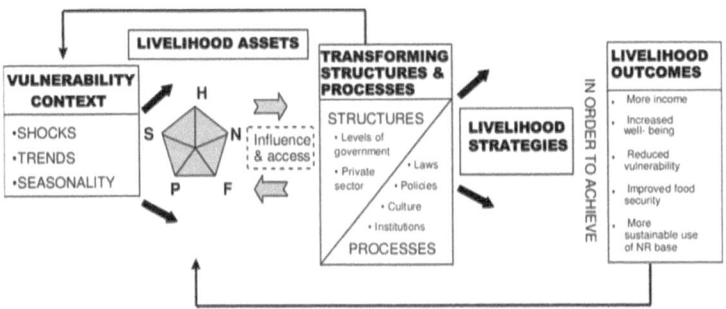

Human Capital

Human Capital is a measure of the skills, education, capacity and attributes of labour which influence their productive capacity and earning of the Khohar population. Among adults, the men were adamant on the fact that the entire family must migrate every time, be it infants or even pregnant women and staying back home is not an option. The females on the other hand stated that sometimes the small children and those who cannot help in the fields do stay back in Khohar with the elderly of the household. One major issue with migration for the women was the education of their kids. Being away for four to five months straight interrupts their studies and they just come back to give the final exams, which they are bound to fail.

The challenges faced by the youth are very different for boys and girls too. While the main challenge for the boys was to get a decent job or employment in or around the village that could help them earn a decent living, all the girls wanted a higher secondary school in the village itself so as to complete their education. As the nearest school is almost 10 kms away and adding to the yearly migration practice, the girls usually drop out of school after 8th-9th grade and are unable to complete their education. The boys contrastingly do manage to complete their schooling and a few of them had even done a technical course or graduated from college, but were still unemployed. Boys and girls both realize the need to migrate with their families as they are aware of the financial constraints existing in the village. Yet they are constantly looking for opportunities to expand their horizon and escape this cycle of migration. Some of the male participants in the FGD were now venturing out into non-agricultural services like driving and stitching, diversifying the opportunities available to them. Like the limited opportunities available to them, the dreams of these girls are also limited. They only dream of fulfilling their very basic and fundamental needs like education, getting married on their own terms or going to college if they like.

Healthcare is another cause of concern for the people of Khohar. The nearest hospital is in Alwar which takes about an hour or longer to reach, that too if they find some mode of transportation for the same. There is no doctor or a Public Health Center in the village, making it increasingly difficult for the villagers to get proper and timely cure and treatment for their illnesses. The situation for migrants is worse as they live in unbearable harsh conditions in the rural areas of Punjab and Gujarat, coming back home with malaria, high fever or other diseases. The women expressed having a hospital nearby and explained how tough it is to take a pregnant woman to the hospital for delivery at odd hours in the day. The migrant women mostly suffer from low blood count or nutritional deficiency.

Natural Capital

Natural capital can be defined as the world's stocks of natural assets which include geology, soil, air, water and all living things. Migrants possess small to negligible acres of land which they are able to cultivate only in the monsoons. Their fields lie fallow the rest of the year due to irrigation issues in the village. The average land holding size of migrants is less than 0.83 bigha and for non migrants is more than 2.6 bigha. Smaller landholdings are one of the primary reasons for migration as well.

The migrants also have to put in a lot of effort in getting water for their households as the borewells in the village are majorly owned by affluent families. One of the borewells is opened for 15 to 20 minutes each day in which the entire village rushes with their pots and utensils to fill water for their daily needs. The women especially take part in this daily activity, earning their share of water from a battle they wage every day.

Forest is also a source of income for the whole community as timber is acquired from the bushy trees near the mountains and sold off by migrants and non-migrants alike. The money is utilised for the community needs like renovation of village infrastructure, temple etc.

Financial Capital

Financial capital is any economic resource measured in terms of money used by the Khohar population and businesses to buy what they need to do agriculture or to provide their services to the sector of the economy upon which their operation is based. Even though, the migrants earn a decent amount of money through agricultural wage labour, at least 2/5th of their earning is spent on medical bills as estimated by the migrating population themselves. They usually migrate at least three times in a year for cotton, wheat and rice cultivation. Table 2 below provides an estimate of the wages they earn daily.

Table 2 - Estimated wages earned by the migrants

Crop	Location	Duration	Wage earned per person
Wheat	Punjab/Palwal	15-20 days	INR 400-600 per day
Cotton	Gujarat/Punjab	4-5 months	INR 350-500 per day
Rice	Gujarat/Palwal	15 days	INR 600-700 per day

Source: FGDs and Personal Interviews

Physical Capital

Physical capital refers to a factor of production (or input into the process of production) which is mainly the capital for agriculture and other livelihood activities. The villagers in Khohar have pucca houses to live in with proper shelter over their head. However, toilets are not functioning due to lack of water. Open defecation is highly prevalent among men and women alike. The migrating women did complain about going out in the open for defecation but were also aware about the financial constraints of getting a toilet built in their homes. Even when the toilets were built, most of them were non-functional due to lack of water availability.

All the groups in the FGDs mentioned similar problems faced at the migrating destination including lack of proper housing as the families had to live on the farms, under a makeshift tent for some shade and sleep in the open fields in extreme weather conditions as well. Water and food issues also exist as the contractors sometime provided them with ration which they had to cook themselves but they needed to fetch water for their daily needs from nearby streams or canals where all animals bathe and germs and mosquitoes are breeding. Thus, people get ill very often when working there, with high fever and malaria being common diseases and low blood count and nutritional deficiency common among females. The intense 12 hour shifts start at 6 in the morning and stretches up to late evenings which contributes to their ill health. The women expressed frustration regarding this and raised grave concerns about travelling all the way with their little children and not being able to take proper care of them. They were also blaming their husbands for being complacent not looking for employment elsewhere or go to an urban setup for non-agricultural daily wage work.

Social Capital

Social Capital includes the networks of relationships among people who live and work in Khohar, enabling that society to function effectively. Conducting in-depth interviews with the villagers including migrants and non-migrants also helped in understanding differences between them in detail. The women belonging to better off households who are not engaged in migration were physically healthier than the women who migrate. Sumitra Bai, a woman living with her husband in Khohar does not need to worry about employment as her two children live and work in Delhi and provide for the family. The woman cultivates a few crops in her small field but is reaping the benefits of educating her children who were able to get away from the vicious trap and make their own living. She herself did migrate with her husband for a couple of years in the beginning of her marriage but was unable to continue, describing it as a highly tedious and challenging task. Women of Khohar thus lead very challenging lives with migration being a necessity for them, and the only possible means to earn a living guaranteeing survival. They have been migrating since they were children and have seen their parents do it as well. Their education was interrupted because of the frequent migration, wherein many of them dropped out of school at a young age and never went back. The same cycle continues with their kids not being able to go to school for similar reasons. All family members who are healthy and are able to participate in the fields, work together in order to earn maximum returns for their labour.

Surviving under such unbearable conditions makes the whole process of migration extremely difficult for all members of the household. However, the burden falls harder on females as they are supposed to perform all household duties, look after their children as well as work in the fields for long hours even if they don't wish to. In a study by Sandhya Mahapatro (2013), it is highlighted how increased female migration is a sign of empowerment for women and that higher migration leads to improved role of women in their households and in decision-making processes as well. Khohar however presents a different side to this. Living in a patriarchal system, their migration trends are not characterized by empowerment but by forced and taxing situations, from which they can't seem to find a way out.

Table 3 - Heckman selection model for seasonal migration

	Total Migration Select Heckman	Total Migration In (tot_annual_inc)
edu_status_HH_head	0.02141 *	0.0234*
agri_equipments	0.14722	0.627960
land_size	0.59613	0.964413
amt_credi	0.58117	0.962029
agri_diversification_index	2.14e-05 ***	0.849314
sources_income	0.39940	0.000152 ***
dependency_ratio	0.54728	0.141791
time_spent_in_day_to_ collect_water	0.00469 **	0.65630
agri_income	0.65630	0.027366 *

livestock	0.67585	0.006036 **
social_part_index	0.59268	0.023185 *

*** p<0.01, ** p<0.05, * p<0.1

Table 3 shows the results of Heckman two step model. From the model it can be said that the main determinants of decision to migrate are the education status of the household head, agriculture diversification index and time spent in a day to collect water. On the other hand, the main variables influencing the total income of migrants are the education status of the household head, total sources of income, agricultural income, livestock and social participation index. Education status of the household head and agricultural diversification index have a negative impact on the migration decision while time spent in a day to collect water has a positive impact.

Conclusion

Gender analysis along with Heckman model helps us to identify the factors responsible for migration in Khohar as well as factors affecting the total income earned by migrants. With the help of Heckman two-step model, we realize the significant differences in the socio-economic variables and livelihood asset components of migrating and non-migrating farmers.

Looking at the issues faced by the migrants in the village, adequate policy measures should be adopted to effectively solve their problems. The statistical results help us to stress on the variables which are highly significant in influencing the decision to migrate. Policies for better access to education and generating employment opportunities in the village would help these villagers to stay back in Khohar and work instead of frequently migrating. As agriculture is the primary occupation in the village and water scarcity is a major problem, a district level Master Plan for small water harvesting structures like check dams or earthen tanks could be developed.

Another policy level change needs to focus on better inclusion of the migrating community all across India. These individuals are often deprived of the basic legal and social protection that could ease the process of migration and help them become recognized and a respected part of the society. This would also provide them relief from living in such unliveable conditions at their migrating workplace.

References:

Aajeevika Bureau (2012), *Creative Practices and Policies* for Better Inclusion of Migrant Workers: The Experience of Aajeevika Bureau. Udaipur.

Census of India (2011), Provisional -D-5 Migrants By Place Of Last Residence, Age, Sex, Reason For Migration And Duration Of Residence-2011(India , States/UTs).

Davis, K. (1951), The *Population of India and Pakistan.*

De Haan (1999), "Livelihoods and Poverty: the Role of Migration, A Critical Review of the Migration Literature". *Journal of Development Studies* 36(2), 1–47.

DFID (1999). Sustainable Livelihood Guidance Sheets. Retrieved from http://www.eldis.org/vfile/upload/1/document/0901/section2.pdf

Deshingkar, P, and Akter, S. (2009), Migration and Human Development in India, Human Development Research Paper 2009/13, *New York: United Nations Development Programme.*

GoI (2017), Report of the Working Group on Migration in India. Government of India: Ministry of Housing and Urban Poverty Alleviation.

International Labour Organization (2015), ILO global estimates on migrant workers, *Conditions of Work and Equality Department.*

Ministry of Finance (2017), Economic Survey 2016-17, Department of Economic Affairs, GoI.

Vulnerabilities of Distress Labour Migrants from North and North Eastern States in South India

P.O. Martin and Smitha Philip

Abstract

Historically, the south Indian states were known for out-migration going abroad, to north Indian states and to neighbouring states within south India. However, in the last two and a half decades, there has been a huge surge in labour migration to south Indian states from north and east Indian states. This trend of migration is triggered by distress, known as distress migration. It is viewed as a strategy for survival and livelihood. In this paper, the myriad challenges and problems faced by distant labour migrants in south India are summed up and analysed under various vulnerabilities. It is done by narrating incidents based on the field experiences of the authors where they encountered various forms of human rights violations in terms of vulnerabilities. The secondary data, including recent news reports, is used to explain the concepts and their implications from global and national perspectives. The paper raises the pertinent question, why are these inter-state distress migrants treated as second class citizens? and, asserts citizens' right 'to move freely throughout the territory of India; to reside and settle in any part of the territory of India'. Finally, the paper concludes with a clarion call to ensure the constitutional and the labour rights of the inter-state migrants in India.

Key words:*Vulnerability, Migrant worker, Distress, Xenophobia, Exclusion.*

Introduction

Migration has been a viable strategy for survival and livelihood for millions globally and there were over 244 million international migrants alone in 2015 (International Migration Report, 2015). In India too, migration has been both a survival mechanism as well as a refuge from turmoil. The findings of Census 2011 point to a decade of rural distress as the major reason for migration. The collapse of the form of livelihoods in agriculture and other related occupations has accelerated the distress migration, especially among the Dalits, Tribals and the marginalised sections in India. It is further evident from the large scale poverty (Socio Economic and Caste Census, 2011), exclusion, hunger, farmer suicides and starvation deaths in rural India. Landless farmers, agricultural labourers and marginal farmers who lose their livelihoods on account of globalised agricultural practices form the bulk of these distress migrants.

The introduction of the New Economic Policy in 1992 through liberalisation, privatisation and globalisation accelerated migration in India. The developmental plans centred on mega cities and negated the countryside which widened the gulf between the rich and the poor leading to large scale distress migration in the country. The masses of dispossessed farmers and labourers were forced to migrate to cities and other parts of the country for survival (Mukherji, 2013). In the Indian rural set up, agrarian crisis has agravated the employment economy. The forced failure of agricultural activities and indebtedness due to loans taken and mass farmer suicides have resulted in marginal peasants abandoning agriculture, landless workers being unemployed and exodus of these groups to other parts of the country for survival (Gopalakrishan & Sreenivasa, 2009).

The Economic Survey of India (2016-17) highlighted the surge in inter-state labour migration towards south Indian states, particularly to Tamil Nadu, Karnataka and Kerala. Since the introduction of the New Economic Policy in 1992, there has been a spate of labour migration to south Indian states from north and east Indian states. For example, labour flow from Gujarat to Tamil Nadu are about seven lakhs annually. Kerala appeared to be a net exporter of migrants in 2011-12, but it appeared importer of labour migrants in 2015-16. Karnataka is also a recent entrant among net in-migration states (Martin, 2017).

The economic development, job opportunities and daily wages in the southern states are considerably higher and act as green pastures. Further, the better education prospects and the possibility of a better life allure the rural populace. Thus, the vacuum created in the manual labour and other works is filled by the migrant workers from northern and eastern states.

Stan Swamy (2016) connects this recent phenomenon to 'the third wave of Adivasi migration' – migration of *Adivasi* youth to the southern states (the first being the migration of young Adivasi women to metropolitan cities and the second being the seasonal migration of whole families to northern states). According to him, deepening poverty and increasing state repression have forced thousands of young Adivasi men and women to migrate to southern states for livelihood and survival. However, these survival strategies and opportunities are laden with vulnerabilities for these distress migrant workers in southern states. These vulnerabilities based on differences in ethnicities, states and races, are serious human rights violations and aberrations of the constitution of India.

Vulnerabilities of Internal Distress Labour Migrants in India

International Organisation for Migration (2011) defines vulnerability as a situation in which individuals or groups are unable to access basic rights and entitlements which are available to them. It is a state of inability of people to withstand adverse impacts to which they are exposed to and a state where persons are in need of special care, support and protection from abuse or neglect. Vulnerability is the exposure to contingencies and stress, and difficulty in coping with them. The social sciences' perspective takes into account various factors and parameters that influence vulnerability such as physical, economic, social, environmental, and institutional characteristics.

Internal distress migrant workers face several vulnerabilities in India. They are forced to live and work in extremely difficult and dangerous conditions. They are very vulnerable as they are on the margins of Indian society both economically and socially, and face unnecessary high costs and risks because of non-recognition at the policy level and faulty implementation of laws. Nearly all sectors employ migrant workers through a complex system of contractors and agents who are well-positioned to exploit these vulnerable distress migrants (Deshingkar and Akter, 2009).

Vulnerabilities faced by internal distress labour migrants in India are summed up under seven areas and explained as follows.

Rights violations

Distress migrant workers in India are very vulnerable to various kinds of rights violations and deprivation of basic amenities. They face systematic violations of their human rights daily. The rights violations include their right to livelihood, residence, food, health, education, social security, equal wages, proper hours of work and freedom from bondage. They remain mostly without identity and so are unable to claim state resources. They have no social security, compensation in cases of accidental injuries and deaths, and access to safe drinking water and heath care. Most of these workers are forced to buy food grains and kerosene at higher market prices as they do not possess ration cards for subsidised food schemes at the destinations (UNESCO, 2013).

Poor living and dangerous working conditions

Vulnerabilities of distress migrant workers include their poor living and dangerous working conditions. Housing conditions of migrant labour are appalling. They live in hovels alongside the heaps of filth and mud. There is no proper arrangement for toilets, drainage, ventilation or provision for clean drinking water or light. Further, they are forced to work under inhuman conditions for long working hours. They are usually in the lowest paid 3D jobs – dirty, dangerous and degrading (Deshingkar, 2010).

Exploitation, cheating and bondage

Distress migrant workers in India are very vulnerable to exploitation, cheating and bondage at the destinations. Employers prefer to hire migrant workers as they are easy to control and exploit. Migrant workers are perhaps the most exploited sector of the entire unorganised sector workforce in India. Multiple methods are used to ensure maximum extraction of surplus tasks from these workers. Employers vanish when the time for payments comes due or pay less than agreed upon. Since workers have no recourse, they are easily cheated. Further, the *thekedars* and contractors operate to break up any possibility of unity between workers and any such unity poses a danger to the worker's livelihoods. So migrants are exploited and cheated more than the local workers (Gopalakrishnan and Sreenivasa, 2009).

Distress migrants are from the poorest section of the society in India. The intermediaries often exploit their helplessness by giving certain advance payments and force them and their families into a kind of bondage or trafficking. Those who have been trapped as bonded labourers work 12 to 16 hours a day with very little or no wages. Some of the employers, particularly the owners of construction companies, brick chambers and quarry chambers exploit and harass the migrant workers as slaves. In some case, extreme exploitation including bonded and child labour are practiced through the grip of labour contractors and money lenders (Haan, 2011).

Accidents and health hazards

Distress migrant workers in India are very vulnerable to accidents and health hazards. Due to dangerous working conditions and lack of safety measures, migrant workers are very prone to accidents. However, in cases of accidental injury and deaths, migrant workers are often denied of rightful compensation. Health of migrants is adversely affected by poor living and working conditions, increased exposure to infectious diseases and lack of access to public health care at the destinations. The employers hardly provide medical and health facilities to the migrant workers (Haan, 2011).

Stereotypes and xenophobia

Internal migrants in India have to adjust themselves in the new locality or state which is linguistically, culturally, geographically and traditionally far from their native place or state. Thus, most of the internal distress migrants in India suffer from stereotypes, xenophobia, harassment, isolation, exclusion and rejection (Mishra, 2016; Haan, 2011).

Women and children face discrimination and violence

Women and child migrants are the most vulnerable sections among the distress migrant workers and they suffer from labour market discrimination and violence. Women's wages are less than those paid to men. They often end up as victims of sexual abuse and harassment. Migrant women and child domestic workers are often beaten up and sexually harassed by the owners. Migrant women and children are also the major victims of human trafficking which is an extreme form of human rights violation. They also battle loneliness and emotional stress (Haan, 2011).

Lack of Legislative Protection

Distress migrant labourers in India face lack of legislative protection due to scattered and dispersed nature of employment and lack of collective bargaining power. The state sees migrants as a low priority and so many social protection schemes tend to have 'sedatory' biases and tending to exclude migrants. The Inter-State Migrant Workmen Act, 1979 remain by and large without teeth (Haan, 2011).

Vulnerabilities of Distress Labour Migrants in South India

Distress labour migrants from north and east Indian states to south Indian states are catapulted into a state of cultural shock. They grapple with alien languages, different cultures, races, climate, food habits, work cultures, etc. These factors at the destinations assume an adverse form and trigger alienation, exclusion and various vulnerabilities despite the same nationality.

The findings from the field show that distress labour migrants from north and east Indian states to south Indian states are vulnerable to various rights violations and they can be summed up and analysed under the following areas.

i.   Language barriers

ii. Exclusion

iii. Xenophobia

iv. Health hazards, accidents and deaths

v.   Exploitation, Discrimination and Non-payment of wages

vi. Human trafficking and Bonded labour

vii. Gender discrimination and Violence

Language Barriers

Learning the local language is a major challenge for the north Indian migrant workers in southern states. Tamil, Kannada, Malayalam and Telugu, the major languages of the southern states, are of Dravidian family. These languages have very little resemblance with the Indo-Aryan languages such as Hindi, Bengali, Oriya and Assamese spoken by most of the migrants. Some of these migrant workers are also from the north-eastern states where they have their own distinct languages or dialects. Further, most of these migrants hail from the rural areas of eastern states such as Assam, West Bengal and Odisha where Hindi is not the state language and they do not sufficiently converse in Hindi. Interestingly, some of these migrants have reported to have learnt to speak in Hindi after coming to south India for work. On the other hand, most of the local population in southern states are not very conversant in Hindi. Thus, language barrier continues to be a major challenge for the migrant workers for their communication with the local population, to understand the instructions of the employers, for travelling and for accessing government schemes and benefits available to them. They acquire limited fluency in spoken form of the language after many years but acquisition of expertise in reading and writing is still a distant dream. Thus, language barrier is one of the reasons for the exclusion of these migrants from the government schemes, entitlements, public health, PDS and membership in trade unions.

Often language barriers create misunderstandings, prejudices and stereotypes between the migrants and the local population. At times, language barrier also causes police and local administration to suspect migrants as criminals, to detain them in police stations for questioning and to even jail them for the crimes not committed by them. For instance, Dipen Konra, a 30-year old tribal from a remote village in West Bengal, was travelling in a suffocated general compartment of the Shalimar-Trivandrum Express to toil at the construction sites in Kerala. At the Aluva railway station, Dipen got down to fetch water and could not get back into the over-crowded general bogey to reach Kollam, his destination. Not knowing what to do and how to ask in Malayalam, the partly and poorly dressed Dipen began to walk. In the late evening, as the strangely appeared Dipen could not answer the Police in Malayalam, he was taken to the Police Station. In the early hours, he attempted to escape and inadvertently entered the adjacent airport compound. He was suspected to be a Maoist or a terrorist and beaten up so brutally that his legs and hands were broken and he became unconscious. The critical Dipen was sent to a central jail. After nine months of the assault, with the intervention of State Human Rights Commission, Dipen was released from the jail and returned home, but with one leg and one hand dysfunctional (Martin, 2017).

Exclusion

Exclusion is a systematic process of segregation and isolation of migrants from social, political, economic and cultural domains creating a system of domination and subjugation by the local population. It is also a process involving systematic denial of entitlements to resources and services, and the denial of the right to participate on equal terms in social relationships in economic, social, cultural or political arenas. The distress migrant workers face total exclusion from local culture and society. They are often kept excluded in order to ensure their social insularity and disempowerment which prevents them from asserting their rights as citizens and labourers. This systematic exclusion works to the advantage of the local population to keep the wage levels low, rent levels high, provide cheap services, and to maintain a labour force that is at their beck and call, and one that can be absorbed and driven out at will. In fact, the local population and government officials refuse to accept these migrants as equal citizens with all democratic rights. As a result, they are excluded from the legal provisions and social security schemes (Martin, 2017).

According to Moses and Rajan (2012), local employers use strategy of exclusion to restrict migrants' entrance to social protection and unionisation. Thus, migrant workers are left on their own to deal with local employers. Also, migrants are physically isolated from the surrounding community which makes it more difficult for them to find out local wage, rights, and support systems available to them.

Their rights are often denied on the political defence of the "sons of the soil" theory. In fact, exclusion of migrants takes place through political and administrative processes. This exclusion results in ghettoisation of migrant population. They are excluded from government schemes to varying degrees, from formal residency rights, identity proofs, political representation, adequate housing, financial services, public distribution system [PDS] and membership in trade unions at the destinations. They are also denied access to public health, education and other basic amenities such as water and sanitation. As a result of these exclusions, migrant workers are prone to several vulnerabilities in southern states.

Xenophobia

Xenophobia can be described as attitudes, prejudices and behaviour that reject, exclude and often vilify persons, based on the perception that they are outsiders or foreigners to the local community, society or national identity. There is a close link between racism and xenophobia, two terms that can be hard to differentiate from each other (International Organisation for Migration, 2011). There is a general tendency among the locals in south India to look down on the distress migrant workers from northern states based on certain stereotypes which seriously affects the perception and treatment towards them. The number of crimes in which these inter-State migrant workers are involved is much less in proportion when compared with the corresponding figures for the general population. However, a few of the crimes in which they are involved get high degree of publicity and adds fuel to the perception that most of the migrants are criminals. This adds to the fear psychosis and strengthens suspicion and distrust which informs the attitude of the authorities too.

North Indian migrant workers are soft targets for the police, administration and the locals in south India. Profiling of these workers by police clearly demonstrates xenophobia based on suspicion and prejudice. They are also targeted by the locals for the crimes as petty as theft and on the grounds of mere suspicion. They are viewed as outsiders who vitiate the traditional culture and unbalance law and order. Further, the constant vilification of the migrant workers often becomes a tool for putting the crimes that are committed by the locals on the migrants.

There are several reported cases where north Indian migrant workers were beaten up, lynched and killed based on suspicion and rumors. In Chennai, police and scores of bystanders watched a migrant worker beaten to death in 2012. A few even cheered and egged on the mob. Some screamed 'north Indian thief" (Dutta, 2012). Kailas Behra, a migrant worker was beaten to death in Kottayam district of Kerala in May 2016. Behra, who was mistaken for a thief, was lynched by a mob of about 50 persons. Some people remained mute spectators watching the young worker slowly die in the scorching sun. In another incident, a young migrant labourer Jagabandha Karkaria from Rayagada district of Odisha was murdered in Thrissur because of certain stereotypes entrenched deeply in the minds of the people (Hudwai, 2016). In yet another case in Chennai, five north Indian workers were killed by police in an encounter which neighbours and human rights activists termed as fake encounter and cold blooded murder (The Hindu, 23 February 2012). There are also several reported cases of north easterners beaten up in Bangalore based on xenophobia. In some instances, migrants also become victims of mistrust and violence by the locals. For instance, in August 2012, thousands of panic-stricken migrants from the northeast, living in Bengaluru, boarded trains towards Guwahati following rumors of violence targeting them. The mass exodus revealed an atmosphere of 'fear and mistrust' felt by them.

Health hazards, Accidents and Deaths

Migrant workers in southern states are vulnerable to health hazards and infectious diseases as their working and living conditions are deplorable. Their poor living and working conditions, increased exposure to infectious diseases and lack of access to public health care deter their health. The employers hardly provide medical and health facilities to the migrant workers. Housing conditions too are appalling. They live in hovels alongside the heaps of filth and mud. There is no proper arrangement for toilets, drainage, ventilation or provision for clean drinking water or light. For instance, 80 per cent of the women garment workers in Bangalore reported their health at risk because of working conditions and 19 per cent of the respondents of the study classified themselves as having bad health (Sisters For Change, 2016).

Due to dangerous working conditions and lack of safety measures, migrant workers are highly prone to accidents and deaths. However, in cases of accidental injury and deaths, migrant workers are often denied rightful compensation. Statistics provided by the police show that as many as 52 migrant labourers have died at the construction sites alone in Bangalore in the first six months of 2015 (Gangadhar, 10 July 2015). Minimum 50 dead bodies of inter-state migrant workers reach the hospitals for post mortem every month in Kerala (*Malayala Manorama*, 28 November 2013). In fact, these statistics account only for deaths in which FIRs have been registered. For example, Dheeraj Kumar, a migrant labourer from Bihar, fell to his death at a construction site in Whitefield on 6 July 2015. Kumar was reportedly lying on the ground, in a pool of blood, for more than two hours, but none of the supervisors or contractors called for an ambulance. Some fellow workers later rushed him to a near-by hospital but he was declared brought dead. According to Ashok, a fellow labourer, Kumar was the fourth migrant worker to die on the same worksite (*Deccan Herald*, 10 July 2015).

Human trafficking and Bonded labour

Evidences manifest that migrant workers are also susceptible to human trafficking and bonded labour in southern states. The intermediaries often exploit their helplessness by giving certain advance payments and force them and their families into a kind of bondage or trafficking. Those who have been trapped as bonded labourers work 12 to 16 hours a day with very little or no wages. Some of the employers, particularly the owners of construction companies, brick chambers and quarry chambers exploit and harass the migrant workers as slaves. There are several recent reported cases of existence of bonded labour in Karnataka, Tamil Nadu, Telangana and Andhra Pradesh.

In Karnataka, a large number of migrant workers have fallen prey to money lenders and become bonded labourers. A total of 7,646 people are being allegedly forced to work as bonded labourers in different districts of Karnataka, according to a report of the Bonded Labourers' Review constituted by the State government (Prabhu, 25 September 2015).

Kaibalya Majhi, aged 40 was one among the 260 migrant men, women and children who were rescued from forced labour slavery in three brick factories in the outskirts of Bangalore on 29 April 2015. The agrarian crisis compelled this poor tribal from Balangir district of Odisha to borrow a sum of money from a middle man on promise of working in a brick kiln near Bangalore. After seven months of hard toil as bonded labourer, through the intervention of a voluntary organisation, Kaibalya along with his wife and two children walked into freedom to rejoin his joint family in rural Odisha.

333 bonded labourers including 75 children were rescued from Tamil Nadu brick kilns in 2015 (NDTV, 12 February 2015). They were all migrant workers from Odisha and were paid just Rs. 200 per week for every ten thousand bricks they made. An agent had brought them to Tiruvallur after paying an advance of about Rs. 14-16,000. They were reportedly housed in thatched sheds with no toilet and some of the children were also made to work.

Phoolmoni Murmu (17), who died in suspicious circumstances in Whitefield in Bangalore on 2 April 2017, was a victim of human trafficking and bonded labour. An agent paid Rs. 19,000 to her father and sold her to a placement agency in Delhi. The agency employed her as a domestic worker in Delhi and later transferred her to Bangalore without informing her parents. According to the police, 150 such trafficked and bonded girls from the same agency are working in Bangalore (Deccan Herald News Service, 8 April 2017).

Gender discrimination and Violence

Women are the most vulnerable sections among the distress migrant workers and they are subject to dual victimisation from labour market and sexual violence. Women's wages are less than those paid to men. They often end up as victims of violence, sexual abuse and harassment. Migrant women workers are often beaten up and sexually harassed by the employers or supervisors. Migrant women are also the major victims of human trafficking which is an extreme form of human rights violation. They also battle loneliness and emotional stress as most of them are separated from their families.

According to Sisters For Change (2016), 80 per cent of Bangalore's garment factory workers are women and these women undergo high levels of sexual harassment and violence at workplace despite the existence of the act: Sexual Harassment of Women at Workplace (Prevention, Prohibition and Redressal) Act 2013. Most of these women garment workers are young, unmarried and are from scheduled castes or scheduled tribes. A good number of them are migrant workers hailing from north eastern states, Odisha, Jharkhand and West Bengal. The study found that one out of every fourteen women garment workers experiences physical violence and fourteen per cent undergo rape or forced sexual act.

Verbal abuse, humiliation and sexual harassment of women garment workers are part of daily life. Factory hostels deprive women and girl workers of their rights to privacy and liberty, and create an enabling environment for exploitation.

Gender discrimination is manifest in organisational structure which usually consists of all-male managers. Despite widespread physical and sexual violence, factory managements hardly punish the supervisors and managers who perpetrate these crimes. As a result, the Study found that 75 per cent of the women garment workers lack confidence that they would get justice if they report the case to the management or to the police. It is substantiated by the fact that only 3.6 per cent of the reported cases of violence resulted in action by factories or police.

The ILO Conventions and Declarations for Migrant Workers

The International Labour Organisation (ILO) works towards upholding the dignity and rights of all workers, including migrant workers. *International Convention on the Protection of the Rights of all Migrant Workers and Members of Their Families, 1990* covers the entire migration process and provides many areas of protection for migrant workers and their families. *International Labour Standards on Migrants' Rights, 2007* provides guidelines for policymakers and practitioners in Asia and Pacific (ILO, 2007). *International labour Migration: A Rights-based Approach, 2010* provides a framework for protection of migrants' rights, the governance of international labour migration, and the role of social dialogue and international cooperation (ILO, 2010). A democratic country like India cannot and should not ignore these guidelines. Therefore, these ILO guidelines should be deployed by central and State governments in upholding the rights of internal migrant workers in India.

The Constitution of India

The Constitution of India [Art.19] (1) (d) and (e) states 'all citizens shall have the right ... to move freely throughout the territory of India; to reside and settle in any part of the territory of India'. Thus, all the citizens of India have the fundamental right to migrate, to work and settle in any part of the country. As such inter-state migrants are not required to be registered in India either at the place of origin or at the place of destination. Therefore, compulsory registration and exclusion of inter-state migrant workers in destination States violate the above mentioned fundamental rights of the citizens of India. Thus, it calls for central and State governments to guarantee the inter-state migrant workers the fundamental rights enshrined in the Constitution.

Conclusion

The central, state governments and the civil society have the duty to ensure the constitutional and labour rights of the inter-state migrants. Therefore, the above narrated vulnerabilities experienced by the distress migrant workers are serious violations of human rights and aberrations of the Constitution of India. Migrants' labour is extracted, but they are not valued and are not allowed to live and work as equal citizens with dignity. Therefore, it calls for greater honesty in the pledge to ensure constitutional rights and labour rights of inter-state migrants for a dignified human life in host states in India.

References

Deccan Herald News Service. (8 April 2017). "3 held from Delhi agency that sent Assam teen to work in city." Accessed on 10 March, 2017, from http://www.deccanherald.com/content/605260/3-held-delhi-agency-sent.html

Deccan Herald. (10 July 2015). "Supervisors left worker to die." Accessed on 10 March, 2017, from http://www.deccanherald.com/content/488632/supervisors-left-worker-die.html

Deshingar, Priya and Akter, S. (2009). *Migration and human development in India.* UNDP Research Paper 2009/13. Accessed on 10 August, 2017, from http://hdr.undp.org/sites/default/files/hdrp_2009_13.pdf

Deshingkar, Priya. (2010). "Migration, remote rural areas and chronic poverty in India". *Overseas Development Institute*, Working Paper 323. Accessed on 10 August, 2017, from http://www.chronicpoverty.org/uploads/publication_files/WP163%20Deshingkar.pdf

Dutta, Madhumita. (9 March 2012). "Come south, young man, but here be dragons." Accessed on 10 March, 2017, from http://www.thehindu.com/opinion/op-ed/come-south-young-man-but-here-be-dragons/article2974594.ece

Gangadhar, Nikhil. (10 July 2015). "City becoming death trap for migrant labourers." Accessed on 10 March, 2017, from http://m.deccanherald.com/articles.php?name=http%3A%2F%2Fwww.deccanherald.com%2Fcontent%2F488631%2Fcity-becoming-death-trap-migrant.html

Gopalakrishnan, Shankar and Sreenivasa, Priya. (2009). *The Political Economy of Migrant Labour.* New Delhi: Sruti.

Haan, Arjan de. (January 2011). "Inclusive growth? Labour migration and poverty in India." *International Institute of Social Studies*, Working Paper 513.

Hudwai, Shafeeq. (14 May 2016). "With no one to address their concerns, migrant labourers in Kerala face tough odds to earn a livelihood." Accessed on 10 March, 2017, fromhttp://twocircles.net/2016may14/1463219290.html

ILO. (2007). *International Labour Standards on Migrant Workers' Rights.* Bangkok: International Labour office. Accessed on 10 August, 2017, from http://www.ilo.org/wcmsp5/groups/public/---asia/---ro bangkok/documents/publication/wcms_146244.pdf

ILO. (2010). *International labour migration: A rights-based approach.* Geneva: International Labour Office. Accessed on 10 August, 2017, from http://digitalcommons.ilr.cornell.edu/cgi/viewcontent.cgi?article=1086&context=intl

International Migration Report. (2015). Accessed on 10 March, 2017, from http://www.un.org/en/development/desa/population/migration/ publications/migrationreport/docs/MigrationReport2015.pdf

International Organisation for Migration. (2011). *Key Migration Terms.* Accessed on 10 March, 2017, from http://www.iom.int/key-migration-terms

Malayala Manorama. (28 November, 2013). Editorial page, Ernakulam edition

Martin, P.O. (2017). "A Study of Human Rights Violations of Migrant Workers in Kerala". (2011-14). *PESQUISA*, 2 (2), 1-7.

Mishra, Deepak Kumar (Ed). (2016). *Internal migration in contemporary India.* New Delhi: Sage.

Moses, W. Jonathan and Rajan, S. Irudaya. (2012). "Labour migration and Integration in Kerala." *Labour& Development,* 19(1), 1-18.

Mukherji, Shekhar (Ed.). (2013). *Migration in India: Links to urbanisation, regional disparities and development policies.* Jaipur: Rawat Publications.

NDTV. (12 February 2015). "75 children among 333 bonded labourers rescued from Tamil Nadu brick kilns." Accessed on 10 March, 2017, from http://www.ndtv.com/tamil-nadu-news/75-children-among-333-bonded-labourers-rescued-from-brick-kilns-in-tamil-nadu-739047

Prabhu, Nagesh. (25 September 2015). "Bonded labour in fresh avatar enters new sectors." Accessed on 10 March, 2017, from http://www.thehindu.com/news/cities/bangalore/bonded-labour-in-fresh-avatar-enters-new-sectors/article7687213.ece

Shaik, Zeeshan. (5 December 2016). "Every 3rd Indian migrant, most headed south." Accessed on 10 March, 2017, from http://indianexpress.com/article/explained/tamil- nadu-kerala-daily-wages-migrant-population-4410694/

Sisters For Change. (2016). *Eliminating violence against women at work.* Study Report Socio-Economic and Caste Census. (2011). Accessed on 10 May, 2017, from http://www.secc.gov.in/

Swamy, Stan. (9 July 2016). *Adivasis leaving their homeland in waves.* Accessed on 10 May, 2017, from http://jharkhandforum.com/node/89

The Economic Survey of India. (2016-17). *Chapter 12, India on the move and churning: New evidence.* Govt. of India.

The Hindu. (23 February 2012). *In the light of day, questions about midnight encounter.* Accessed on 10 March, 2017, from http://www.thehindu.com/news/cities/chennai/article2922641.ece?mstac=0

UNESCO. (2013). *Social inclusion of internal migrants in India.* Accessed on 10 August, 2017, from http://unesdoc.unesco.org/images/0022/002237/223702e.pdf

Migrant Workers in Sanitation Work:

Vulnerabilities of Inter-state Migrants in India

Ratnesh Katulkar and Paul D'Souza

Abstract

Migration to cities in search of employment is an age old need of the people from rural India. The stories and legends of the labourers of India who went far to off nations like Mauritius, Fiji as migrant labourers are well known in fictional as well as in academic writings. However, the inter-state migration from the times of British India to the contemporary times in sanitation work has not been studied seriously in the academia.

Based on an empirical investigation of the migrant workers engaged in sanitation work in Madhya Pradesh and Chhattisgarh, this paper focuses on the inter-state migration and the vulnerabilities deriving from their social status. In the state of Madhya Pradesh, particularly in Jabalpur city, and in Chhattisgarh, the cities of Korba and Bilaspur, sanitation work is predominantly occupied by the migrants from Andhra Pradesh and Uttar Pradesh respectively. In Jabalpur, the Malas and Madigas and a few other Andhraite castes are engaged in sanitation work from the pre-independence era. On the other hand, the Domars of Uttar Pradesh have been migrating to Chhattisgarh over the last few decades for livelihood, especially seeking jobs as sanitation workers. The "discriminative" state policies regarding the social status of the migrants from other states have serious implications for their citizenship. The paper further highlights the need for a policy change in order to reduce the vulnerabilities of inter-state migrants, especially those engaged in sanitation work across states.

Introduction

Migration to cities in search of employment is an age old need of the people especially from countrysides or the places that lack employment opportunities. The stories and legends of the labourers of India who went to far off nations like Mauritius, Fiji as migrant labourers are well known in fictional as well as in academic writings. However, the inter-state migration from the times of British India to the contemporary times particularly in sanitation work has not been studied seriously in the academia. The present paper is an attempt to discuss the vulnerabilities of inter-state migrants. This paper is based on a recent study conducted by the Indian Social Institute; New Delhi[1] reveals such vulnerability of the migrants of Andhra Pradesh and Uttar Pradesh engaged in sanitation work.

INTER-STATE MIGRATION AND SANITATION WORK

The Occupation of Sanitation

There are many varieties of work involved in sanitation work such as scavenging, sweeping, garbage collection, engagement in post-mortem, cleaning of septic tanks, gutters, drainage, tanning, pig rearing etc. This job is performed both in the government sector as well as in private sectors. In government offices, the nature of employment could be on permanent or contract basis while housekeeping is purely an informal job. The second most prominent type is sweeping, mainly they are employed in Municipal

Corporations, Railways and other governmental sectors. Before 90's the migrants had opportunities to become permanent staff in government sectors. This sort of employment is available in both Jabalpur and Chhattisgarh. In Jabalpur, army cantonment, Gun carriage factory are also service providers to the migrant Andhraites. While in Chhattisgarh, thermal plants, mines and public sector industrial units are the main service providers. The municipality was of course one unit in both the regions. However, with change of time permanent jobs are no more available in this sector. Despite implementation of 'The Prohibition of Employment as Manual Scavengers and Their Rehabilitation Act, 2013'; the mines still issue tenders to hire even manual scavengers for cleaning septic tanks in Korba!

In the state of Madhya Pradesh, particularly in Jabalpur city, and in Chhattisgarh, the cities of Korba and Bilaspur, sanitation work is predominantly occupied by the migrants of Andhra Pradesh and Uttar Pradesh respectively. In Jabalpur the Malas and Madigas and a few other Andhraite castes are engaged in sanitation work from the pre-independence era. On the other hand, the Domars of Uttar Pradesh have been migrating to Chhattisgarh over the last few decades for the search of livelihood, ends up in involving in sanitation work and other 'Unclean' occupations.

Migrant Sanitation Workers in Jabalpur

In Jabalpur city, sanitation work is carried out by individuals belonging to various castes such as Dumar, Valmiki, Chamar, Kori, Basor, Dom, and individuals of a few other castes belonging to other SCs and in a fewer instances OBC and general caste categories.

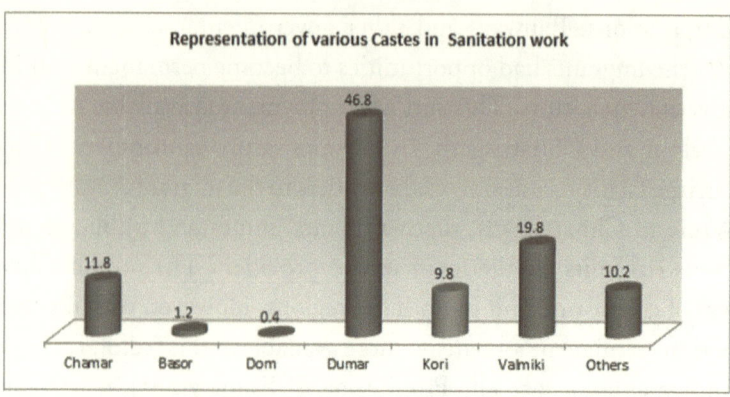

All these castes other than the Kori are locals of Madhya Pradesh, some of them are from Jabalpur and some are from the neighboring districts. However, none of the Koris who are involved in these occupations are domicile of Madhya Pradesh; they are all migrants of Andhra Pradesh. The Koris in Madhya Pradesh and elsewhere are in fact now associated with sanitation work. The Kori in different states are called by different names such as Bunkar, Julaha, Vankar etc. The caste occupation of Koris is weaving. But despite this fact, the migrant Andhraites involved in sanitation confidently claim their caste in Jabalpur as Kori. This claim is made by all the migrant Andhraites despite diversity of castes in their own region.

The Andhraite Castes and its Local Synonyms

S.No.	Caste in Andhra	Equivalent caste in Jabalpur*
1	Mala	Kori
2.	Madiga	Chamar
3.	Yanadi/Chamla	Mehtar/Valmiki
4.	Golla	Yadav
5.	Yerukella	Basod
6.	Chakalli	Dhobi
7.	Reddy/Kamma	Thakur

This is however a strange claim on two grounds, firstly the Koris in Madhya Pradesh or elsewhere are no way associated with any sanitation work including scavenging. Secondly, in Andhra Pradesh there is no presence of Kori caste. But despite these facts the migrants of Andhra Pradesh for past three generations are confidently claiming 'Kori' identity. The reason for this new caste identity is basically to claim the Scheduled Caste stature in Madhya Pradesh, which is available only to the native residents of Madhya Pradesh. The migrant Andhraites thus in order to access the entitlements for the Scheduled castes, devise this tactic. The dominant migrant castes such as 'Kamma' and 'Reddy' also use the same 'Kori' identity to claim these entitlements. There is a tactical reason behind choosing Kori nomenclature instead of the Valmiki, or Mehtar, the castes which are predominantly in the scavenging occupation nationwide traditionally. First, the migrants at the time of their settlement wanted to claim their separate identity from the traditional scavenging castes either to maintain their ritual superior status or more practically that they do not want to fall in conflict with the local Valmikis or Mehtars by claiming their caste. Thus to identify themselves as Koris was the easiest and cleverest way for getting the entitlement of the Scheduled Caste without falling into any socio-political conflict.

The Koris are largely settled in Sarvodaya Nagar and Chandal Bhata, which offer residence to both the Dalit castes such as Mala and Madigas and dominant castes such as Kamma and Reddy of Andhra Pradesh. All these residents are engaged in sanitation work mainly in Municipal Corporation. But despite engaged in the same sort of "Unclean" or Polluting work, the Reddis and Kammas still maintain caste arrogance and social distance from Malas and Madigas who in their eyes are untouchables, "Unclean" and of lower caste. The relation between the Malas and Madigas does not seem to

be antagonistic as it prevails in their home state. The reason
behind this is unlike in Andhra Pradesh, as at Jabalpur both
the castes are engaged in the same occupation and are living
closely. However, being two different castes, they do not
have inter-caste matrimony between them but sharing of
food and visiting homes of each other is a normal practice.
The Kammas and Reddis, unlike the Mala and Madigas claim
Thakur status amongst local community. As they find Thakur or
Rajput caste equivalent to their domicile social status. It is however,
a question that how far this claim makes them comfortable in
maintaining normal relation with the caste/ communities that are
not involved in sanitation work including the Rajputs or Thakurs
of Jabalpur. The engagement in sanitation work despite their
claim of Kamma, Reddy alias Rajput or Thakur would certainly
be an obstacle. There is also a small chunk of Golla, Yerukella
and Chakalli castes among the migrants. Most of these castes do
claim Kori identity. It is an interesting fact that none of these
migrants whether Dalits or non-Dalits do have marital relations
with the local community. There is a tradition of going back to
Andhra Pradesh for the selection of life partners for marriages in
among these migrants to ensure maintenance of endogamy. The
practice of going back to Andhra for marriages thus ceases the
challenge of inter-caste marriages.

Miigrant Sanitation Workers in Chhattisgarh

The castes in Chhattisgarh which are engaged in the sanitation
occupations mainly include Domar, Valmiki, Makhiyar, and
Hela. In some areas tribes such as Gonds, Kharias, and Oraons
which are classified in state's ST list are also found to be engaged
in this work. Apart from these marginalized communities, there
are also individuals of other castes such as Yadavs, Teli, and a
few others who are found to engage in sanitation work. In one

or two instances, *the Brahmins* are also said to be engaged in this job. But they are migrants of far off states, who claim that they are hiding their occupation in their home state to maintain their ritual superiority.

However, the main chunk of workers in this sector are migrants of Banda districts of UP hailing from Domar caste. Their share in the sanitation work in the cities of Korba and Bilaspur is 39%, which is highest among all other individual castes. No other castes share such a huge representation, singly. Others share their presence only in the range of 1 to 6.4 % only. The Domars are generally known as a sub-caste of Dumar and Dom. But the migrant Domars vehemently deny their caste as a sub-caste of Doms. The reason for this is the potential claim for their higher ritual status. However, the Domar without any hesitation accepts Dumars as their sub-caste. They also accept the Valmikis into their caste stating that Valmikis and Domars are of same origin. They continue to argue that those Domars who gained occupational mobility started adopting Valmiki nomenclature. Some of the Domar respondents claim that in their city, there are a few Domars who, after attaining occupational mobility start using the Valmiki title. This shows the ritually higher position of Valmiki caste over the Domars. This is however a local understanding among the migrants of Domar from Uttar Pradesh, in other places for instance in Madhya Pradesh the Valmikis maintain their independent identity and do not want to associate with Domars. However, in the eyes of laypersons both Domars and Valmiki are equally low as both the castes are ex-untouchables who traditionally engaged in sanitation work.

The reason behind the mass migration of Domars from Banda district to Chhattisgarh and elsewhere is that at one time the elder women of this caste used to get a contract of cleaning human excreta of a particular village. This work was then transferred from a woman to daughter-in-law in the family. Thus it was a very well-managed caste occupation but as with the change of time and increasing of family size it resulted in a situation where this traditional caste occupation was no more available to the younger generation. Therefore to meet the adequate minimum survival need of the families, they are bound to look for the alternate occupations. Secondly, with the introduction of modern toilets, the traditional dry latrines are also being replaced. This technological change also has led to unemployment among the Domars who at the time were getting contracts in manual scavenging. Thus, because of unemployment and family pressure they have no other option than to move out of their town and state in search of new jobs. Since, manual scavenging was their traditional caste occupation; the migrant Domars do not find difficulty in getting the scavenging and allied occupations in the states like Chhattisgarh--as most of the local Dalit castes of this state have not been generally involved in sanitation work. The poor local Dalits and Adivasis of Chhattisgarh are hardworking traditionally involved in the construction sectors. They often migrate to far off places like Punjab, Delhi and elsewhere for this work. Among the local community, there are a few castes that have been into occupations of scavenging thus there is ample opportunity available in this sector. This is easily availed by the migrant Domars of Uttar Pradesh. Therefore, they easily get employment opportunities in Chhattisgarh. There are many families and individuals of Banda district who are still coming to Chhattisgarh seeking these jobs.

The local Satnamis, a sub caste of Chamar, who are traditionally not associated with sanitation work, are now engaged in sanitation work due to financial constraints but they are very small in number. The major chunk of Satnamis have gained occupation mobility thus they are moved of their traditional caste occupation of leather tanning. A fewer Satnamis who are in the sanitation occupation/work are mainly working in government schools as part time labourers. They are protected by a union *anshkalin mazdoor theka kamgarsangh*. They are not involved in hazardous work but they get meagre salary. The other castes such as Yadav, Teli, Kalar which are traditionally dominant castes are involved in rearing cattle, tilling, and vending of oil, and brewing indigenous liquor respectively also have a minor representation in the sanitation work. These individuals are also both inter-state and intra-state migrants. It is however, difficult to ascertain whether their claimed caste identities are real or fake. There is a possibility that in order to show higher ritual superiority, some of the migrant sanitation workers other than migrants Domars of Uttar Pradesh do claim a false caste identity.

Overall the highest number of single caste involved in sanitation work in Korba and Bilaspur is the Domars migrants of Uttar Pradesh. They are settled in the outskirts of the city in the settlements of Oriya Basti, Pragati Nagar and Dipaka.

POLICIES AND THE CITIZENSHIP OF INTER-STATE MIGRATION

Migration and Caste Identity

The Government of India has made a special clause for the castes categorized in erstwhile untouchable communities into SC category and has provided the facility of reservation in government services, affirmative action in educational institutes and mandatory representation in politics. And in order to boost and support SCs and to raise its level to the rest of the population there are schemes and policies such as scholarships etc., so that they get the support and motivation which was denied to them for centuries, as reparation since they had been discriminated and excluded from the mainstream. Various studies suggest that positive discrimination has played a pivotal role in uplifting this community and the rampant occupational mobility is primarily the result of the reservation.[2]

The migrants in both Madhya Pradesh and Chhattisgarh are however not entitled for reservation. The reason for this is their migratory status. In Jabalpur as discussed above the adoption of Kori caste was a successful attempt. This strategy worked initially, when many Andhraite migrants were successful in getting the caste certificates. This was however short lived and they were not able to get much benefit out of it. Because in the initial days there was lack of opportunities for them and their children, firstly because of their poor educational qualification compared to the native SCs of Madhya Pradesh. Secondly, at that time there were very few schemes being implemented by the government for the upliftment of the Scheduled Castes. However, in the 90s, when both the central and state governments introduced many new welfare schemes and opportunities for the Scheduled Castes, a new problem emerged. The government of Madhya Pradesh in subsequent years introduced many changes in the issuance of caste certificate. Initially the caste certificate was issued by simple attestation of local political representatives, but in later years such certificates lost their authority and a new regulation was imposed that in order to avail SC status one has to produce the documentary evidence of local residence in Madhya Pradesh for the past fifty years. This new rule created difficulty for the migrant Andhraite sanitation workers as they lacked documentary domicile evidences in Jabalpur. Many of them had the records in Andhra Pradesh but that could be accepted since it was showing their migratory status. A few of the old migrants who got *patta* in their names were successful in getting the caste certificate but the large chunk of migrants whether they had been settled from the time independence of the country or in recent past lacked any documentary proof.

Thus despite their presence in Madhya Pradesh for more than fifty years, the biggest problem for the migrant Andhratites who did not want to conceal their caste identity was that their real caste, such as Mala, Madiga. Yanadi, Chamla etc, were listed in the SC list of Madhya Pradesh. Thus despite fulfilling the technical obligation of being a domicile of Madhya Pradesh for the past fifty years, they are bound to hide their caste identity under the Kori mask.

Being denied the SC status, they are now treated as a general caste in all official records. Therefore the younger generation is denied with the facility of scholarships in schools and colleges and other facilities including reservation in admission and services. Despite their hardship due to occupation which leads them to live in poor habitation and many other disadvantages. However, it is strange that they are not even listed in the OBC category. They are thus bound to compete with the most privileged communities of the state. Such uneven completion naturally results in their failure and loss. Thus there is no scope available of them for their occupational mobility and growth. They fall in such a trap that their coming generations will have no other choice but to involve in scavenging and allied occupations. Despite the fact that even among Dalits the worst sufferers of exclusion and untouchability are those who involve in "Unclean" occupations. A few studies suggest that they are even more untouchable among the untouchables. Therefore, it is beyond doubt that these castes deserve the first right in the reservation. However, in the selected universe, it was found that the castes such as Domars of Chhattisgarh, Malas, and

Madigas and other Dalit migrants of Andhra Pradesh in Jabalpur are not entitled to reservation in the states of Chhattisgarh and MP.

There is a legal reason behind this denial. As a circular issued by the GoI, Minister of Home Affairs dated February 22, 1985 states:

> It is also clarified that a Scheduled Caste/Tribe person who has migrated from the State of origin to some other State for the purpose of seeking education, employment, etc. will be deemed to be a Scheduled Caste/Tribe of the State of his origin and will be entitled to derive benefits from the State of origin and not from the State to which he has migrated.

Therefore, under this clause, the migrant Dalits from the other states such as the Dumars of Banda district of Uttar Pradesh (UP), and the Mala, Madigas of Andhra Pradesh, who are actually listed as SCs in their own home states are denied SC status in their new states, where they migrated for seeking employment opportunities and continued with their traditional caste occupations. The matter is not simple as it seems. In the Chhattisgarh state government list of SCs, the Domar caste is listed in the Third Schedule (section 19) amendment of the Constitution (Scheduled Castes) Order, 1950. The Domar caste is listed in the 23rd number along with the Dom, Dumar, Dome, Domar, Doris. Thus, on the one side the migrants from Domar of UP should not have any difficulty in ascertaining their rights as SC. However, the problem comes with their migrant status which is in the range of between 15 years to 1-2 years. As stated above in the Ministry of Home Affairs order dated February 22, 1985. Therefore for the entitlement of SC status in Chhattisgarh, one has to produce the documentary evidence of his residence of the past 50 years. There has been a continuous discrepancy in dealing with their matter therefore; the Chhattisgarh government specifies its stand clearly on this issue in its official website in the following words:

भारत सरकार, गृह मंत्रालय के निर्देश एवं माननीय
सर्वोच्य न्यायालय के 5 सदस्यीय संविधान पीठ के
निर्णय के अनुसार अनुसूचति जाति/जनजाति जिनिके
पूर्वज 1950 को तथा अन्य पछिड़ा वर्ग जिनके पूर्वज
1984 को छत्तीसगढ़ के भौगोलिकि सीमाके मूल निवासी
नहीं थे, उन्हें जातिप्रमाण-पत्र एवं आरक्षण की
पात्रता उनके पिता/पूर्वजों के मूल राज्य में आयेगी,
छत्तीसगढ़ राज्य में नहीं।[3]

Because of the state government's clear stand, the migrant Domars are denied of the reservation provision despite the fact that they are the most deserving case. However, they easily get temporary caste certificate simply by getting the signature of elected municipal leader but this document is valid in the schools only up to 9th standard. Trouble starts from 10th class onwards when one has to produce a proper caste certificate issued by the SDM office. At this juncture because of their migratory status they are unable to produce the documents, thus denied of SC status. As a result they lose the eligibility of concession in fee and scholarship facilities. This brings additional financial burdens to the family. Thus, in many cases it results in the dropout of students from schools.

A respondent, Bhola is working in Korba for the past for 12-13 years. He has three children: two daughters studying in 4th and 5th standard respectively and a son enrolled in 2nd standard. His salary is about 7000-8000 per month. These children are studying in government schools; and they are getting scholarship, stationary etc. He says:

> I have to spend money for other expenses. I am facing problem of caste certificate. Up to 9th and 10th standard everything was ok, but from 11th standard onwards we need to produce caste certificate signed by District Magistrate.

Religion and Social Status

In Jabalpur the migrants of Andhra Pradesh particularly Koris alias Malas and Madigas largely follow Christianity. There are four Churches in their locality belonging to different groups of Protestant sects. This community was affiliated with Christianity from their home states and they continued to follow this even after migration. In most of the cases however, at the time of their grandparents, the association with Christianity was for the name sake only, as they hardly visited churches or participated in religious ceremonies. The community was then in transition between Hinduism and Christianity. But after being settled in Jabalpur the then younger generation who are now in the stage of parenthood started taking interest in the religious activities. And they have become Christian practitioners.

Conversion to Christianity however becomes another reason for denial of SC status in many cases. When these individuals and castes engaged in santiation and allied occupations and of Dalit origin are converts to Christianity, automatically they lose the rights of reservation. As the Constitution Order affirms : (Amendment) Act 1956 says:

> No person who professes a religion other than the Hindu or the Sikh religion shall be deemed to be a member of a Scheduled Castes.

This Act was amended by the Scheduled Castes Order (Amendment) Act, 1990 which provides those members of SCs included in the President's order and converted to Buddhism, who shall continue to be deemed to be a member of SCs. Thus, those who are claiming the Christian identity in the field are denied the facility of reservation. Therefore many families and individuals are confused with their identities. Some are following Christianity but in records they are Hindu. Some who are strict in religious practice of Christianity are thus losing the protection granted to SCs because of their conversion.

There are ample numbers of Dalit Christians among the migrant Andhraites, who lost their claim in SC because of their religion despite their continuous engagement in the sanitation occupation.

VULNERABILITIES OF INTER-STATE MIGRANTS

Exploitation of Labour

The persons involved in sanitation work or other "Unclean" occupations are not protected by any labour laws. The workers start their work early as they used to reach the site early in the morning at 4.30 hours, when there are no public transport facilities. This results in the extra spending on petrol for fuelling their bikes. The Sweepers also have to show their presence twice in the office to get attendance for a day. Lalla, a contract worker says:

> During Swachh Bharat Mission we have to work even at 2 0'clock in morning…this happened to be a tedious work as our contractor used to call us at such odd times.

In other government offices, the working hours of a sweeper is more than other staff for the reason that he or she has to clean the office premises before its formal time of opening. However their work doesn't end here, as in most of the cases the locking of the office is also an extra responsibility of the sweepers. Thus, in such a case the working hours of an employee surpasses the maximum work hour. Thus, in many instances the labour laws are not applied to the people engaged in "Unclean" occupations. The extra and strenuous work affects the family life,and the parental care is affected.

In case of religious gatherings, they are even more exploited and forcible manual scavenging is imposed on them. On religious occasions, the government takes a pro-active role by fixing the duties of sweepers working in Municipal Corporation, who was posted at the sites of religious functions which are generally located far off from the main cities. As a result they have to be out of their home for 5-6 days but they are neither compensated with any leave nor provided any over time. And in case of Jain' religious retreats, the sweepers are forced to perform manual scavenging.[4] During the mass gatherings of Hindus, the sweepers are transferred to the sites, no matter how far is that place from their own home town.[5]

The scavenging work also requires one to clean septic tanks and gutters manually. Unfortunately despite strict provision the contractors do not provide any safety gears, gloves and gum boots to the workers. In the absence of these, the workers have wounds, cuts and skin infections. These physical problems are not minor in nature, but are openly visible. A manual scavenger is easily recognizable by his infected hands, body smell and other outward appearances. Further the meagre salary adds more wound to their looks. They hardly get enough money to spend on their dress and other basic necessities. The lower income is thus easily reflects in their personality. A respondent narrates:

> I used to clean gutter by getting down inside it. I use spades to lift the dirt of gutter on a pan, and then I pass this pan to another labourer who stands outside the gutter. This work involves direct contact with dirt and human excreta. We have not been provided any safety gears, gloves or even gum boots. Even the contractor does not provide soap and water to wash ourselves. We have to depend on the nearby houses for water to clean ourselves. Sometimes there are blades, glass pieces and other sharp objects which cut our hand.

Working in such unhygienic and hazardous condition lowers the age of workers; sometimes they even lose their life while performing such works. The sudden death of the family head leaves the family in such a crossroad where they are unable to move. This has often resulted in the discontinuation of schools for children in the past. The deaths due to sickness as a result of skin infections and respiratory disorders are not uncommon in the community. There are frequent occurrences of such instances. Many young contract workers share the reason of their dropout because of this. Lalluram a contract worker at Korba says:

> Four to five years ago, my father was working as a contract worker. He used to work in gutter and drainage. Once while coming out of drainage, he fell down and suddenly lost his consciousness and after a while he was dead. Nobody knows the reason of his sudden death. His co-workers informed the contractor and dead body was brought home. That time I was in 7th class in a government school. I was the eldest among my four siblings. We suddenly lost our family head, that time there was no financial security for us. My family was not provided with any sort of financial assistance, there was neither Provident Fund nor any fund available to us. We were left with no security. The contractor provided us a meagre amount. Then I left the school and later I got engaged as a contract worker.

Loss of Labour Bargaining Power

Sanitation workers are the least paid labourer in India but the problem increases with their migratory status. Employment is the basic need of the migrants which forces them to work for low wages. The domicile workers are generally in better bargaining position than the migrant workers.

The income of the selected household in these states varies from below 5000 rupees a month to high as 35,000. Those who are employed as a contract labourer or working in private sectors earn daily wages. They get the least salary while those migrants who settled for a longer times and successful in getting permanent jobs are getting better salaries. However, as said there is no hope for the recent migrants owing to the changing recruitment policy of the government. The individuals employed on contract as a sweeper or garbage collectors are getting very less salary without any social security. The poor income and lack of social security results in the poor admission rate of their children in school and high dropout.

A respondent Bodhdas describes his financial position and the problems faced in education his children:

> My daily income is ₹100-150. I have three children and all are going to school, studying in the Karma Bharati School in class 2, 3 and 4 respectively. I think they are doing well in studies, I cannot say much about it because I am not educated enough to understand their actual performance. All what I can say is that they are regular to school and are taking an interest in studies.

Impact on Higher Education

The poor students in the migrant community who are able to complete their higher studies in absence of caste certificate have to write the competitive exams in the general category. It is most shocking that they are not even included in OBC category. Due to lack of background support and unavailability of minimum resources, it becomes very tough and difficult for these students to clear the exams, and they often fail. These unsuccessful attempts de-motivate the community's students who begin to think that earning degrees and education is of no use.

Thus it demoralizes them to continue their study. Most often such failure becomes a role model for the younger generation, who concludes that education is meaningless for them, thus they prefer to discontinue their study and ultimately fall in the trap where the scope of occupation mobility of the community ends.

During FGDs and personal interviews many children who dropped out school narrated that financial problem was the key reason behind their discontinuation. In some of the cases the children had to get involved in the family trade of pig rearing which took a lot of their work and disturbed the time schedule, which ultimately led to their dropout. As Lakhan a drop out of Bilaspur narrates:

> I was the eldest among my siblings. My parents used to leave home early for their works therefore I was taking responsibilities of my younger brothers and sisters. I also had to take pigs for grazing… this was a tedious and time consuming job. This affected my school attendance. I used to be absent from school regularly and subsequently I stopped going to school. I was only in 5th class that time. You can assume how much responsibilities I was carrying at that tender age.

The meagre income results in their poor housing in the periphery of city. This also results in lack of basic amenities like water, sanitation and electricity.

Conclusion

The people who are employed as sanitation workers and allied occupations are the most vulnerable people in the country. In most of the cities, this work is carried out by the migrants of other states. This migratory status adds more wound to their vulnerability as it ceases their citizenship rights, further it also rejects their claim in Scheduled Caste status. Thus despite their unprivileged status they are even neglected with the privilege of OBCs. This results in their identity as a general category. The most vulnerable and weakest community thus loses all sorts of opportunity and concessions and falls in to a vicious trap that doesn't allow even their younger generations to move out of these works.

It is a legal fact that they are denied their rights on the basis of provision to safeguard the domicile Dalits of respective states but it is equally true that the migrants involved in the sanitation work are the most unprivileged even amongst the Dalits. In this case their caste becomes secondary and legally ceases its relevance and significance because of their migratory status. Therefore, to provide justice to this community and to make them avail the benefits meant for the other deprived communities such as SCs, STs and OBCs there is an ardent need of creating a separate category based on the occupation of sanitation and "Unclean" works and to provide them entitlements based on their involvement in these occupations irrespective of their caste and the state in which they work.

Endnotes

[1] Discrimination and Exclusion in Education: A Study of the Children of Households Associated with "Unclean" Occupations of Madhya Pradesh and Chhattisgarh, Indian Social Institute, New Delhi

[2] For instance, Thorat and Senapati (2006), Reservation Policies in India Dimensions and Issues, IIDS http://www.dalitstudies.org.in/download/wp/0602.pdf

[3] http://cgsccommission.com/caste_certificate.php

[4] Discrimination and Exclusion in Education: A Study of the Children of Households Associated with "Unclean" Occupations of Madhya Pradesh and Chhattisgarh, Indian Social Institute, New Delhi p. 34.

[5] *Ibid.,* p.35.

Status of Rural Migrant Workers in Ranchi City

Sweta

Abstract

Migration has been a perennial problem all over the world. As yet, in India it has been a feature that is continued by caste, class and the informal employment opportunities added to which are seasonal migrations. This paper envisages to analyse the various aspects of migration to Ranchi city as Urban migration has been a unique feature all over the World.

Introduction

In our economy, labour is abundant and capital is scarce...Yet, over the years, the Indian economy has witnessed a disturbing shift towards greater capital intensity in production. This has led to distortion and avoidable hardship in cases where labour is replaced, or employment potential reduced, by resort to capital intensive methods of production, even in cases where such a shift is not justified on other economic and technical considerations. (1991 budget speech)

These words of the then finance minister Dr. Manmohan Singh during the presentation of Budget seems to appear that the Liberalization policy would be concerned with the welfare of the labourers rather than with the capital. But in later periods it was clear that Liberalization did not show conducive result of the welfare for the labourers. This speech does not refer to any specific kind of labour such as formal labour or informal labour, but later periods have shown that informalization of labour increased due to adoption of liberalized policies. Labourers from the rural area involved in agriculture sector were forced to move out and work in informal sectors mainly in urban areas. A significant number of workers have not completely moved out of the rural sector but they are in circulation. They are the same labourers who work in the agriculture and allied sectors and urban informal sectors as well. A government report on "Conditions of Work and Promotion of Livelihoods in the Unorganized Sector, 2007" highlighted that informal workers constituted 92% of the total workforce and they do not have employment security, work security and social security. The report also noted that,

> At the end of 2004-05, about 836 million or 77 per cent of the population were living below Rs.20 per day and constituted most of India's informal economy. About 79 per cent of the informal or unorganized workers belonged to this group without any legal protection of their jobs or working conditions or social security, living in abject poverty and excluded from all the glory of a shining India. (p.1)

Jha(2016) notes that, the major premise to bring neoliberalism was that inward looking capital was resulting in bias against agriculture and other employment intensive activities with respect to both domestic and external markets. But after liberalization was adopted, it tended to less utilize the labour which was well below the potential. The pro liberalizations advocated that through market reform investment from domestic and foreign sources it would surge but in reality it happened the other way. The economic reform thus could not utilize the labour to their full potential.

Informal Sector

Although the informal sector in India grew exponentially after liberalization but the term gained currency in 1970s. Informal sector was identified as urban self-employment and also viewed as a solution to the crisis of unemployment generated by industrialization. The formal sector had shown a healthy growth till 1960s but by the 1980s the crisis in it was apparent. Hitherto there were two kinds of sectors where in the labourers were engaged; one, traditional i.e. agriculture sector and second, modern i.e. industrial sector. Then this dualism was replaced by formal sector and informal sector where the former meant secure, well paid, skilled and unionized jobs and the latter meant insecure, low-paid and unskilled work. (Behal, Joshi & Mohapatra, 2010)

However, Breman (1996) argues that the distinction between formal and informal cannot be restricted to urban labour only. All the activities of rural economy are not the part of agriculture economy and non-agricultural activities are not entirely related to urban locations only. He argued that even agriculture should be included in the informal sector as the Indian agriculture system completely lacks the formal working arrangements. The Government report on employment-unemployment survey 2013-14 notes that more than 90 per cent of the workforce and about 50 per cent of the national product are accounted by the informal economy. A high proportion of socially and economically underprivileged sections of society are concentrated in the informal economic activities. At the macro-level the presence and increase of the daily-wage labourers or informal sector labourers in cities can be analyzed as an inevitable outcome of the urbanization process, a consequence of industrialization and economic development that induces migration of the rural poor to major cities. (Bora, 2014)

Migration from rural to urban areas

Over the period of time people have devised alternative livelihood pattern apart from agricultural activities. One of these is working as daily wage labourers in urban spaces. Due to the seasonal limitation in agriculture and non-availability of irrigation facility in the villages have made them to migrate to the cities. The phenomenon of migration is not new. Working-class people have left their homes in search of jobs elsewhere for a shorter or longer period of time. In late-colonial period, it became necessary for the landless or small landholders to migrate to seasonal or semi-permanent worksites. In post-independent period, however, this type of mobility increased due to huge expansion of the building trade in towns and cities. A large segment of the mobile labour go to nearby towns or more distant cities in the expectation of better payment, less fluctuation of employment and easy access of jobs. Due to modernization of transport and communications, labour migration shows a circular character. They leave their home for work and may come back again, which also provide the informal sector an almost inexhaustible reservoir of labourers. (Breman, 1996) L. P. Vidyarthi (1970) called these labourers as 'auxiliary industrial labour'. They belonged to Oraon and other Chhotanagpur tribals who provided their labour in tea plantations, jute mills, mines-mining operations and railway track and road constructions.

The report on "Conditions of Work and Promotion of Livelihoods in the Unorganized Sector, 2007" noted that large scale migration of unskilled wage labourers is not necessarily due to native place being poor in terms of resources but poverty, low demand of labourers are also the reasons. They prefer to go to the areas where unskilled labour is more in demand. Migration becomes imperative to survive for these economically and socially deprived groups of rural areas such as tribals and other groups. The report further notes that migration rose in nineties due to structural changes in availability of employment opportunities which was largely generated in urban areas. The improvement in infrastructure and connectivity also led to the mobility of workers from far-flung areas to urban locations. It also had impact on the nature of migration. The report mentions that the number of seasonal migrants increased due to this which the official sources underestimated. The National Commission on rural labour 1991 estimated the number of seasonal migrants around 10 million in rural areas alone. But according to the reports other estimates suggested that the range could go higher up to 30 million. The rising unemployment also has accelerated the process of migration.

The report recognizes the plight of the migrant workers and describes the factors behind labourers' migration. They belong to the poorest section of the society characterized by meager human capabilities and capital assets with lower education level, lower income from agriculture. They primarily belong to socially deprived groups such as Scheduled Castes and Scheduled Tribes. The seasonal migrants also tend to be the least educated. The report also noted that migrants working in the formal sector are in much better position than migrants working as casual labourers. And the unemployment rate among migrants is much higher than the non-migrants.

Jha (2016) has argued that the study of the impact of liberalization mobility of labour has become very important. He points out that the existing data sources for internal migration in India do not capture the short time migration efficiently. But the fact that internal migration has increased in the last three decades cannot be denied. Nevertheless the occupation structure and wage structure has not changed much. With the process of urbanization growing up, the rural-urban migration also increased such as 307 per thousand moved in 1993-94 and 354 per thousand moved in 2007-08. The internal migration for Scheduled Caste group and Scheduled Tribe group is the highest among all social groups. NSSO 2013 also showed that as more and more women are entering in the job market, the internal migration of Scheduled Caste and Scheduled Tribe are increasing only.

In this context, I studied the socio-economic status of labourers of *mazdoor bazar* (labour markets) of Ranchi City. There are twelve bazars in Ranchi with varying number of labourers in each bazars. Five of these markets are the biggest ones where around 500 labourers come and wait daily. In other four markets, around 200-350 labourers would be found daily. Rest of the three markets have very less strength of 50-100 labourers.

There are various patterns of migration in these bazars: some come from adjoining areas of Ranchi and some even commute from adjoining states, for eg. from West Bengal. There are mainly three categories of migrant labourers- first, those who come to the city for a season; they go back to their respective villages. Second category is of those who come in the morning and go back by the evening. And there is a third category of those who have moved with their family to the city from their villages but they have not broken their ties with the native place. They also do go back to their native place in agricultural season.

Ranchi City

Ranchi is the capital city of Jharkhand which was formed in 2000 after a prolonged struggle for a separate state. Until the early 20th century, Jharkhand was part of Bihar and mainly inhabited by indigenous people who had a self-sufficient economy. In the post-Independence period, when Nehru-led industrialization began, some industries were set up in Ranchi also. It accelerated the process of urbanization in the region and non-tribal communities migrated to this place. Gradually the industrialization process intensified in the region along with non-tribal migration to the region.

Ranchi has a very significant position with reference to the state of Jharkhand as it lies almost at the center of the chief mineral belt of the Northeast upland of India, which covers Jharkhand, West Bengal, Orissa and Chhattishgarh. Further, its close proximity to coal and iron mines has specially facilitated the course of industrial development in the area. All these factors have favored Ranchi in attracting the attention of the Government of India as one of the most suitable places for concentrating some major industries.

Ranchi city is situated almost at the center of the Chotanagpur plateau. According to 2011 Census, the city covers about 216 sq. km. with a population of 1073427. Spatially, the city is located at the convergent point of national highways connecting Hazaribagh, Daltonganj, Jamshedpur and Muri. It is well connected to other districts of Jharkhand by road.

Migration to Ranchi City

The process of urbanization in Jharkhand began in the 17th century. There were several local chiefs who used to rule over the region. Due to its rugged topography and dense forests, the Chhotanagpur plateau was a virtual 'no man's land'. It is said that during the reign of Ashoka, this region was known as 'Atavi' or 'forest states'. During the Mughal period this region was known as the 'Kokrah' region. During the British period there were several small princely states such as Ramgarh, Kharagdiha, Kendy etc. The British began the construction of roads and railways to exploit the minerals and forest products in the region. It also led to further development in the area and some new settlements emerged in the region. The British Raj also developed new administrative centers in the region which led further to urban development. Prior to the 20th century, Ranchi was only a tribal settlement, which was transformed into an administrative and defense center by the British Raj. In the first half of the 20th century, Ranchi became an important educational and commercial center of this region. Even after Independence the city retained its importance due to several major industries being established there. Due to all these developments, people were moving to this city and tribal and non-tribal cultures were found to exist side by side. One is the indigenous culture of original inhabitants and the other is the culture brought by the migrants who came later to settle here.

The growth of Ranchi city reveals that it has been exposed to several forces of change over time. From its evolution till now, Ranchi has seen and absorbed many vital changes. Since Ranchi's formation as capital, the city has witnessed massive construction activities. The construction activities is booming in the city as it includes various activities such as formation of roads, flyovers, Sarkari Bhavan (government institutions such as high court, legislative assembly etc.), private residences, real estate construction etc. These construction jobs of the city are done by the workers of *mazdoor bazar*. The jobs are those of masons, carrying bricks, painting houses, cleaning drainage, cooking food for gatherings, cleaning utensils etc. The Master Plan of Ranchi developed by Ranchi Municipal Corporation and Urban Development Ministry of Jharkhand, shows that various kinds of construction activities were planned for the city such as: Integrated freight Complexes, District Commercial centers, Convenience stores, local shopping centers, neighborhood parks, residential colonies, bus depots, hospitals, schools, ring road, inner circle roads, radial roads, overbridges etc. Apparently these activities attracted a lot of labourers from other areas than Ranchi. They were mainly rural migrants.

Socio-economic Status of the labourers from *Mazdoor Bazar*

I interviewed around 200 labourers with the help of an interview schedule which had open ended and closed-ended questions. These are some of the issues that came out of the interviews which are discussed below.

* Not recognized as labourer: First of all, these migrant labourers are not recognized as labourers. When asked about them possessing any kind of identity card of a labourer, most of the labourers said that they do not have such a kind of identity card. Very few responded in the positive. When enquired about how they got the cards made, they said that they were approached by labour union who told them about the labour card. The labourers who do not have the identity card were asked about why they have not got it made if others have. Some said they are not aware of it and some said it will take days to make the cards. And if the card is made, then that put an obligation on one to associate with labour union and take part in protests and other activities. If they participate in union activities they would lose the days of work and in turn wages. One of the markets is located in Doranda just beside State labour office. The irony is most of the labourers coming to this market haven't got their identity card made.

* No job security: Except in agricultural season, the markets are full to their capacity. There is not a single day when labourers are not present in the market, but this does not guarantee work for them everyday. In an entire month, the maximum a worker would get the work for 10- 15 days. In rest of the days, they have to go without any job. Unlike MGNREGA

these labourers do not have any job security for a minimum of 100 days. Enquiring about them possessing MGNREGA card, they denied it. So for the days when there is no employment they remain empty handed. If their days of jobs are calculated annually, they get to work for 120-150 days in a year, which is near to the formal sector employees' days of job. But their wages are not comparable. Job security is very different. So the conditions of formal workers and these daily wage labourers are not comparable.

- Low wages: Although the minimum wages are fixed but most of the workers are not paid that. Especially the rural workers who commute daily from their village. Since they spend money on transportation they do not want to miss a single opportunity to work so they choose to work instead of bargaining with the employer. The employers take benefit out of their situation and pay them less. Even though the union has fixed the minimum wages, they do not get paid in these situations.

- No Social Security: Despite the existence of Unorganized Sector Workers' Social Security Act (UWSSA), 2008 the labourers are not availing any benefits under it. This act provides for the construction of a National Social Security Board. Which shall recommend social security schemes such as life and disability cover, health and maternity benefits, old-age protection, and any other benefit as may be determined by the government for the unorganized workers. The National Social Security Board has also been constituted in the year 2009. The board recommended that the Rashtriya Swasthya Bima Yojna (to provide health and maternity benefits), the Janshree Bima Yojna (to provide death and disability cover) and the Indira Gandhi National Old Age Pension Scheme be extended to certain categories of unorganized workers.

During the interviews when asked about the awareness of any of these schemes, they responded that they are not aware of any of these schemes.

- Security to women workers: All the markets have equal number of women workers as men. Usually they get to work as *reja* labour which means they would carry bricks-cement-sand-water, prepare the sand-cement mix and do other works which a mason asks. They do not get to work as the main labourer who is paid the highest. So their employment depends on the male labourers' employment. But it is not considered good if a woman worker gets ready to work alone with other male members. During the field study, in one of the markets when one woman labourer went alone with the employer, other women laborers started discussing about her character. When enquired further, they said the woman who goes alone works as a prostitute. What else work she could do if other labourers are not there. The problem with this is they are not recognized as sex workers.

- Also some labourers shared about the sexual harassment by employers and fellow workers they face at work places. They do not have any other mechanism than police to go to, which they want to avoid.

- Problem of accommodation: There are workers who migrate to Ranchi seasonally. They have rented accommodation. There are those who come to city every week. They do not rent the place rather they choose to stay at temples or shelter homes. According to a NGO staff working with the State Labour department, there are 5-6 places of accommodation in the entire city for the labourers. But these shelters are certainly not sufficient for the large number of labourers.

- Blurred identity of the labourer: Since they are migrants, they do not hold right to exercise their democratic right of voting in the city where they work. Most of the workers have their voter id card made of their native place. So when it comes to decide for choosing the political ideology during election time, their ethnic, caste or other ascribed identity overwhelms them. The identity of a migrant worker hardly matters at that time of exercising their citizenship rights.

Conclusion

The precariousness of the migrant labourers can be resolved through welfare measures by the state. An effective and active state intervention through labour regulation and providing the job security-social security can generate gainful employment with decent working conditions. All paid and unpaid workers should be recognized as 'workers'. They should also be made part of decision-making so that their citizenship as labourers could be ensured.

Bibliography

Agarwala, R. (2008). "Reshaping the social contract: emerging relations between the state and informal labor in India." *Theory and Society*, 37(4), 375-408.

Banerjee-Guha, S. (2011). "Status of Rural Migrant Workers in Chinese Cities." *Economic and Political Weekly*, 33-37.

Behal, R.P., Joshi, C. & Mohapatra, P.P.(2010). India. In Campbell, A., Allen, J., & McIlroy, J. (Eds.). (pp. 290-314) *Histories of labour: national and international perspectives*. Aakar books.

Bora, R. S. (2014). "Migrant Informal Workers: A Study of Delhi and Satellite Towns." *Modern Economy*, 5(05), 562.

Breman, Jan. (1996) *Footloose labour: working in India's informal economy.* Vol. 2. Cambridge University Press.

Haberfeld, Y., Menaria, R. K., Sahoo, B. B., & Vyas, R. N. (1999). "Seasonal migration of rural labor in India." *Population Research and Policy Review*, 18(5), 471-487.

Jha, P. (2016). *Labour in Contemporary India.* Oxford University Press.

NCE, U. (2007). "Conditions of work and promotion of livelihoods in the unorganized sector." *Report of the National Commission for enterprises in the unorganized sector, Reuters, 10.*

NSSO. (2013). Migration in India July 2007-June 2008. Report No. 533.

Ranchi Master Plan 2037

Singh, A. K. (2007). *Patterns and process of urban development* in Jharkhand: a case *Study of Ranchi city.*

Singh, M. (1991). Budget 1991-92 speech of Shri. Manmohan Singh, minister of finance. *Ministry of Finance (Union Budget), 24.*

Vidyarthi, L. P. (1970). "Socio-Economic Implications of industrialization in India: A Case Study of Tribal Bihar." *Planning Commission, New Delhi.*

Politics of Saptial Governmentalities: Migrants and their Right to the City

Teena Anil

ABSTRACT

The migrants in India are excluded from the economic, cultural, social and political life and are often treated as strangers and second-class citizens. They are looked down as 'outsiders' by the local population as well as host administration. Their right to the city is often denied on the political defence of the "sons of the soil" theory. Looking at the data on urban poor migrants from 1975–2007 in New Delhi, who have gone through seemingly relentless series of evictions of their 'illegal settlements' (colloquially known as bastis) ordered by the Delhi High Court and the Supreme Court of India in Public Interest Litigations (PILs), one draws a premise that space and community are mutually constituted. It is in this context, the paper explores the mechanisms through which democratic urban polities produce, maintain and reproduce inequality in urban India.

The workers who migrate to the urban areas do not remain unattached to the city ... they become part of the city as citizens and thus belong to city's socio-economic, political and physical space. However, they remain 'outsiders' and at the margins of the city. In this context the paper develops a critical reading of the politics of housing in general and politics of resettlement in particular as a very critical site of the politics of citizenship. The empirical study of the resettlement project for the urban poor reveals the impoverishment of urban citizens in contemporary India, manifested in access to resources and entitlements as well as a place within the narratives of belonging and personhood. The paper highlights the plight of those once migrants but now trying to occupy urban space officially through resettlement project claiming for inclusive citizenship.

Introduction

Rapid liberalisation of the Indian economy in recent years and increasing inflow of foreign investment for major infrastructural projects including investments by the World Bank and international financial institutions has led to widespread displacement and loss of access to traditional resources and means of livelihood of many in the country. In the years, immediately after Independence, the overarching ideology of nation building favoured a development model of accelerated economic growth through the agency of a mixed economy, combining centralized planning and command investment with capitalist free enterprise. Equity concerns were pushed to the backburner and it was believed that growth would itself take care of poverty and unemployment, hunger and inequality.

Quite contrary to that in case of poor migrants who had come to city for better life, left to illegally occupy space in the city, considered as urban poor, and became part of unintended city space and seeking integration in the planned city spaces to be gradually treated as legitimate citizens. Our analytical focus, then will not be on urban 'poor' but on migrants and the underlying issue on othering as experienced by the migrants during the process of becoming informal citizens of "unintended city" (see Ashish Nandy, 1998) space.

Governmentality, Production of Space and Reproduction of Social Inequality

When the object of the claim is land (for housing), then the target of the claim ultimately is the State, as in the Indian context land is regulated by the State. It is hence essential to understand how state understands urban poor squatting illegally of government land and their rights to the city, co-constitutive of space and community. In order to characterize this relationship, an articulation of the concepts of governmentality (Chatterjee 2004) and Lefebvre's ([1974] 1991) notion of production of space is useful.

Governmentality, a key notion in Foucault's work, can be "understood in the broad sense of techniques and procedures for directing human behavior" (Rose, O'Malley and Valverde 2006). More specifically governmentality describes mechanisms of linking forms of power to processes of subjectification through techniques of domination anchored in a certain regime of rationality (Lemke 2000:2, 7). In this sense governmentality helps to articulate the strategic character of government. Foucault paid little attention to Empire (Prakash 2010) and hence did not explicitly articulate governmentality with the imperatives of colonialism. Building on Foucault's work, Chatterjee embraced the concept in his seminal book *The Politics of the Governed* (2004) to describe state-society dynamics in the post-colonial world. He argues that the particularity of the post-colonial context is that techniques of governmentality predate the nation-state. Rather than securing state legitimacy by citizen participation, the state apparatus claims to provide entitlements to certain populations (Chatterjee 2004:34). Populations have the status of subjects, rather than citizens. This framing makes available to governments "a set of rationally manipulable instruments for reaching populations of a country as the target of their policies" (Chatterjee 2004:34).

Drawing from the above discussion, the paper attempts to understand how the resettlement policy as part of spatial practice of state becomes an instrument of reaching to the migrant population as the target of their policy. An attempt in this regard further enable us to critically understand how spatialized notion of governmentality, its desire/ an obsession of planned development is fraught with conflict. Delhi's, and urban India's particular predicament, today is not the dispute over its linear perspective of planned development which has been so fixated with its modernising gaze on the city as the pinnacle of a nation's socio-political development but the conflict internal to it-between the planned development of urbanization and socio-spatial organization of the urban environment. Ashish Nandy defines it as the "city that was never part of the formal 'master plan' but always implicitly in it". The unintended city consists of the growing number of poor houses in slums and streets, who provide the cheap labour and services without which the official city could not survive. Exploited and disenfranchised, the existence of this other cannot be acknowledged by the official part of its self. This reflects that how the very idea of planned/formal development created unplanned and informal development of its own kind, resulting in geographical segregation.

The nature of geographical segregation in general and the role of resettlement policy enabled one to understand the processes of regularisation of informal land which lead to more legalised planned space, stigmatising the squatter (migrants) for illegally occupying the city space perpetuating the very process of othering of the migrants (squatters) and denying them from their rights to city. This process can be understood with Lefebvre's theory of "production of space," which lends itself to understand the relations between space and social change (Buser 2012:2). Similarly, in order to understand how the inherent biases of resettlement policy perpetuates othering of the migrants, one explores by drawing from the conceptual triad which expresses the interaction between spatial *practices, representations of space* and *spaces of representation* to trace the production of space (Buser 2012:6).

A) Representations of space **relates** to a rationally abstracted space, defined or *planned* by technocratic agents who hold power and knowledge. *Representations of space* are a frame of references, which permit spatial orientation and thus co-determines activity. They are held in verbal descriptions and the written word (Buser 2012:6). Within techniques of governmentality, *representations of space* are defined within the geographical purview in which policy targets are situated and to which the benefits pertain.

The Resettlement Policy acted as a key process to affirm the positioning of these settled populations / migrants within the city space. Families who were originally living in informal settlements across the city were brought together within the Resettlement Colonies and subsequently classified as residents of legal residents of the colony. Over the years, many waves of resettlement have attempted to integrate these informal city dwellers into the governable domain of legal housing, using their documentation as criteria of eligibility.

It is to be noted that prior to resettlement, despite living in informal and illegal settlements, these settled populations / migrants were able to collect proofs of residency and citizenship such as ration cards, voter ID cards and licenses. The key difference for these was that such documents labelled their residences as 'T-Hut' or 'Temporary Hut', demarcating their residence as temporary, having limited authorisation over their place of residence However, documentation collected over the years cemented their claim to space within the city, but not of the claim over their place of residence, reinforcing discriminatory practices against the poor migrant.

Let us look at how this process of "representation of space" occupied by the poor migrants has evolved from 1976, at the time of inception of Jahangirpuri, to the recent decade, when Savda came into being in 2006 compelling squatter's evictions from the old settlement.[1]

Representing Space Eviction from the Settlements

Eviction in cities is usually done when the land is needed for developmental purposes. However, as will be seen in the examples that follow, the reasons for eviction varied from period to period, and also from one eviction site to another. From the point of view of the evictees, however, the process was one of displacement from their homes, their place of community as well as livelihood. As will be seen from the narrations of respondents, the implementation of policy was done in a haphazard manner, often with little prior notice, which led to it being a distressing process for the evictees.

There are two views to understand the process of eviction: One is from the government's side, and the other is the lived experience of a slum dweller of being evicted from their home. In the context of older colonies such as Jahangirpuri and Seemapuri, eviction was said to have occurred as part of a welfare initiative wherein urban slum dwellers living in inhospitable conditions were granted land free of cost, on a 100-year lease, in order to help them achieve stability and economic progress. This was thus meant as a positive gesture for the beneficiaries

On the other hand, in the case of newer colonies such as Bawana and Savda, the reason for eviction varied from one location to another. While in Khan Market, eviction was done suddenly due to a gas pipeline explosion, for a location like Laxmi Nagar, eviction made way for a metro station. The Nizamuddin *basti* and the Yamuna Pushta areas were cleared for beautification purposes, the latter reportedly in order to put up a tourist pavilion in view of the upcoming Commonwealth Games.

Eviction for Welfare

The narrative of most original residents of Jahangirpuri follows the story of migration to the city in search of employment, residence at multiple places across the city for a number of years, culminating in an eviction and relocation to the JJ Colony. Among the original allottees of Jahangipuri, a large number of respondents had originated from slum locations such as in Majnu ka Tila, Gur Mandi (Ghanta Ghar), Kewal Park and Yamuna Pushta. A typical story of resettlement for a number of original respondents from Jahangirpuri was as follows:

> People lived on the banks of Yamuna River or Yamuna Pushta on an uneven land that had been left vacant due to its instability. Every few months, the river would rise and dislodge the straw, tin and mud houses on the edges, destroyed all the work put in by the impoverished residents who could not afford to pay rent or buy land in the already overcrowded and overpriced spaces in the city. One fine morning, some years after people began living in Pushta, government officials came around and took down the names of all the families living there. They counted the number of families who had ration cards. Since a number of families had been in Delhi for only a few years, they did not have a ration card. Nonetheless, their names were noted down. After some time, the people were told that Indira Gandhi was giving them land in a new colony built for them, and they were going to be moved there. Soon, bulldozers came and demolished all the houses, and trucks carried the people to their new home in Jahangirpuri.

Quite differently, the residents of Khan Market *jhuggi* were not evicted from their homes. They were forced to leave because half of their settlement was destroyed in a gas explosion in the underground pipelines. The survivors were initially housed in a nearby park, and eventually offered the option of either remaining where they were, or receiving allotment in Savda or Bawana. Realising the danger to their lives, most choose resettlement and praised the government for its efforts to rehabilitate them. Following the above discussion one could suggest that how the politics of spatial governmentality regularised the land for its developmental project, informalised the people residing on those areas, perpetuating hierarchy leading to the othering of the squatter (poor migrant). As Ravi Sundaram argues, by Independence, urban development projects such as the drafting of master plans redirected the moral imperative of social reform to one of redressing the inequities of the colonial city through planning, Where information gathering and mapping techniques, long associated with planning, were significantly altered in their orientation by the 1990s.

B) Spaces of representation on the other hand engages with spaces that are lived and formed by human experiences, memories and feelings (Buser 2012). To articulate the effects of governmentality with spaces of representation is to decipher the changes in the lives of the individuals targeted by policy. For example, to ask: Once a locality is targeted for slum-redevelopment what chain of events does it trigger and how does it change the urban experience for the inhabitants?

Regularizing Space and Informalising Squatters (Poor Migrants)

A variety of experiences were captured when discussing the lived reality of squatters who were being infomalized by the state machinery within the process of regularizing the land for city's development. These experiences can be categorically divided into two: short term and long term experience of traumatic stories of injury, loss and disruption in life. The short term experiences of informalisation were a function of a combination of factors - the amount of information and notice given to the slum community, one's financial resources, social capital as well as one's willingness to relocate.

Overall, when asked if the entire process of obtaining a plot at the JJRC was difficult, within the wider sample, 54 per cent, of the Original Residents stated having had no difficulty in gaining the plot in the resettlement colony. However, the difference between the colonies was especially stark here: For Jahangirpuri residents, as was clear from the resettlement process highlighted by them, that there was hardly anything to do to gain allotment in the JJRCs. This is because plots were given easily to the slum dwellers. This was the complete opposite of Savda, where people were forcefully relocated after being rudely and violently evicted from their previous homes.

It then comes as no surprise that 93 per cent of Jahangirpuri residents state that they faced little or no difficulty in getting the plot, an answer matched by only 30 per cent of Savda residents. On the other hand, 60 per cent of Savda residents report facing extreme difficulty in the process, an experience which was shared by only 6 per cent of respondents from Jahangirpuri (see table 1).

Table 1: The Legal procedures – Difficulties in getting the plot

Was the process of getting a plot here difficult?	Jahangirpuri	Savda	Total
Extremely difficult	6%	60%	32%
To some extent	2%	10%	7%
Not much	9%	4%	7%
No difficulty	84%	26%	54%
Total	100%	100%	100%

In case of long term effect a particularly horrifying story of loss comes into the memories from a resident of O-block in Savda who was evicted from Raghubir Nagar, whose elder son committed suicide due to the stress of the process, leaving behind two children, and whose younger son lost his arm in a factory accident not long after, leaving the family traumatised and with a severely reduced earning capacity.

> Suddenly one day they put up a notice that they are going to break the *jhuggi*, it was the winter season and we were left out in the cold. And the next day they broke the *jhuggis*. Who can find another place in one day? Some found, some didn't. They just broke the *jhuggis* in one day, and everyone was crowded into the nearby park. It was extremely difficult.

> In Raghubir Nagar, my husband used to sell vegetables, my sons used to drive cycle rickshaws. Even I used to work. Now, here, there is no employment. How much will a poor person be able to invest in construction? My son committed suicide by hanging himself. Everything got left behind. When we came here our cycle rickshaw was stolen, and my son had an accident—his arm got cut off while working at the factory. This just added to our troubles. My other son died. Now I just have one son who earns. He goes back to Raghubir Nagar to work.

Lakshmi's story reflects many of the difficulties ailing the new residents of Savda—dislocation of employment, as well as the stresses of the entire process, which eventually led to her elder son committing suicide. Her story also reflects the inherent distrust that many of the urban poor have of the government/ welfare state. For instance, she believes the poor in city/cities have been the victims of state violence.

That the state is a 'distrustful partner' and cannot be relied upon is the prominent feeling, memories and human experience and, to a large extent, is what pains them the most. This feeling comes from the experiences of the squatters (urban poor) being treated unequally, of not being given correct and proper information, where they are considered as objects in the process of negotiation and not citizens to be in dialogue with.

A careful analysis help us to explore the way poor migrants engage with space from which they were evicted, these brought forth and critiqued the role of international financial agencies like World Bank (WB), which subsequently came up with stringent guidelines, to be adhered to by the state which seeks money from the bank for the development projects. 'The World Bank's new position was that no project site could be cleared without a resettlement and rehabilitation component' (Burra, 2005: 71). Nonetheless, these newer guidelines further perpetuate the squatter as "other" who could be shifted anywhere with proper rehabilitation and resettlement without any subsequent feeling, memories and experience. With this, one can see the how conceptualization of the space of representation in the context of selected resettlement colony (JJRC) has helped us to understand the process of othering as experienced by squatters (poor migrants). This further reaffirms that state and other international agency's unwillingness to treat squatters (poor migrants) as equal citizens.

C) *Spatial practices* relate to people's *perceptions* on the basis of their experiences of daily life. Perception not only relates to materiality, but also to the processes by which materiality is produced. Hence, the networks of social relations that mediate these processes and make up daily life (Buser 2012).

An important component of citizenship of any political entity is its power to include some while excluding others. Citizenship simultaneously creates an in-group to which people can prescribe, and leaves an out-group to treat as the other. Inclusion in the in-group of the city was a primary desire for the slum dwellers that migrated to Delhi many decades or even a century ago. It was a desire to be included in the city's spaces as participative and productive citizens, and to improve their socio-economic conditions as well as overall standard of living.

The inclusion of these slum dwellers was limited in many ways: They have poor access to facilities, no security of tenure, and often faced harassment from authorities and fellow citizens. Despite this, they were able to build their communities, find employment and earn their living. The JJ Resettlement Policy, by allotting space to beneficiaries, claimed to offer slum dwellers a way out of their difficult circumstances by granting a greater degree of legality to their presence within the city, thereby opening up many new possibilities for advancement.

However, the validity of this claim has been questioned repeatedly over the years. Has the resettlement colony truly given its residents greater legality and legitimacy in the city? Has it given them any power over their lives or choices of how to live it? And has it granted them the full citizenship that is the right of every citizen of the country? For residents of Savda and Jahangirpuri, it was discovered that these benefits have been limited in scope, especially with respect to their legitimacy within the city space. Narratives of discrimination were widely acknowledged by respondents at both sites. These expressions reveal both the pain of being perceived and identified as 'stigmatised,' being discriminated and differentiated unfairly by others in the city spaces outside the colony.

This question was also posed in the context of five major areas of day to day life, i.e. 'officials treating residents of the locality as equal with all,' 'outsiders' negative view of the colony,' 'differential treatment of colony residents in public areas outside the colony,' 'difficulty in securing a job outside the colony.' The

strongest expression of discrimination and rejection came from
a youth leader of Savda:

> When the government created these, "Resettlement colonies," why
> have they retained this "*jhuggi jhopri*" status? Why is it still called
> JJ colony & not resettlement colony? You have been to so many JJ
> Colonies—have you ever seen this word '*punarvaas*' [resettlement]
> used anywhere? No, we are still called '*jhuggi jhopri*'. We should
> be allowed a new identity. They say we are legal residents, we are
> living in a *pakki* [cemented] colony, and then why are we still
> called JJ? (...) We have got the 'JJ', but we have yet to receive
> *punarvaas* [resettlement].

Jhuggi-jhopri is the colloquial term used in Delhi for both the
slums and their illegal inhabitants. The *jhuggi jhopris* are described
by some as the 'warts on the beautiful skin of the city that must
be gotten rid of—not by making them equal to the other citizens,
but rather by expelling them altogether' (Verma, 2002). The
title 'JJ resettlement colony' today has become a derogatory and
stigmatised term and is seen to seep into many aspects of life for
the residents. Officials and those in positions of power therefore
tend to avoid any association with the locality.

In these cases, the blame was attributed directly to the actions
of the government representatives, who treat the residents of the
JJ Colony as lesser citizens, and have distorted the image of the
Resettlement Colony by labelling it 'JJ Colony'—which is the
colony's official name, even mentioned on the signboard at Ghevra
Mor ("Sawda JJ Colony").

Outsiders' Negative View of the Colony

As stated earlier, personal identity is a function of how we view
ourselves as well as our perception of how others view us. In this
respect, it is important to consider the experiences of residents of
the JJRC with other residents of the city, in order to understand

their experiences of inclusion in the in-group of the city. Pavitiri of Jahangirpuri resettlement colony mentioned the following with regard to weddings and functions:

> My daughters' in-laws out-rightly rejected coming to Jahagirpuri with the wedding procession. They didn't have a problem marrying into Jahangirpuri, but the problem was with having the function inside the colony. I don't quite feel the same, but to maintain our pride we did agree to do the functions outside the colony. There is always a fear, what if a drunkard or hooligan happens to come and ruin the event? That kind of thing can easily happen in Jahangirpuri. Plus the lanes are quite small, so other people would also get disturbed; there is not much space for such functions.

For Pavitiri and others, the negative element of the colony lay in its lack of safety, which has been emphasised by almost all residents from the colony. As she and others mentioned, people from outside the colony, including from the immediate neighbourhood of Adarsh Nagar (which is considered an upper-class area), had no problems in marrying their children into the colony, however, when it came to hosting functions, they refused to do this inside the colony due to the high possibility of thefts or hooliganism.

As long-term residents, Pavitiri feels that they live in a good locality, and hold themselves as honest citizens. However, they accept that outsiders view the colony as an undesirable place to live; that the colony contains anti-social elements; and that because of this, people may not want to be associated with it.

Differential Treatment of Colony Residents in Public Areas Outside the Colony

Differential treatment in city spaces, Shashikala from Savda narrated her experience at the bank near the colony:

> We JJ Colony residents can never get our work done easily. We keep standing in the line, and a person from the village will come

and they will let him in instantly, saying, "He is from my area."
So why does that matter? Aren't we all customers? Why does he
get special treatment and we are treated like dirt just because
we are from the JJ Colony? How is this fair? Speaking of the
discriminatory gaze of outsiders towards colony residents.

Difficulty in Securing a Job outside the Colony

An area where respondents felt strongly discriminated against was in
the job market outside the colony. Discussions with young people
in both colonies led to similar narratives where employers, upon
learning that the applicant lived in a JJ Colony, made an excuse
to reject them regardless of their qualifications, thus depriving
them of equal opportunities. For instance, Gaurav, a 21-year-old
resident of Savda, confessed:

> I apply for many jobs; a few times I've even been called for
> interviews. But the moment they see my address on my CV as
> 'Savda Ghevra JJ Colony', they say, "Oh that's so far away, how
> will you travel? What if we need you to stay late?" Even if I tell
> them that it's not an issue for me, they hold on to it and I've never
> been offered a job. Obviously, they don't want to hire anyone from
> a JJ Colony. Even if I lie to them and tell them I live in Mundka,
> it is still there on my papers, right? I can't hide it forever.

A Jahangirpuri policeman also pointed towards the factors
concerning different socio-cultural groups present within the
colony and his perceptions about different communities:

> There are many communities here but among them *Balmiki*
> and Muslim, both are mostly illiterate. Anywhere you go in the
> country, *'Balmiki'* meaning the one who slaughters pigs, the *safai*
> *karamcharis* [public sweepers] and all, they are only *Balmikis*.
> Others don't go into these professions. Women go to clean in the
> houses. They don't feel the need for education—they just pick
> up the broom and start cleaning. They don't study, that's why
> the situation is bad in Jahangirpuri. (...) However much may
> you try to educate them—Delhi police has a program for them
> about addiction, about education, all the facilities are provided to

them—but they are not interested. The children beat up teachers and the parents even support their children. Parents are also just as likely to beat up teachers, so the teacher is wary. The children may go to school or may not. Another parent takes care of whether the child is going to school, doing homework, eating etc. Here that cannot happen. When a child says "I am going to play"—the parent must know where the child is going. But they don't pay attention and the child falls into bad company, and eventually falls into alcoholism and addiction.

However, the narratives of 'outsiders'— the policeman—express the general perceptions of those outside the colony as to how they look at the colony and its residents. It reveals the identity of the insiders and who they are for outsiders; in public areas outside the colony, government appointed official from the colony, the residents finding difficulty in securing a job outside the colony because of stigma of JJ colony etc. express the negative stereotype attached with the colony. Not only is it a painful experience that one must live with, but the helplessness experienced by the residents in not being able to change their identities is more agonizing. An analysis of this data suggests spatial practise or governmentalities are unequal in nature creating a hierarchy of citizenship.

Conclusion

The aim of this paper was to explore techniques of governmentality coupled with the production of space, that shape experiences of the poor migrants and their citizenship rights. Within the framework of systems of governmentality and production of space, I argued that there is a total disconnect between the planned, lived and perceived which shape the process of continuous othering or exclusion an poor migrants

Foucault's theory of governmentality, with an extension of Chatterjee's extension of colonial governmentality applied along with Lefebvre's theory of the production of space was used to examine the co-constitutiveness of space and community targeted by policy. The National Rehabilitation and Resettlement policy markedly influenced the built us form and experience of it and the social relations in the slum in particular and city in general. This conceptual approach pinpointed the tension between the scale of public policy intervention that targets a spatially constituted community denying urban poor and their citizenship rights. A closer reading of this tension within the presented episodes leads me to identify outcomes affecting the community targeted by policy. This forms the hypotheses that could be tested through further empirical investigations.

The (logical) consequence from perceiving the dissonance between planned and lived as a citizen, having very low social skills and no social network, could lead to total exclusion from the community and the geographical space. New migrants into the city would be particularly vulnerable to the third situation.

Within the discussion of production of space, it is also important to note the perceptions held by government agencies about the capacity of the poor to endure hardships. In none of the localities where Resettlement policy leading to eviction of poor migrants and regularization of land were realized in-situ were adequate arrangements for transit housing made treating them as 'other' assuming that community they members could put up their tents and tin-sheets, as they were accustomed to living in abysmal conditions. Moreover, it was taken for granted that they could and would start from scratch building a livelihood, enrolling their kids into new schools, and organizing for other lacking amenities, leaving the urban poor to "their own devices" (Berner and Phillips 2005).

These two episodes show how the eviction of urban poor for land, allotment of land for housing at the fringe of the city is conflictual, i.e. to what means the communities can resort in order to assert a claim equal citizenship status not for housing but also to their citizenship rights. Even though the resettlement policy recognized to a limited extent the right to the city's materiality in the form of the provision for adequate housing and urban services, ignoring the continuous stigmatization of the community were still markers of the inhabitants' citizenship status. Both the resettlement colonies were officially recognized (declared) JJRC, which makes the State "see" (Scott 1998) these communities.

On the basis of two case studies, this article attempted to shed light on the politicized processes of housing. By spatializing the concept of governmentality, I argued that the gross dissonance between the planned, the lived and the perceived triggered discriminatory forms of citizenship. In this sense, urban citizenship defies governmentality mechanisms that identify beneficiaries without feelings, memories and experiences and calls for more attention to the co-constitutiveness of space and community. The displaced urban poor are struggling to validate and prove their claim to citizenship on an everyday basis. Thus the politics of housing can be argued to be the single most critical site of politics of citizenship in this city' (Appadurai, 2004:72).

References

Appadurai. (2004). 'The Capacity to Aspire: Culture and the Terms of Recognition', in Rao, V. and Walton, M., (eds.) *Culture and Public Action*, Stanford University Press, Palo Alto, California, pp 59-84.

Berner, Erhard and Benedict Phillips. 2005. "Left to Their Own Devices? Community Self-Help between Alternative Development and Neo-Liberalism." *Community Development Journal* 40(1): 17–29.

Burra, S., S. Patel and T. Kerr. (2005). 'Community-designed, Built and Managed Toilet Blocks in Indian Cities'. *Environment and Urbanism* 15 (2): 11-32.

Chatterjee, P. (2004). *The politics of the governed: reflections on popular politics in most of the world*. Columbia University Press.

Lefebvre, H. (1991). *The production of space*. (Vol. 142). Blackwell: Oxford.

Lemke 2000 Lemke, Thomas. 2000. "Foucault, Governmentality, and Critique." Presented at the Rethinking Marxism Conference, September 21-24, University of Amherst, MA.

Nandy, Ashish, (1998). "Introduction: Indian Popular Cinema as the Slum's Eye View of Politics" in Ashish Nandy ed. *The Secret Politics of Our Desires: Innocence, Culpability and Indian Popular Cinema*, Oxford University Press, Delhi.

Prakash, G. (2002). 'Urban Turn', in Vasudevan, R, R, Sundaram, J, Bagchi, M. Narula, G. Lovink, and S. Sengupta (Ed) *Saria Reader 2002: The Cities of Everyday* Life. New Delhi: Saria- The New Media Initiative& CSDS

Rose, Nikolas, Pat O'Malley and Mariana Valverde. 2006. "Governmentality." *Annual Review of Law and Social Science* 2(1): 83–104. Retrieved March 2, 2013 (http://www.annualreviews.org/doi/abs/10.1146/annurev.lawsocsci.2.081805.105900).

Scott, J. (1998). *Seeing like State: How Certain Schemes to Improve the Human Condition Have Failed*. New Haven: Yale University Press.

Endnotes

[1] This study was conducted by DDS at ISI Delhi, which the journey of two *Jhuggi Jhopri* Resettlement Colonies (JJRC) of Delhi, i.e. Jahangirpuri established in 1976 and Savda Ghevra established in 2006. It is a recording of the process of their establishment, development and the lived experiences of their residents.

Post Liberalization, Dalits and Large Scale Industry: Experiences of Labour who migrated from Coastal Odisha to Other Parts of India

Dhaneswar Bhoi and Neelima Rashmi Lakra

Abstract

This paper is based on the experiences of the people migrated from Odisha to Mumbai, Surat and Hyderabad for their livelihood by losing their agrarian occupation of their village. This study captures how the free trading of liberalization has reached every corner of Indian economy, trying to take over the space of agricultural occupation and the occupation of agricultural labourers. The objectives of the paper are to explore how migration compels to shift Dalits from rural occupation to another occupation outside the village, city and state; how their personal, social, cultural and educational life get affected due to the shifting of their occupation, and how they live-in the congested city due to the liberalization forced migration.

Keywords: *Post Liberalization, Forced Labour Migration, POSCO, Life Condition of Dalits.*

Introduction

The situation of labour is undergoing a big change because of liberalized world today, inspite of the demands which make trading or business easy and free from the rules and regulation of the State, labor reforms have become obligatory along with the structural and administrative reforms in the liberalized world. In this economic reform after 1991, the most vulnerable unit of the production is labour. Due to increased technology, installation of outsourced skilled labour suffers a lot in the Indian labour market. Specially with the instruction of World Bank and International Monetary Fund, India has started reducing labour affecting the service sector. New employment was not promoted by all most all states including center. Many states were awarded budget allocated money, some of the states were also awarded as economical states did not spend money on government employment. Employment sector was managed mostly by contractual position (Bhoi and Lakra 2018). According to the National Sample Survey Organisation, in 2009-10 there were some 46.5 crore workers out of which just 2.8 crore workers had been in the organized sector – a mere 6 per cent are working in organized sector. The differentiation of the lifestyle was clearly visible among them. While workers in the organized sector get decent wages accompanied by a high standard of living, those in the unorganized sector don't even get minimum wages, leave alone social security. The social security and social welfare modes were drawn from the citizens as well as the employees. Even, pension system was also withdrawn in a few new employments in the government sector. The promotion of private sector also indirectly withdrew the rights of socially backward communities (Bhoi 2013).

An NSSO report of 2011-12 says, in India 68 per cent of the workforce has neither a written assurance about jobs nor do they enjoy paid-holidays. Today, the availability of jobs in India is so wobbly and so little that workers are ready to do any kind of work in exchange for even very small wages. No wonder then that India is counted – and advocated – as one of the most profit-giving countries in the world.

History of Liberalisation

The history of Liberalisation is based on many-folded privatisation policy in Western countries. It started in a large-scale sector between 1922-1925 in Italy, in 1923 in France and between 1934-37 in Germany to build the nation differently. The most important public debate on privatisation started in the early 1920s with the proposal of privatisation of railways in Switzerland, Germany, Belgium and Italy. After a long gap it was started in the mid-1970s in Chile and in early 1980s in the UK. Even if the privatisation was applied in 1929s in Italy and 1930s in Germany, interestingly neither the Fascist nor the Nazi policy implied the liberalisation or the withdrawal of state control over the market. There was a strong control of the market by the state. The study of interior privatisation in Europe gives increasing lessons, how authoritarian and the totalitarian government implemented their policies (Bel, 2011). In the late 1980s, the modern neoliberal economic reform policies stated structural adjustment and promoted privatisation in most of the developing countries (Richardson & Haralz, 1995 cited by Bhoi 2013).

The theoretical connection to the privatisation emerged from the idea that the wealth of the nation (proposed by Smith as this theory invitees thriving capitalist system in the world), defines the governments' and individual's perspective about the formation and distribution of wealth. In this concept, individuals are fully capable to regulate prices for goods and services in the nation. The idea that the wealth of the nation believes in free trade and the market economy (Smith, 1776), is strengthened by the argument that the absence of belief in freedom is the base idea of Friedman towards opponents of privatization. His theory is based on the principles of a truly liberal society, *underlying most arguments against the free market is a lack of belief in freedom itself* [normals us] (Friedman, 1962, p. 15). On the contrary, the idea of welfare concept came to economics with the effort of Alfred Marshall, who emphasizes study of wealth and the human rather wealth alone, *political economy or economics is a study of humankind in the ordinary business of life; it examines that part of individual and social action which is most closely connected with the attainment and with the use of the material requisites of well-being.* There are some goods which are meant for the welfare of the human and society that cannot be considered as economic goods for profit [normal are us] (Marshall, 1890, p-1). The capitalistic mode of production challenged by Karl Marx, who argued about structure of production in an economy is based on class division and class struggle and rooted in the capitalist social relations of production, *the wealth of those societies which is the capitalist mode of production prevails, present itself as an immense accumulation of commodities* [....] *Each individual commodity, in this connection, is considered as an average sample of its class.* He suggested the socialist mode of production for the equity in society (Marx, 1867, p. 1& 6). Keynes Theory also defies the idea of privatization. He claimed, government regulation is needed in the production process where people can enjoy the completely absence of the laissez-faire economy in the state. He suggested that the government can take part in a constructive role in protecting citizens' interest from most terrible harms of capitalism, especially as it concerns unemployment (Keynes, 1926). Supporting this, the cultural hegemony of social structure was argued in the line of institutional form of the state where class struggle and political struggle spin into the institutional form of the state which promotes the formation of institution/firm and structure in the society for capitalistic base (Gramsci, 1971 cited by Bhoi 2013).

New Economic Policy and LPG in India

The new economic LPG policy of the Government of India announced in 1991 has brought in drastic changes in the way in which business is organized and managed in our country. Prior to the reforms of 1991, statesmen had a very firm grip on factors of production through license and permit. After reforms not only this vice-like grip has loosened; many such powers have slipped from their hands and are now controlled by the market forces. The process of liberalisation has had the maximum impact on industries, as it had drastically changed the business environment and future growth dynamics. As India adopted the agreement of WTO, every phenomenon of privatisation appears in the basket-case situation of Indian economy. In the process of privatization, the government transfers the authority to the private where the private players are paying power-play against public to set a complete capitalist world. Like other countries, India is trapped into the policies of *the WTO* in 1994 and *GATT* in 1996 to adopt the privatisation of her economic system. With the effect of *LPG,* the world is now moving towards a wide- spreading common platform for free trading (Bhoi 2013). Structural changes in the Indian industrial sector and globalisation were initiated because the government wanted to encourage growth by doing away with supply bottlenecks that stopped efficiency and competitiveness. Turning to the industrial sector, reforms which encompassed removal of industrial licensing, de-reservation, the substantial opening of foreign direct investment and trade liberalisation have imparted a competitive edge to Indian industry (Bhoi and Lakra 2018).

The LPG had come to India with the New Economic Policy of India in 1991. There have been many structural changes brought by the LPG and come to the life of people with huge character of negativity and little positivity. This process of *Liberalisation* is defined as making economics free to enter the market and establish their venture in the country. Likewise, *Privatisation* is defined as when the control of economic activities is shifted from a public to a private hand. Then *Globalisation* is described as the process by which regional economies, societies, and cultures have become integrated through a global network of communication, transportation, and trade. However, the free entry and abolition of state control over trade and tariff takes India in different directions (Bhoi 2011).

One-way the LPG promises growth and development of and inclusion in the societies in other ways is found in the practices which create gaps between the rich and poor and create problems for the labour which is an important aspect of the production process. India was bound to sign the LPG because of the Government borrowed money from the International Monetary Fund (IMF) and the World Bank as a result they signed fiscal and economic reform policy through LPG. Again, the impact of recent economic changes due to reforms in the labour market reveals a mixed picture. While the pace of employment-generation picked up after the initial years of reform, recent years have witnessed a reduction in employment growth. Even the most ardent supporter of liberalization would agree that, regardless of how well a Government manages the transition from a regulated to a liberal economy, its immediate impact is bad and unjust for the society and nation. It is bad because it reduces economic welfare, and unjust because the costs of adjustment fall disproportionately on the poor. Despite liberalization of trade, industry and finance, no law relating to labour has been amended much less repealed so far for the benefits of the citizen of India. This shows that the basic material conditions of labour in India will continue to be determined primarily by the macro-economic processes rather than by worker-specific legislation (ibid.).

Post Liberalisation and Labour Migration

The New Economic Policy in 1991 of LPG has ruined the labour and specially the marginal community for accessing their life and culture, health and education both and social and personal level. The market-driven development model makes conflict in the village and forces the Dalits to search for jobs in another state to earn their livelihood. In India, much of the labor force is unorganized. According to the National Sample Survey Organisation, in 2009-10 there were some 46.5 crore workers out of which just 2.8 crore workers had been in the organized sector or a mere 6 per cent were in organized sector and having a decent job. In the organized sector get decent wages accompanied by a high standard of living, those in the unorganized sector don't even get minimum wages, leave alone without social security and social welfare. According to an NSSO report of published in 2011-12 the do not have job security and any job benefits. In India mostly 68 per cent of the workforce have neither written assurance about jobs nor they enjoy paid-holidays. There are more than 30 million people in India are seasonal migrant labourers. Among all states Odisha shares is 2.5 million and considered as a key state for the supply of migrant labour to the workforce. Remittance from migrants from Surat stands high which counts at 2000crores, every second day there are news about how migrant workers are harassed, abused, less paid and exploited in various part of India. It is a small effort to deliberate and advocate on the issue of migration, its impact, development, policy framework and search for alternatives to the challenges of new liberal policy in India. The basic question here is how much the Dalits suffer due to the liberal policies in India. Where does their life style stand in the installation process of large scale industry?

Objectives

1. To find out the impact of LPG and large-scale industry influence in rural villages of Odisha.

2. To explore the vulnerability of Dalit labours due to forced migration of POSCO in Coastal Odisha.

3. To explore the forced migration of Dalits and their social, economic, education and health access in their present living place.

Methodology

This is an exploratory study based on qualitative research where 25 migrated family's in-depth interviews were gathered from different places of India. The interviews were conducted from the migrated labour who are currently working in Mumbai, Hyderabad, Surat. It mostly covers the workers in the construction field and brick labourer and cotton mill labour. This paper has collected data from the migrated Dalits families of Coastal Odisha. The research design for this study was purposive and snowball sampling, where the information is gathered from one Dalit family to other Dalit families. The sources of data collection were both secondary and primary. Secondary data were gathered from newspapers, books and journals and websites. Primary data were collected from the Dalit families who migrated or displaced by an installation process of POSCO a large-scale industry at Coastal Odisha. Semi structure in-depth interview schedules were the tools for data collection along with the case study guide and focus group discussion. The analysis method was based on thematic analysis which follows single and cross-case analysis. Analysis and conclusion were drawn on the basis of the case study findings and the content of theoretical and secondary data-based matter.

Migration and Labour in Odisha an Overview

More than 30 million people in India are seasonal migrant labourers. Orissa's share is 2.5 million and considered as a key state for a supplier of migrant labour. The remittance from migrants to Surat stands at 2000 crores across the country, every second day there are news about how migrant workers are harassed, abused and less paid, exploited in various part of India. Through this paper, it is a small effort to deliberate and advocate the issue of migration, its impact, development, policy framework and search for alternatives. The secondary estimates on the number of migrants from Odisha are largely informed by the Census and NSS, the two largest data collection exercises pursued by the Government of India which shows a large number of the labourers migrated after 1991.

The NSS 64th round which was conducted in 2007-08 defines migrants based on usual place of residence where the person had stayed continuously for a period of six months or more. In other words, a migrant is defined if he or she had stayed continuously for at least six months or more in a place other than the village or town where he or she was enumerated. As per this data there are 94,495 rural households and 25,590 urban households are reporting themselves as having migrated to different places in search of their livelihood means. In rural areas, the total number of migrants comes to 88 lakh persons, 92 per cent of them are female migrants. In terms of migration rate - number of migrants per 1000 persons from rural areas, 218 persons reported migrating to different places. The further sub-division of migration rates among men and women was 43 (per 1000) and 514 (per 1000) respectively. The dominance of women in the migration estimates is largely explained by large scale movement of women for marriage purposes and to earn more money, though there are scholars who argue that NSS definitions tends to *camouflage* some labor movement as within the larger category of marriage migration (Mazumdar et al, 2013).

According to the last round survey of NSS, where it introduced a special typology of migrants called short-term migrants, a migrant is defined as a person who had stayed away from the village or town for a period of one month or more but less than 6 months during the last 365 days for employment or in search of employment. Calculations on number of short 1.3 term migrants show that there is a total of 4.17 lakh short term migrants from rural Odisha. Eighty-two percent of the short-term migrants are men. Only 72,000 women workers are reported to have migrated as short-term migrants. Notably, there is a stark difference in migration numbers across northern, southern and western regions of Odisha. The majority of the short-term migrants (71 per cent) are from the southern region, followed by northern (19 per cent) and coastal (10 per cent). The short term migrants come close to the nature of migration being profiled in this report. However, there are serious limitations with this definition as well, which leaves a large group of workers moving for a period longer than 6 months. These figures are serious underestimates. Especially, when we look at the number of women migrants in the short-term category, the discrepancies become apparent. Odisha is known for sending a large number of women (with family as a unit) to brick kilns, a fact that is well documented. The above numbers do not support this observation well. Further, women are also known to feature more in short-term migrant streams; however, the NSS estimates again do not corroborate this. Framing this study it was trying to find out the how the people from one part started migrated to some other parts, even the job duration was for one month. They do not bother whether it is for one month or one year. They need money for their survival. How the coastal Odisha people struggle to get jobs and lose livelihood due to the installation of large scale industry. This study is based on the coastal migration, those who are migrating from coastal Odisha to other parts of India in search of their livelihood means.

OMEGA and Distress Migration in Odisha

Migration from the Odisha to other parts of the country was checked by the programme *Odisha Modernising Economy, Government and Administration* (OMEGA). This programme was initiated by the Government of Odisha with the support of DFID of the United Kingdom to reduce migration from Odisha to other parts of the country. Thousands of workers from Odisha started to move to states like Andhra Pradesh, Tamil Nadu, Karnataka, Gujarat, Delhi and even Kerala to work as construction workers or unskilled labourer. Out of them, very few earned good wages, most would slave away for a pittance. It was slightly reduced with the introduction of the scheme under the Mahatma Gandhi National Rural Employment Generation Act (MGNREGA), there has been a sharp dip in migrations from the state, especially from the migration-prone Kalahandi-Balangir-Koraput belt. The enormous potential of MGNREGA and meticulous execution by the Odisha government has paid off and translated into an additional source of income for families below the poverty line in tribal areas. Now, they have at least 100 days of guaranteed employment for the people who work. Taking a cue from the central scheme, the Odisha government in 2012 launched its own initiative on similar lines - the Odisha Modernising Economy, Government and Administration (OMEGA) through this scheme the government is trying to revive the economy as well as to reduce out the migration by providing job opportunity in the state.

The pilot project was launched in eleven blocks of two districts, ensuring more effective implementation of MGNREGA by exploring the best possible options for streamlining processes, and improving transparency and accountability. The pilot project introduced in the two districts has been able to hold back over 60 per cent families from the migration by engaging them in MGNREGA and other livelihood-related activities. It assures 150 days of employment for households in migration-prone areas of Nuapada and Balangir districts. The project, thus, added another 50 days to the central scheme which guaranteed 100 days of unskilled jobs per rural household. "The migrant labourers generally move to other states from the beginning of November until June-end. A corpus of Rs 300 crore has been proposed in the budget for 2017-18 to ensure timely payments as there are often delays in receiving payments from the Centre. Even if OMEGA has announced and planned a budget for 150days plan for the people of migrated prone areas, however the migration is still rampant and many people migrated from different part of Odisha to other parts of the county for better jobs. Likewise situation also exists with the coastal Odisha people where the installation process of POSCO started land airing and forced the local people migrating to other states.

Pohang Steel Corporation (POSCO) and Labour Migration from Coastal Odisha

The internal distress migrant workers are subjected to several vulnerabilities in India. They are forced to leave their original habitation and work in extremely difficult and dangerous conditions. They are very vulnerable as they are on the margins of Indian society, both economically and socially, and they are facing risks because of non-recognition at the policy level and faulty implementation of laws. Pohang Steel Corporation (POSCO) has signed MoU with the government of Odisha to establish integrated steel plant in Jagatsinghpur district of Odisha in 2005.

In the initial phase, they started land acquiring, the project was planned to install in the coastal district of Odisha. The details of the project are given below;

- Investment: Rs. 51,000 Crore (USD 12-billion)
- Land Requirement: 2700 acre
- Allotted: 500 acres
- Capacity: 12 million tons per annum
- Now they are again demanding total 4004-acre land to produce 12 MTPA steel.
- POSCO will pay Rs. 30/ton compared with the commercial value of Rs. 7,000/ton for iron ore extraction.

In the beginning of the land acquiring process, the company acquires the land through there was protest from POSCO Pratirodha Samiti and the people who affected directly or indirectly in the process of POSCo installation. Because of the land acquiring many of the people (farmer) lose their agricultural land and they became jobless, allowing the farmer many of the agricultural labour lost their occupation. The agricultural labourer those who are from Dalit background they becoming the more sufferers in this process of land acquisition. By losing their job they migrated to other states for searching job to run their livelihood.

Socio-economic Vulnerability

Mostly, those who are migrating from the Coastal Odisha are from Dalit background who worked as agricultural lalour there. Because of land acquisition of POSCO, they migrated in search of jobs or means of livelihood at Mumbai, Hyderabad and Surat. After coming to the new place, they lost every benefit from the government as do not have any identity card and ration card from the presently staying state. A family head Ramakant aged 42 narrates;

> I came to Hyderabad to get a job for my family livelihood and came here through a contractor from upper caste, when I share caste and economic condition instead of helping him try to exploit me, he did not give me my wage for three months, I migrated with my family all of my family members also support me my brick field work. I was also debarred from getting the ration items as I do not have that state specific identity card to avail the facilities. Not getting any sufficient money for the train ticket, I was also not able to come back to my native place. Before coming to Hyderabad, I was and my family working in agricultural fields as agricultural labour we move to Hyderabad because of the POSCO installation process.

The process of Installation of POSCO and the Agricultural Occupation in Odisha

In Noliasahi and Nuagaon villages, land has been acquired by force and deception, and the approach road was being constructed from IOCL side. They deliberately choose not to visit Dhinkia Panchayat and interact with our people. This is quite bizarre as we have been opposing the project from its inception in 2005. The whole visit to the area was completed in just about an hour. The 2000 acres which is in Dhinkia Panchayat, which could not be usurped by the government due to opposition from our people, is the key to the project due to its landscape. It is 3.5 km x 3 km, whereas the width of the land which has been acquired is barely half a kilometre. The team also did not visit the proposed port site at the mouth of river Jatadhari. Without visiting such key sites and taking the opinion of the key people, the report, which will be given by such committee, can only be eyewash and would be to the taste of central and state governments and the IDCO, which are hell bent upon implementing the project despite stiff opposition from people. Interestingly, the beneficiaries of the project eying on contract and construction work seem to have enjoyed the confidence of the committee as they were the privileged people who could talk to visiting members. The situation of the of the landless agricultural labourer was very pathetic when the installation POSCO process started a migrant Sukant aged 45 in Surat said;

> Because of the POSCO installation process they lose their occupation and forced to move Surat to a cotton mill and worked then initially for one year, then I bring all my four younger brothers and we all are working here for one more year the experiences were good and then suddenly we are exploited by our own village supervisor who brought us to the city here. As all come here are exploited by our supervisor, by to getting money my younger brother got sick and we did not give treatment to him. Back in my home also my wife and my old parents who are dependent by us became clueless to run the family and subsequently my children were also dropped from school and suffer due to our migration. Ultimately, we felt we were not of the village as well as not of the city. We were becoming the bonded labour in Surat worked with only get food and accommodation, other than that they were not given money for their treatment. We do not have any health insurance and also because of us our family suffers and denied many accesses in the village, their life was miserable in our village.

Initial Struggle Against POSCO and Agriculture Labourer

Initially the struggle against the POSCO was supported by the civil society and the victimized local people with the installation of POSCO in Jagatsinghpur, under the banner of the POSCO Pratirodh Sangram Samiti (PPSS). PPSS is a community based anti-POSCO movement who fought to give justice to the people who affected by POSCO. Why they are protesting? They are protesting to safeguard the right of the people by opposing to forcible land acquisition. To save the local betel farm, fishery and agriculture and livelihood displacement and fake job promises.

Education, Health and Social Security of POSCO Displaced People

Forced migration affects the life and livelihood and access to education and health. In spite of protest, the pre-works of the installation process of POSCO happened in the Jagatsinghpur district and they forced migrated people suffered in many angles of their life. There is a case where a family come from the Jagatsinghpur and worked in Mumbai in as construction labour and debarred to access education, health and social category. A household head named Prasant, aged 35 moved to Mumbai to a construction site and work there with his family, he explains;

> When I moved to the Mumbai with aspired a better life in Mumbai, however, after reaching working in Mumbai, I lost all my aspiration except Vodapao and daily food, I was getting good money in my work, my family members were engaged the same job, but what we loose that my children drop out from their school and they faced problem in enrolling either in Marathi or Hindi medium school and the enrolment process of the student in Mumbai was also not possible. Due to the inappropriate staying, deprived of sleeping and not getting good food my children and other family member usually faced problem being well, usually they fall in sick and not able to get better treatment or may medical facilities. Due to the identity card we were not able to access to ration and other benefit from the government in Mumbai. After deprived from education my children were only getting the opportunity to teach in their study with the efforts of students of Tata Institute of Social Sciences, Mumbai. They used to teach my children in tutorial class with the aim of that our children should get in touch in their study. All the discontinuity in their children's education, health hazards and deprived of government facility was only because of the POSCO installation process and they used to happy and manage their livelihood, provide education for their children and getting government facilities in their home at village before coming to construction side.

Conclusion

One-way development welcomes many for the growth of the nation as a gate-way for development. But it also affects the life and destiny of many specially those at the margins. In post liberal era the problem of marginal and detached Dalit communities from their own habitation displaces them into a separate place. This type of displacement is happening because of the LPG driven industrialisation in India. In a post liberalization era, the Dalit communities are badly affected as labour migration. As a result, the process of installation of POSCO in Jagatsighpur, Odisha has forced the agricultural labour and nominal farmers from the Dalit communities of Odisha. The land acquisition process indirectly forced the Dalits from the coastal district of Odisha. In this process, Dalits who working in the agricultural field of upper caste earlier or sharing cultivation and engagement of agriculture related work in the agricultural land. When the POSCO started acquiring land and Dalits became jobless, to maintain and earn their livelihood they migrated to Hyderabad, Mumbai and Surat as a construction worker, brick worker and cotton mill worker. After starting their lives in out of state they firstly loses the welfare benefits as they do not have presently staying ration card and other identity car on welfare benefits. They were deprived of education as language barrier and they also dropped out from their school and were not enrolled in the other state education system. The children of migration workers supported their parents in the brick and construction labour field. Emotionally, they were detached from their other family members and relatives, they lost the support system from their home state. They also worked in unsafe work situations, as the paper found a few of them are dying during unsafety working field. Their health and living style was in a very miserable situation, they stayed very congested and unhealthy environment. They were also victimized by contractors and petty contractors, because of their socioe-conomic status their contact or not given them money even for years, they gave money just maintain daily food only. Because of no money they did not move to their home town even they wanted also. At the end it can be argued that the liberalisation policy of India has created disparity of income, displaced the Dalits and other marginal in a systematic way and the life of Dalit migrants has become more vulnerable due to the market driven large scale industry (POSCO) installation process.

References

Bhoi, D and Lakra, N. R. (2018). Post Liberalisation, Land Encroachments by Large Scale Industry: Evidences from Dalits of the Coastal Odisha. In Labour Migration in Post Liberalisation Era, National Conference, 18th & 19th August 2018, Indian Social Institute, New Delhi.

Bhoi, D. (2011). Globalization and Socio-educational Inequalities: A Study of Privatization of Higher Education in India, Sociology Study, 1 (2): 121-142.

Bhoi, D. (2013). Educational Privatisation and Access to Higher Education: Experiences of Scheduled Caste Students in Odisha, Social Change, 43 (3): 341-363.

Government of India (2012). Report on Second Annual Employment and Unemployment Survey 2011-12, Vol. I, Ministry of Labour and Employment, Labour Bureau, Chandigarh.

Government of Odisha (2005). Review of Annual Plan 2004-05, Report of Adviser (State Plans), Shri Chandra Pal, October 2005, Accessed on 28th July, 2014.

Government of Odisha (2012), Economic Survey 2011-12, Odisha, Planning & Coordination Department Directorate of Economics & Statistics, Government of Odisha, URL: http://www.odisha.gov. in/pc/Download/Economic_Survey_2011_12.pdf, Accessed on 24th July 2018.

Government of Odisha (2013). Economic Survey 2012-13, Odisha, Planning & Coordination Department Directorate of Economics & Statistics, Government of Odisha, URL: www.odisha.gov.in/pc/Download/

Economic%20Survey_2012-13.pdf, Accessed on 10th August 2018.

Jha, Vikas (2005). Migration of Orissa's Tribal Women: A New Story of Exploitation, Economic and Political Weekly, April 09, 2005 Vol. xl No. 15.

Mahadevia D. (2002). The Poverty and Vulnerability of Migrant Workers in India: A Post-earthquake Study in the State of Gujarat, Report prepared for International Organization for Migration (IOM), Centre for Environmental Planning and Technology Ahmedabad, India, URL: http://aajeevika.gov.in/studies/understanding-poverty/29-The-Poverty-and-Vulnerability-of-Migrantsin-India.pdf, Accessed on 22th July 2018.

Mishra B. (2010). Agriculture, Industry and Mining in Orissa in the Post-Liberalisation Era: An InterDistrict and Inter-State Panel Analysis, Economic and Political Weekly, May 15, 2010 Vol. xlv No. 20.

NCEUS (2007). Report on Conditions of Work and Promotion of Livelihoods in the Unorganised Sector, National Commission for Enterprises in the Unorganised Sector.

Sainath P. (2009). More Migrations, New Destinations, The Hindu, July 11, 2009, URL: http://www.thehindu.com/todays-paper/tp-opinion/more-migrations-newdestinations/article226404.ece, Accessed on 25th July 2018.

Sainath P. (2011). Decadal Journeys – Debt and despair spur urban growth, The Hindu, September 7, 2011, URL: http://www.thehindu.com/opinion/columns/sainath/decadal-journeys-debt-and-despairspur-urban-growth/article2487670.ece%20-%20The%20Hindu%20 2011/, Accessed on 21th July 2018.

Teamlease and IIJT (2009). India Labour Market Report, The Geographic Mismatch & A Ranking of Indian States by their Labour Ecosystem (Labour Demand, Labour Supply, Labour Laws), Accessed on 28th July, 2018.

Tumbe, Chinmay (2011). 'Remittances in India: Facts and Issues', Indian Institute of Management Bangalore Working Paper No. 331, Bangalore IIM. UNDP, (no date), Orissa Economic and Human Development Indicators, United Nations Development Programme URL: http://www.in.undp.org/content/dam/india/docs/orissa_factsheet.pdf. Accessed on 12th August 2018.

Graveyard of Inter-state Migrant Workers on Gujarat's Alang Beach: An Inquiry into How Migrant Workers Constitute a Community of Fate

Gopal Krishna

Abstract

The paper examines how local political ecosystem shaped the movement of workers from villages of Gorakhpur, Uttar Pradesh in 1880s in the Ganga river basin, how similar situation engineered their movement in post 1980s and continues to do so. Ancestors of V S Naipaul, the author had migrated as indentured farm workers to Trinidad and Tobago from one of these villages. The villagers in the vicinity of Naipaul's village Mahadeva, Kampiraganj also work in the ship-breaking yards of Alang beach, Bhavnagar, Gujarat. The paper will draw on field visits to these villages and to the ship-breaking yards in Alang located on the Gulf of Khambat, a bay on the Arabian Sea coast. The paper will examine the parallels between the journey of the indentured workers and inter-state migrant workers. In the former they traversed the path towards an uncertain future. In the latter they embrace degrading, dangerous and hazardous jobs that makes their life's future uncertain. Villagers from this region left their village where they could not earn a living to work. In the case of the former they did not come back to their country from the foreign countries to which they departed. In the case of the latter many never came back to the village because the graveyard of foreign ships became their grave yards. The paper will share findings about how Gorakhpur and Alang have emerged as a site of convergence of economic forces that sculpt the present and the future of migrant workers in a global economy.

Key words*: Gorakhpur, river basin, Alang, indentured worker, migrant worker, foreign country, foreign ships, beach, global economy*

Introduction In the ongoing saga of death toll of migrant workers on Alang beach, Bhavnagar, Gujarat, the bodies of two migrant workers who were killed in the ship-breaking yard due to a toxic gas leak on plot no. 32 were taken to Talaja Civil Hospital, Bhavanagar where they were declared brought dead on 14 March, 2018.[1] Prior to this incident Ashok Yadav, who was a migrant worker employed in the ship breaking activity at Alang was killed in sector plot no. 14.

The owner wherein he was employed as a helper gave his family members Rs 25, 000 for his cremation. The deceased worker is survived by wife and three sons. The dead body of the worker reached Chidaiyawad village under Bariyaarpur police station of Munger, Bihar after 72 hours of his death.[2] A complaint has been filed with the National Human Rights Commission (NHRC) in this regard.[3] This paper provides the testimony of victims from Alang's ship-breaking industry and the names of villages of the migrant workers from the Bhojpuri speaking region of Bihar and Uttar Pradesh. Approximately 10 km long sea front on the western coast of the Gulf of Cambay adjoining Alang-Sosiya village is developed as ship recycling yard. Alang / Sosiya Ship recycling yard is located 50 km from the city of Bhavnagar, Gujarat.

This year till April 2018, some 90 end-of-life ships have entered Indian waters for dismantling by these migrant workers. The end-of-life ships are hazardous wastes under the international law. The global shipping industry is dependent on the developing countries like India to dispose of their retired deep-sea ships through the process of ship-breaking.[4] The illegal shipment of hazardous waste "from industrialized countries is being shipped to less developed countries under the listed intention of recycling and reclamation," is a serious problem. According to World Customs Organisations' Green Customs Initiative, national and international crime syndicates earn 20-30 billion US dollars annually from hazardous wastes dumping and smuggling proscribed hazardous materials.

Ship-breaking[5] is an integral part of shipping business. Ship-breaking is the process of dismantling ships and selling their parts - primarily the secondary steel.

More than 80% of international trade in goods by volume is carried by ships. All these ships have a life span after which they become obsolete and waste like all end-of-life products. The average age of ships is 30 years. There were some more than one lakh commercial ships in the world fleet. All these ships after their average life is over will become end-of-life ships and are likely to be dumped on South Asian beaches like Alang either through linguistic corruption wherein waste is defined as non-waste or non-new good or in the name of recycling.

Eight of the top ten ship owning countries use foreign flags for more than half of their tonnage. The top 35 ship owning countries have an estimated market share of 95.6 per cent of the world tonnage. About a third of this tonnage is controlled by developing-country owners, about 66 per cent by developed-country owners, and 1.56 per cent by Russian Federation owners. Out of the top 35 ship owning countries and territories, 17 are developed and 17 are developing countries. Out of which 17 countries or territories are in Asia, 14 are in Europe and 4 are in the Americas.

Around 70 per cent of the world's tonnage is registered under a foreign flag.[6] The flag providing countries seem to provide flags of convenience to ship owners who routinely attempt to escape their past liabilities connected to their ships. This appears to be an exercise in hiding behind the corporate veil using foreign flags as veils. The ship owners escape their liability towards workers by transferring the end-of-life ships to shipbreakers in countries like India where labour and environmental laws are lax.

Most of these major flags of registration are not host to any significant national ship owning interests, but mainly provide their flag to vessels owned by nationals of other countries. This is the case for the three largest flags of registration, notably Panama, Liberia and the Marshall Islands. The largest ships are flagged in Panama. These flag providing countries seem to provide flags of convenience to ship owners who routinely attempt to escape their past liabilities connected to their ships to make ship owners immune from legal responsibility for deleterious impact on worker's occupational and environmental health.

South Asian beaches in India, Pakistan and Bangladesh account for 70–80 percent of the global ship-breaking market. In these countries, it is the migrant workers who dismantle the end-of-life ships in primitive conditions without any occupational safety. The ship-breaking industry contributes to country's secondary steel production, a hazardous industrial activity wherein migrant workers are employed, are made to adopt flawed method of breaking ships by "beaching" them in fragile ecosystem of a beach to cut and split the ships wide open on tidal flats. The containment of oil and toxic contaminants is not possible. These toxins enter the marine environment. Such working space cannot safely use cranes alongside ships to lift heavy cut pieces or to rescue workers or to bring emergency equipment (ambulances, fire trucks) to the workers or the ships. A large percentage of these migrant workers come from Bihar, Jharkhand, Uttar Pradesh, Odisha and Madhya Pradesh.

The scope of this paper is confined to native villages of migrant workers from Bhojpuri speaking region of Bihar and UP who work in Indian ship-breaking industry in Gujarat.

Migrant workers of Bhojpuri region of Bihar and UP

This paper focuses on the migrant workers from Bhojpuri speaking region of Bihar and UP because they constitute a community of fate. Workers from villages of Saran district like Domaeegarh who have been working in the ship-breaking Alang beach have been traced. Migration of workers from this part of the state is not a new phenomenon. The origin of modern day migration goes back to the colonial period, with the dispatch of indentured labour to erstwhile British colonies. This happened because the British wished to replace Black slave labour with the indentured labour after the abolition of slavery. Thousands of migrant workers who are mostly from the Bhojpuri speaking (a dialect of Hindi) belt of from UP, Bihar, Jharkhand and Madhya Pradesh, one of India's most backward states, work at Alang. These are people mostly from farmer families who choose to endanger their life to earn their livelihood instead of committing suicide as is being witnessed in most of the prosperous states like Andhra Pradesh, and Maharashtra.

International Labour Organisation (ILO) has noted that historically migration was predominantly from this very area. The plight of migrant workers of this region is yet to be fully documented. Given the fact that the worker's body is a laboratory of occupational and environmental health in particular and the ecological space in general, documentation of these workers who work in hazardous ship-breaking industry is significant to prevent public health disaster amidst globalisation of hazardous industries and their waste.

Neither religion nor the freedom struggle brought any noticeable change in this part of Bhojpuri region, which represents a region that has been under absolute desolation from the influences of modern socio-economic metamorphosis. The interdependency of the factors responsible for its abysmal plight has formed a horrendously shocking interaction matrix. Fast growing population, galloping unemployment and poor resource management- all have synergistically contributed to the present form of the economy of this region. They are always content with their present possessions and are oblivious of their future. They seem to be destined to have succumbed to the immortality of age-old poverty and deprivation. Agriculture has been, and still is the mainstay of this territory and the cottage and the tiny industries continue to serve as the hub and the head and shoulders of its industrial economy. Employment opportunities have almost dried up and the youth are left staring at the monster of jobless growth with horror and despair. Many of these variables are chronic, obdurate and die-hard. This situation compels people from the villages of this Bhojpuri speaking region to migrate to work in hazardous ship-breaking industry as casual and contract workers in Alang.

Alang beach in Bhvanagar, Gujarat has turned into the graveyard of migrant workers and one of the most occupationally and environmentally destructive, dangerous and degrading places in the world. But it is business as usual for the Indian ship-breaking and global shipping industry. Each plot on the beach employs 150–200 workers when industrial activity on Alang beach is in full swing. The number workers employed depends on the arrival of end-of-life ships on the beach. These workers are mostly unorganised and illiterate.

Dead and injured migrant workers of ship breaking industry: Stories of some victims and their families

Given the fact that Prime Minister **Narendra Modi as Chief Minister of Gujarat was also the Chairman of Gujarat Maritime Board, the observation of Rahul Gandhi[7] claiming, "GGG गुजरात"[8](In Gujarat's Alang, no labour laws are complied with because of which after the death of workers their bodies do not burn due to radioactive chemicals) assumes significance.**

Speaking in the Rajya Sabha, Ahmed Patel, a Member of Parliament from Gujarat said that the circumstances in the ship-breaking yards are horrible for the employees, and the regulators have all turned a blind eye. I urge the Government to take mandatory steps to guarantee the essential rights of these labourers safeguarded, and the most primary human dignities are afforded to these individuals. He expressed the hope that Swachh Bharat Abhiyan reaches Alang as well.[9]

Several of them work in the ship-breaking yards as unskilled and semi-skilled workers. Families of workers from villages like Rasulpur, Kisanpur Dharan, and Dumai Garh in Saran district and villages like Pokharbhinda, Nathbaba, Gaunar and Gaunarkhas in Gorakhpur have a story of injury, accident and death to narrate due to the hazards involved in working at Alang. Several of their family members left the village where they could not earn a living to work in the ship-breaking yards but they never came back.

This paper focuses on Dumai Garh village located in Manjhi Block of Saran district, Bihar and Gaonar village of Charui Chaura tehsil (block) of Gorakhpur, Uttar Pradesh. The distance between

Chhapra to Gorakhpur by train is 179 kilometers. The travel time from Chhapra to Gorakhpur by train is 2.75 hours.

Dumai Garh has some 550 resident families. The Dumai Garh village has a population of around 3700 people. Out of which some 1200 are workers. There are some 700 marginal workers. Out of which some 550 are male workers and 150 are female workers. In Dumai Garh, male literacy stands at 83.93 % while female literacy rate was 59.38 %, which is higher given that literacy stands at 61.80 % in Bihar. This village is located on the banks of Saryu river.

Testimonies from Dumai Garh

Janak Singh: A 56 year old resident of Dumai Garh used to work in Plot No. 18 in Alang ship breaking yard as a gas cutter. He was not given any Identity card as long as he worked there. He says, *"pet ke bhukh ke karan barso loha katni, jab sharir thik naikhe rah gayil to majduran ke kaun puchhewala ba."* (He cut iron for years. Now that his body is not well who will pay heed to workers.). He suffers from eye-related diseases because of working in extremely hot conditions. Prior to working in Alang he used to do iron cutting in a dock yard of Kolkata. He informed that some 20 people of Rasulpur, Ekma are currently employed in Alang.

Nagina Singh: He worked as Mukadam of Plot No. 14 and 18 for more than 20 years. The ship breakers have withheld Rs 7 lakh of his. He was given an Identity card by his employer, the shipbreaker. He is struggling to get it back. While working at Alang he suffered as he was exposed to hazardous substances. He also had rupture in his stomach due to such exposure because of he had remained unconscious for some seven days. He recovered later after medical treatment.

Ram Kumar Rai: He expired while working at Alang ship-breaking yard. He worked there for more than two decades. He used to live in Alang with his wife and two children. After his death about a year ago, his family has returned to the village. He had chest related problems but it was never diagnosed properly by an occupational health doctor.

Gaonar has some 2100 resident families. Out of which some 4500 are workers. There are some 2500 marginal workers. Out of which some 1500 are male workers and some 1050 are female workers. In Gaonar village, male literacy stands at 78.33 % while female literacy rate is at 50.96 % which is lower in comparison to Uttar Pradesh. The literacy rate of Gaonar village was 64.75 % compared to 67.68 % of Uttar Pradesh. The village is located in the Gandak river region.

Testimonies from Gaonar

Lalji Gupta: Lalji is dead. The wife and son of Lalji, Panmati testifies about his life and death. Panmati says, "He went to Alang because of debt I had adviced him not to go to such a dangerous place but he went. I have no agricultural land." Subhash, his son informs, 'He was only 40 years old. He died in 1995 in Plot No. 29. He was cremated in Talaja, Alang. We did not understand the language of the ship-breakers. Once he was dead an attempt was made to destroy his identity as to whether or not he worked there. A court case was pursued in the matter and a compensation of Rs 1 lakh was won. Out of which the lawyer took Rs 30, 000." Subhash, his son also wished to work in Alang but in his wife did not let him go.

Zhinak Prajapati: Zhinak used to work in Plot no. 136. He suffered serious spinal injury and incurred a medical expense of Rs 1.96 lakh due to his two and half month of stay in hospital but he was paid Rs 5, 000 as compensation. He used to work under one Dilawar Seth and he is pursuing a case against him since his Provident Fund has been withheld.

Ram Vilas Viswakarma: Ram Vilas worked for four months in Alang in Plot No. 98 under one Nathu Seth. He suffered injury in leg and due to some exposure lost his eye-sight.

Rampad Gaur: Bindu Devi, wife of Rampad testifies: "Seven years ago he used to work in Plot No. V-2 and 35 as a Mukadam (Foreman). The accident happened at the time of cyclone and he suffered exposure to some chemical gas, which led to his death after two months. He was cremated in Talaja. The compensation money was Rs 25, 000. He left behind two boys and a daughter. His identity was destroyed so that no one could claim right compensation and his Provident Fund money". Rampad's elder brother Jaswant also used to work there but after this death he came back due to fear of accident. He is now in farming. After the death of Rampad, his children had to leave the pursuit of education.

Besides these, there are several such stories of the likes of Ram Sajan of Lus, Sambhu and Mewalal of Gaura village, Rajindar of Belakatta village. Babulal of Bhathat near Chakia village used to work in Plot No. 32 during 1984, Except for Ram Sajan who fell down from a height and became incapacitated, all the others are dead.

Ganesh who used to work in Plot No. 35 got his four fingers slashed, Begalal got his leg broken, Rajesh who worked in Plot No. V 2 got his hand burnt, Madan Singh who worked in Plot No. 52 suffered chest injury and Chotelal who worked in Plot No. 35 suffered head and hydrocil injury. They were not paid any medical cost.

Sambhu who currently works in Plot No. 35 in the ship-breaking yard on Alang Beach suffered in such a manner that his stomach got ripped which was later restored. But he continues to work there.

These narratives fit into the official narrative. The ship-breaking industry is already known to have a higher accident rate (2 workers per 1000) than the mining industry (0.34 per 1000).[10] This narrative is also corroborated by UN reports and reports submitted in the Supreme Court. The hazardous substances and wastes which the workers handle include asbestos and its dust, heavy metals like lead, mercury, cadmium, copper, zinc etc, organomettalic substances like tributyllin, persistent organic pollutants (POPs), PCBs and Polyvinyl Chloride (PVC), welding fumes, volatile organic compounds and inhalation of gases in confined and enclosed spaces. These workers suffer from repetitive strain, awkward postures and excessive workload besides temporary employment.

In response to a Right to Information (RTI) application[11], NHRC replied saying, "The final report of research study entitled 'Governance Challenges for Implementation of Workers' Rights in Hazardous Industries: A Study of Alang-Sosiya Ship-breaking Yard, Gujarat' is awaited from Tata Institute of Social Sciences (TISS), Mumbai"[12] (NHRC, 2017). NHRC had provided financial support to TISS for this research work during 2013-2014.[13] But this NHRC sponsored study is yet to see the light of the day. Most public institutions have responded to the plight of the migrant workers in ship-breaking industry in a similar manner. They either choose not to acknowledge the existence of such precarious workers or they ignore them even after acknowledging their existence and their sufferings in general and their occupational health status in particular.

After a complaint,[14] a team of NHRC led by its Chairman visited the Alang-Sosiya ship breaking yard on May 26, 2014 to witness the deplorable working and living conditions on Alang beach where hazardous industrial activity for dismantling of end-of-life ships takes place. Pursuant to the complaint, NHRC issued notices to Union Shipping Secretary and Chief Secretary, Gujarat over the death of 5 persons in gas leakage at Alang port.[15] NHRC issued the direction on 25 February, 2016 saying, "From the reports received, it is seen that the next of kin of the diseased workers were paid Rs. 5 Lakhs Thirty Five Thousand each and the injured workers were also paid Rs. Five Thousand each. It is also seen that criminal case has been filed against the Safety Supervisor of the Plot by the Marine Police, Alang and the case is pending before the Court. In such circumstances, no further action is called for. The case is closed."[16] In such cases these court cases remain pending in the same way as it remained pending in the case of initial cases of accidents in the factory of Union Carbide Corporation in Bhopal. The death of the migrant workers' monetary compensation is hardly enough to set matters right to bring industrial peace.

The correspondence with regard to the plight of the migrant workers from the villages of Uttar Pradesh did elicit some response from the Chief Secretary, Government of Uttar Pradesh. He replied, "We are taking necessary action in the matter."[17] When response was sought from the Principal Secretary, Government of Bihar with regard to the plight of the migrant workers from the villages, he wrote back saying, "We will take necessary steps to help our workers."[18] But although several years have passed since this assurance "necessary steps" and "necessary action" are still awaited.

It was in such a backdrop that UN Special Rapporteur's report[19] recommended that regulatory authorities in Alang/Sosiya and the ship-breaking industry should step up their efforts to improve health and safety in the yards of critical concerns regarding "the health and safety situation prevailing at the shipbreaking yards.[20] The report states, "Health facilities in Alang/Sosiya do not possess sufficient human, technical and financial resources to provide any treatment other than first aid for minor injuries. The nearest hospital equipped to deal with life-threatening conditions is in Bhavnagar, more than 50 kilometers away. The Red Cross hospital in Alang, which the Special Rapporteur visited, can count on only four medical doctors and nine beds to provide health care not only to some 30,000 workers in the yards, but also to the neighboring villages of Alang (which has a population of about 18,000 people) and Sosiya (4,000 people)".[21]

Despite Supreme Court's orders and the recommendations of the Court constituted Inter-Ministerial Committee on Ship-breaking, Ministry of Steel, there has been not even an iota of improvement in the working and living conditions of the workers. In name of health care, Alang only has First Aid facilities.

Status of implementation of laws for safeguarding migrant workers

Following Supreme Court's order dated October 13, 2003, the Union Ministry of Labour constituted a Special Committee to examine "Impact of Hazardous Wastes on Workers' Health" under Chairmanship of Director General, Directorate of General Factory Advice Service and Labour Institute (DGFASLI) on the issue of medical benefits and compensation to workers affected by handling of hazardous waste, toxic in nature. The DGFASLI Committee's report mentioned lung cancer and mesothelioma caused by asbestos in all work involving exposure to the risk concerned among other occupational diseases caused by hazardous waste generating industries. This report is an acknowledgement of the grave occupational health condition of the workers but no relief has reached the workers. So far the Court too has not done anything as per the recommendations of its own committee. The authorities in Alang and Gandhi Nagar rarely permit entry of researchers for fear of negative publicity. This has created a compelling logic study the plight of the migrant workers in their native villages.

The Government of India has prepared a Ship Breaking Code 2013 in compliance with the Supreme Court's order dated 6 September, 2007. But this Code has not incorporated the recommendations of the Court constituted Inter Ministerial Committee (IMC) on Ship breaking. The Code refers to "worker" as defined in Section 2 of the Factories Act, 1948 DGFASLI, an arm of the ministry of Labour and Employment. It also refers to factory inspector, safety officer and supervisor as per the provisions of the Factories Act. Chapter VI of the Code provides general instructions for safety, health and environmental compliance for stakeholders involved in ship breaking/recycling. Its chapter VII refers to management of occupational safety and health (OSH) under which there is a requirement emergency preparedness, The ship recycling facility is supposed to comply with relevant OSH national laws and regulations, voluntary programmes, collective agreements on OSH including notification of work-related injuries and occupational disease under the Factories Act. Chapter VIII of the Code has penalty provisions wherein actions is required to be taken in the event of an accident on any plot and/or on the ship or for non-compliance of any of these regulations as per Factories Act. While these provisions of the Code are hardly adequate to bring relief to these most vulnerable workers, compliance with even these regulations is an exception and their violation is a rule.

The ship-breaking operations expose workers to asbestos used in the hanger liners, mastic under insulation, cloth over insulation, cable, lagging and insulation on pipes and hull, adhesive, gaskets on piping connections, and valve packing. As per the directives of the Supreme Court's Technical Expert Committee, this epidemiological study was planned to find out the magnitude of asbestos related health problems and other disorders among ship-breaking workers. The examination of the medical records supplied by Directorate Industrial Safety and Health (DISH) and medical examination of the asbestos handlers identified by Gujarat Maritime Board (GMB) was carried out. It was observed that 15 (16 %) of 94 workers occupationally exposed to asbestos showed linear shadows on chest X-rays, and 26 workers (39%) showed restrictive impairment. The medical examination of 44 workers carried out by National Institute of Occupational Health (NIOH), Ahmedabad revealed that only 35 workers were handling asbestos containing materials. About 65% of the workers have handled asbestos for less than five years and only 3 (8.6%) workers gave history of handling asbestos for more than 10 years. This study by NIOH was submitted in the Supreme Court.[22] All efforts to get the names of these workers exposed to carcinogenic fibers proved futile. The RTI applications did not provide their names which can be used to seek compensation for these migrant workers as per Supreme Court's verdict in the Consumer Education and Research Centre V Union of India case.[23] One of the six directions of the Court reads: "The appropriate Inspector of Factories in particular of the State of Gujarat, is directed to send all the workers, examined by the concerned ESI hospital, for re-examination by the National Institute of Occupational Health to detect whether all or any of them are suffering from asbestosis. In case of the positive finding that all or any of them are suffering from the occupational health hazards, each such worker shall be entitled to compensation in a sum of rupees one lakh payable by the concerned factory or industry or establishment within a period of three months from the date of certification by the National Institute of Occupational Health." Referring to the same NIOH study, the report of Indian Council of Medical Research (ICMR)[24] published a paper which concluded: "The ship breaking workers are exposed to asbestos dust" besides heavy metal like lead and intermittent noise. Despite such official acknowledgement by the concerned public institution, the Court's order in the matter of these migrant workers is not being complied with impunity.

In pursuance of the Supreme Court's order dated October 14, 2003, and at the request of Ministry of Environment and Forest, Ministry of Steel had set up an Inter-Ministerial Committee (IMC) on January 12, 2004 under the Chairmanship of Additional Secretary with members of Ministry of Shipping, Ministry of Environment and Forests (MOEF), Ministry of Labour, GMB, Central Pollution Control Board (CPCB) and others for the implementation of Court's orders and other related functions. IMC held several meetings; coopted members of other organizations; discussed various issues pertaining to ship breaking industries and issued a large number of directions in line with the court's orders. In all these meetings the IMC made recommendations with regard to worker's safety and welfare but till date the concerned ministries and agencies in Gujarat besides ship breakers have failed to comply with them.[25]

The Minutes of the 17th meeting of the Inter-Ministerial Committee (IMC) on Ship breaking held on June 24, 2014 under Chairmanship of Additional Secretary and Financial Adviser, Ministry of Steel and Chairman, IMC on Ship Breaking reveals that it dwelt on the issue of "Safety of workers." In the minutes it is recorded that the representative of GMB stated that DISH has uploaded the report of the accident in their website. For ensuring the safety of shipbreaking workers at Alang GMB has identified a list of common hazards that are likely to cause work related injuries, ill health disease and deaths among the labours. The list has been circulated amongst DISH, DGFASLI, Ship Recycling Industries Association (SRIA) and GPCB. In this case, DISH was asked to provide Standard Operating Procedure (SOP) to prevent accidents. However the SOP is still awaited from the DISH. The representative of Directorate General of Shipping suggested total quality management systems for safety of workers could be adopted and periodical safety audit will ensure strict compliance of the same. It was decided that DISH will make available the SOP to GMB within one month's time. GMB will issue necessary instructions for implementation of SOP in shipbreaking activities and conduct periodical third party audit of shipbreaking yards for ensuring compliance[26]. Similar pious wishes have been expressed since 1983 but to no avail.

The Minutes of the 16th meeting of the IMC on Ship breaking at Gandhinagar, Gujarat convened by Chairman, IMC on Ship Breaking reveals that it also dwelt on the issue of "Safety of workers." The minutes states that the IMC was informed that the accident at Plot No. 82, killing 7 persons occurred due to the presence of oil and its vapour in the pipeline of the ship, while cutting the oil pipe flanged with LPG gas cutting equipment....Chairman, IMC enquired whether criminal prosecution was launched against people who were responsible for loss of life in this accident. GMB may provide details in the next meeting. DISH was asked to place the report of action taken in respect of the accident on the website of GMB and prepare Standard Operating Procedures (SOP) for preventing such incident in future.[27] These recommendations have not been complied with till date. The migrant workers in the ship-breaking industry are deemed a replaceable commodity with no human dignity and natural rights. The employers feel that if one worker dies there will be numerous others willing to take his place. These workers are unorganised and invisible to the law with limited bargaining power.

Conclusion

It emerges from the literature survey and interview of the workers and their family members that the ship-breaking industry that enjoys the patronage of central and Gujarat governments which is more concerned about the profit of the ship breakers at any human cost. They have done little to ensure safeguard the health of these non-Gujarati migrant casual workers who live and work in a slave-like condition. These workers do not constitute a vote bank for the ruling or opposition parties in Gujarat, the ship breakers and the beneficiary local communities do.

So far state governments of Bihar and Uttar Pradesh have not attended to the concerns of these migrant workers from their states. The implementation of Inter-State Migrant Workers Act, 1972 enacted to protect such vulnerable worker has remained a non-starter.

Such concerns have been raised at least since 2004 when IMC convened its first meeting but there has not been even an iota of change in the working and living condition of the migrant workers on Alang beach in Gujarat. GMB (Conditions and Procedures for Granting Permission for Utilising Ship Recycling Plots) Regulation, 2006 has not been revised in the light of Supreme Court's order and the recommendations of Court's Inter Ministerial Committee (IMC). In case of fatal accident, permission holder, the ship-breaker is required to pay Rs one lakh to the GMB by way of penalty which is deposited in the Workers Welfare Fund maintained by GMB. The permission holder is also required to pay Rs.2-00 lacs to the heirs of deceased person who has lost his life in the accident. The "Permission holder" means a person to whom permission is granted for utilizing ship-breaking plot for beaching and recycling ships.

Successive central and state governments have been deemed friendly to the ship-breakers but not to the migrant workers. Meanwhile, the issue of ship-breaking-which entails secondary steel production, has been transferred from IMC, Ministry of Steel to Ministry of Shipping although the latter has no competence over issues of secondary steel production. The latter has set up an inter-ministerial Ship Breaking Scrap Committee a committee under the Ministry of Shipping in this regard.[28]

This 17 member Committee is headed by a Joint Secretary, Ministry of Shipping and includes a representative of the Ministry of Labour and representative of workers in the ship-breaking yards. The latter is nominated by the State Maritime Board by rotation on annual basis. It is supposed to meet at least once in every three months. Its terms of reference with reference to workers reads: "It will review and institute measures to improve working conditions of labourers as well as provisions of residential housing and attention to their health needs, educational needs etc. subject to availability of funds". Although this committee administers the Ship Breaking Scrap Fund, so far it has done nothing to improve the working and living conditions of the workers. It is apparent that the Ministry of Shipping has adopted a business usual status quoist approach. The composition of the committee does not hold any ray of hope for the migrant workers. Steel Ministry's IMC used to publish the minutes of its meeting on its website.

But Ship Breaking Scrap Committee of Ministry of Shipping is totally opaque with regard to its meetings. Although sunlight is the best disinfectant, the non-transparency of this committee too is taking its toll on the migrant workers.

One UNESCO study observed: "Considering the industry is highly unorganized, safety measures required by the Factories Act (1948 – Second amendment 1987) are not being implemented."[29] It had recommended that hazardous industrial operations like ship-breaking should be directly under the Department of Factories but it has not been paid heed to.

The Employee's Compensation (Amendment) Act, 2017 provides that every employer is supposed to inform the employee of his rights to compensation immediately at the time of the employment. Interviews with the workers have revealed that it is not being complied with.

The Ease of Compliance to Maintain Registers under various Labour Law Rules, 2016 provides that combined registers is required to be maintained either electronically or otherwise under the Inter-State Migrant Workmen (Regulation of Employment and Conditions of Service) Act, 1979. As per this provision the employer has to keep an employee register, a wage register and an attendance register in a specified format. This requirement is also not being fulfilled to escape liability for workers' injury, disease and death.

Field visits to villages and to Alang have revealed that the migrant workers employed in this industry are not covered even under Employees' State Insurance Corporation. They do not have basic housing and sanitation facilities. It has also come to light that these workers are not treated as fellow citizens and non-Gujarati migrant workers face discrimination also because of difference in language. In order to send remittances to their families in their native villages, the migrant workers reduce their own expenses and remain callous towards their own health conditions.

The narratives from the native villages of the workers of ship-breaking industry make a case for amendment in the Inter-State Migrant Workmen (Regulation of Employment and Conditions of Service) Act, 1979 to incorporate provisions for easy access to basic entitlements like health care, registration of migrants both at the source and work-site besides safe and healthy living and working environment to make it effective especially for hazardous industries.

The tragic deaths and injury of migrant workers is part of a pattern that has been crying for attention since 1983 because Alang has become the graveyard of workers and toxic ships by externalizing occupational and environmental health cost.

Alang beach has turned into the graveyard of migrant workers and one of the most occupationally and environmentally destructive, dangerous and degrading places in the world. But it is business as usual for the Indian ship-breaking and global shipping industry. The relationship between the employer and the employee is deeply exploitative. The latter suffers the fate of dehumanization and has become the most vulnerable workforce in the world. Their condition is admittedly worse than the workforce in the worst industrial sector-the mining industry. This dehumanization linked to the externalization of human cost by ship-breakers and global shipping companies have made these migrant workers part of the community of fate to which all wretched of the earth belong.

These narratives reveal that public institutions cannot feign to be surprised whenever accidents happen. The beaching of the first end-of-life ship M.V. Kota Tenjong on Alang happened without any planning.[30] The ad hoc approach continues to plague the industrial activity on Alang beach with no relief for the migrant workers. The absence of doctors trained in occupational health and paucity of environmental and occupational health infrastructure facilities makes diagnosis of enviro-occupational diseases difficult.

Even the training of doctors leaves a lot to be desired. As part of MBBS course, the students are supposed to study "Occupational Health" so that the student is able to describe the common industrial and occupational diseases, to describe the feasible methods of control of occupational diseases and to describe the important features of the Workman Compensation Act and provision of health services and health insurance to industrial workers. The content of their course includes study of working environment, health hazards of industrial and agricultural workers, common occupational lung diseases, common occupational skin diseases and cancers, industrial toxic substances, principles of prevention of occupational diseases, legal status in relation to Workman Compensation Act, Employees' State Insurance Act and a visit to a factory. The medical students are supposed to learn about environmental carcinogens besides Occupational lung disorders like asbestosis and mesothelioma as part of their respiratory pathology study. But this sketchy approach to occupational health in the medical syllabus fails to prepare required competence for diagnosis and treatment of the occupational and environmental diseases. This impedes any scope of preventive and remedial action for the protection of workers health. The medical study does not pay attention to ILO Convention on Occupational Health Services (No. 161) and ILO Recommendations on Occupational Health Services (No. 171) which were adopted in 1985 which requires surveillance of work environment, workers' health for preventive steps. The workers' health must be assessed prior to their joining the work, periodically during the work and after the work on retirement or when they stop working or after their termination to detect exposure levels and early biological effects and responses. The lack of adequate documentation of occupational injuries and diseases and lack of competent occupational health personnel and services does not mean absence of gnawing unaddressed occupational health needs.

The callousness towards migrant workers' health amidst weakening of existing national and international legal regulations has been imposing an unacknowledged disease burden on the present and future generations with no structural remedy in sight.

Photo: Dead body of a migrant worker being taken out of an end-of-life ship at Alang ship breaking yard[31]

The narratives of the migrant workers points out that there is a growing tendency among them to naturalize these abnormal and inhuman living and working conditions as if this is the "new normal" which is going to be their fate for all times to come.

Endnotes

[1] (2018), 2 labourers die of suffocation, *The Times of India*, Rajkot, March 15

[2] (2017), *Hindustan,* Bhagalpur, September 18

[3] The complaint has been filed by the author.

[4] (2000), Rousmanier, Peter et al. Shipbreaking in the Developing World: Problems and Prospects, *International Journal of Occupational and Environmental Health*, Volume 13, No. 4, October-December

[5] Till 1980s, ships were dismantled in Japan, Korea and Taiwan. But since 1980s, South Asian beaches of Chittagong, Bangladesh, Gadani, Pakistan and Alang, Gujarat, India have become the graveyard of end-of-life ships. The ship-breaking operations happened in Kolkata and Mumbai in 1912.

[6] (2011), Review of Maritime Transport, United Nations Conference on Trade and Development, p. 36, 46-47, Available at http://unctad.org/en/docs/rmt2011_en.pdf visited on May 2, 2018

[7] The author has briefed him in person about the condition of workers in Alang prior to his visit while meeting him with a delegation of trade union leaders.

[8] Gandhi, Rahul, (2015), Speech at Ramleela Maidan, Delhi, 20 September

[9] Patel, Ahmed (2015), Speech in Rajya Sabha, 8 May 2015

[10] It has been disclosed in the report of the Technical Experts Committee on Shipbreaking in Writ Petition (Civil) No. 657 of 1995.

[11] The RTI application was filed by the author.

[12] Bhakhry, Savita (2017) Reply of National Human Rights Commission, 10/10/2014 PRP &P, January 27

[13] This unpublished research work has been done by TISS, Mumbai.

[14] The complaint was filed by the author.

[15] (2014), Case Details of File Number: 1167/6/6/2014, July 11, http://nhrc.nic.in/disparchive.asp?fno=13288

[16] *Ibid*

[17] Ranjan, Alok (2014) Chief Secretary, Government of Uttar Pradesh, *personal communication*, July 18.

[18] Mishra, Vyas (2012) Principal Secretary, Health Department, Government of Bihar, *personal communication*, November 13

[19] Report of the UN Special Rapporteur on the adverse effects of the movement and dumping of toxic and dangerous products and wastes on the enjoyment of human rights, UN Human Rights Council, Fifteenth session, Agenda item 3, September 2, 2010

[20] The author accompanied the UN Special Rapporteur's team during the site visit to Alang.

[21] (2010), Report of the UN Special Rapporteur on the adverse effects of the movement and dumping of toxic and dangerous products and wastes on the enjoyment of human rights, UN Human Rights Council, Fifteenth session, Agenda item 3, p. 9, 12, 14, September 2, Available at http://www2.ohchr.org/english/bodies/hrcouncil/docs/15session/A.HRC.15.22.Add.3_en.pdf visited on May 2, 2018

[22] The author was an applicant in the case Writ Petition (Civil) No. 657 of 1995.

[23] Writ Petition (Civil) No. 206 of 1986.

[24] The Annual Report of Indian Council of Medical Research (ICMR) 2007-2008.

[25] (2014) Minutes of IMC, Ministry of Steel, June 29

[26] (2014) Minutes of the 17th meeting of the Inter-Ministerial Committee (IMC) on Ship breaking, Ministry of Steel, June 24

[27] (2013) Minutes of the 16th meeting of the IMC on Ship breaking, Ministry of Steel, October 1

[28] (2014) Order, Constitution of Ship Breaking Scrap Committee, MG Section, Ministry of Shipping, July 22

[29] Joshi, Vidyut (2001) Environment and Development in Coastal Regions and in Small Islands papers 17, UNESCO

[30] It was beached on February 13, 1983.

[31] This photo was shared with the author by an anonymous person.

Annexure

Inaugural Address

Dr. George Pattery SJ

Labour Migration in the Post Liberalization Era

I am glad that we are reflecting on this vexing issue of our times as a joint venture of ISI Bangalore and Delhi. I look forward to meaningful discussions in the next two days.

This is an international issue cutting across nations and regions. We talk about forced migration, either for jobs or for political asylum. It is estimated that we have 232 million migrants today which is equivalent to the fifth most populous country in the world. Over 65 million people are forced to leave their homes due to armed conflicts, generalized violence or natural disasters. Sadly it is said that the Mediterranean sea has become the greatest cemetery in the world. On a similar note one may say that with outright rejection of Rohingya migrants, India has joined the exclusive club of 'militant nations' and stopped short of the great nation that welcomed the Tibetans 60 years ago. As Shiv Viswanathan wrote: "Jawaharlal Nehru, defying the Chinese, offered refuge to Dalai Lama and let him set up his government in exile. It was a moment of hospitality and generosity, a Nehruvian moment which one senses as lacking today in this time of Rohingya crisis and the National Register of Citizens threatening to extern lakhs of people." (**The Hindu**, "Lessons in Alternative histories" 16 August, 2018). We cannot ignore this larger and international context of migrants' issue in this debate.

However we are discussing about 'Labour Migration' and within the country in particular, rather focused and limited issue. There is something common in any form of migration. It is this sense of being perceived as 'the other.' Labour Migrant is perceived as 'the other' - seen against the settlers. Settlers are those who own, and claim to belong; migrants do not belong. 'We own up a nation or state' and define nationhood and statehood in terms of religion, caste or ethnicity and consider 'others' as alien who do not belong. A labourer who speaks another language, from another state or territory is an alien in his own country.

In a liberalized economy, capital transfer and technology transfers are welcome; human resource transfer is suspect, especially when it comes to 'labour'. This is compounded by the fact that 'labour' is migrating often due to development induced displacement, or due to natural disasters or due to better prospects/wages. In all such cases, it is the lower strata of the society that is affected. It looks that 'labour' carries with him/her caste, religion and social status wherever they go. When a capital or technology is transferred, it has no caste or religion. But not so with 'labour'! In spite of the talk of one nation, a labour is almost without identity; ration card is not respected in another state; *aadhaar* card is used to identify and segregate. 'Identities' are employed in order to reinforce 'alien-ness'. State machinery is employed in order to identify the alien.

This happens "in a world and at a time when globalization and interdependence affect every person, community or nation in the world."(p.22, Sons and Daughters of a Pilgrim," Alberto Ares Mateo, 168. Booklet - Barcelona). The evolutionary theories, electronic advancements and ecological thinking all highlight the fact that we are living in an inter-connected global world, affecting millions of life in one way or another. 'The flutter of a butterfly affects the harmony of the universe'. We live in a world where intense human labour benefits and reaches across the world. In such a world we are creating 'exclusive theories and policies' within a country to segregate 'migrant labour' force! This is unscientific.

While we rightly discuss rural and urban migrants, caste and gender, dalit and tribal issues of migrant labour, I suggest that along with these, we take up advocacy to bring in comprehensive legislation to support migrant labour across the country. 'One nation one law,' could be applied to migrant labour. Similarly we need to build linkages with origin-states of migrant labour and destination states.

I wish you well in these reflections and am sure that Fr. Martin's many initiatives will bear much fruit. This joint venture of ISIs could focus on net-working with other like-minded agencies who work in this area. After Pedro Arrupe's prophetic call to work with refugees and migrants, the Jesuits across the world have received this mandate with enthusiasm to work with migrants. Today, we begin this seminar with blessings of Chilean St. Alberto Hurtado to become a fire that kindles other fires. I look forward to very engaging discussions and deliberations during these days.

Contributors

Dr. Notan Bhusan Kar is an Academic Counselor of IGNOU in Sociology, Kolkata, West Bengal.

Mr. Atlanta Talukdar and Ms. Deepshikha Malakar are Research Scholars at Tata Institute of Social Sciences, Tetelia, Jalukbari, Guwahati.

Sukanya Kakoti is a Research Scholar at Tata Institute of Social Sciences, Guwahati Campus. Raju Saikia is a Research Scholar at Gauhati University.

Richard Gonsalves is presently employed as the Programme Manager in Labour & Migration Unit, Indian Social Institute, Bangalore.

Ms. Bhumika Sharma PhD, is a Research Scholar in the Department of Laws at Himachal Pradesh University, Shimla. (H.P.)

Ms. Mamta Kashyap PhD, is a Research Scholar in the Department of Laws at Himachal Pradesh University, Shimla. (H.P.)

Ojasvi Goyal is a student in the 2nd year, M.A Economics, GGS Indraprastha University, Dwarka, Delhi.

Prof. Saikat Roy is an Assistant Professor for the Department of Political Science at St. Xavier's College North Bengal.

Ms. Aparna Radhakrishnan and Ms. Niti Saxena are from SM Sehgal Foundation, Gurugram and   Ms. Vrindaa Sharma is from TERI School of Advanced Studies.

P.O. Martin heads the Labour & Migration, Unit of Indian Social Institute Bangalore

Smitha Philip is a Associate Professor, Department of Social Work, CMR University, Bengaluru.

Mr. Ratnesh Katulkar Social Scientist in the Department of Dalit Studies

Mr. Paul D' Souza Head of the Department of Dalit Studies.

Ms. Sweta is a Ph.D. Research Scholar, CSSS, SSS, JNU, New Delhi.

Teena Anil is a Assistant Professor, School of Global Affairs Ambedkar University.

Dr. Dhaneshwar Bhoi PhD, Tata Institute of Social Sciences, Mumbai, Social Scientist, Department of Dalit Studies, Indian Social Institute, New Delhi. Email: dhaneswar.bhoi@gmail.com

Dr. Neelima R. Lakra PhD, School of Management and Labour Studies, Tata Institute of Social Sciences, Mumbai. & Consultant, National Institute of Educational Planning and Administration, New Delhi-110016, Email:neelimalakra@gmail.com

Dr. Gopal Krishna is with the Tata Institute of Social Sciences (TISS), Patna Centre and is editor of www.toxicswatch.org